IN PURSUIT OF THE PAST

Decoding the Archaeological Record

IN PURSUIT OF THE PAST

Decoding the Archaeological Record

Lewis R. Binford

with the editorial collaboration of
John F. Cherry and Robin Torrence

with 147 illustrations

Thames and Hudson

This book is dedicated to the memory of François Bordes. It remembers the many hours of our joking, arguing, and enjoying each other's minds. Our field has lost a major contributor and I have lost a very good friend. I deeply regret that I will not hear Bordes' reply to this book.

First published in the USA in 1983 by Thames and Hudson Inc., 500 Fifth Avenue, New York, New York 10110

First paperback edition 1988

Library of Congress Catalog Card Number 82–50816

Printed and bound in the USA

Contents

Foreword

The work of Lewis Binford establishes him as the outstanding archaeological thinker of our time. His influence, as the senior and most original figure in the intellectual developments of the 1960s which came to be called the 'New Archaeology', has arguably been greater than that of any other writer this century concerned with the understanding of man's early past.

In writing this Foreword I have the privilege of saying why the thinking which this book expresses and represents is so important for the development of modern, processual archaeology, offering, as it does, the opportunity of defining more clearly man's place in the world. For many people the most obvious attraction of archaeology is the excitement of discovery – unearthing the lost treasures of the past. The adventure of making new finds in distant lands is indeed one of its pleasures. But that is only the beginning, and as Binford so clearly shows here, that is not the most important or the most interesting part of the enterprise. For the task of archaeology is not simply a matter of 'piecing together the past' – as if the bits and pieces, the material data, could be fitted together in some painless way to make a coherent picture, as soon as they are dug up. The real task is, on the contrary, a challenge and a struggle – a sustained struggle to devise meanings and interpretations which can be related to the finds, the data, in a coherent and justifiable way. The real intellectual excitement – and the exasperation – of the practice of archaeology comes from the tension between the abundance of the evidence on the one hand, and the very real difficulties in formulating warranted conclusions from it. This is an intellectual adventure which is ultimately more rewarding than the pursuit of new finds by continuing excavation.

I regard this book as outstandingly important because it brings out so clearly – indeed more clearly than any work before it – that this struggle for meaning has always been and remains the fundamental challenge of archaeology. Only by undertaking that struggle can we attain any worthwhile understanding of man's early past and of the developments which shaped its transformation into the present. The book has moreover another – and quite separate – merit: it is enjoyable to read.

Lewis Binford is a man who lives his archaeology with considerable intensity – and archaeology is one of those subjects which is very much an *activity* as well as an area of thought. When this activity involves not simply excavation and research of the familiar archaeological kind, but ethnoarchaeology – living and working amongst contemporary hunter-gatherer groups and others with non-western, subsistence economies – there is scope for a rich variety of experience.

I well remember the author's first academic visit to Britain, to the Sheffield archaeological conference in December 1971. His session at the meeting was devoted to the interpretation of the evidence of the Mousterian period in France (discussed here in Chapter 4), and very lively it was, if decidedly technical at times. But at home in the evenings prior to the conference, four of us sat and talked around the dinner table. The candles, which had been lit at the beginning of dinner, burnt lower and lower as Lew described his experiences among the Nunamiut Eskimo. None of us showed the slightest inclination to move until, one after another, the candles guttered out, around three in the morning, and we decided to call it a day. I recall those interesting and lively evenings with great pleasure now because they had a quality of archaeology *experienced*, archaeology that is lived through – the actual process of ideas and understandings of the past taking shape, and being changed by experience in the field. Such a sense of the immediacy of personal experience is best expressed by the spoken word, yet I believe that it is conveyed here also, by many of the chapters in this book, most of which in fact did take shape as the spoken word, as the editors indicate in their introductory note. All of us in the Department of Archaeology at Southampton were greatly stimulated by, and learnt a great deal from, his teaching with us in the autumn term of 1980, when these chapters took shape. I think that this book does indeed retain much of the urgency and the attack and the force of argument which came over so well in person. It can be read, therefore, as an account by one of the world's leading archaeologists of some of the principal pieces of work which he has undertaken. No one will read it without gaining some fresh insights into the life of early man, and the evidence upon which our knowledge of it rests.

The importance of the work does not, however, lie primarily in the interesting account which the author gives of his individual research projects. It rests rather in its restatement and exemplification of some of the fundamental tenets of the New Archaeology which Binford has consistently propounded since 1962, and which have so significantly influenced much later work.

The most important thing to realize about the New Archaeology – or processual archaeology as it is better called now that the newness is wearing off – is that it started as, and to a large extent remains, a series of *questions* about the human past. It was not initially a coherent body of theory – and this is a point which has often been misunderstood, indeed misrepresented – and only slowly, gradually and painfully is such a body of theory now being generated. It entails, on the contrary, a very frank realization that there is no easy and ready-made way by which we can have a valid knowledge about the past. As Binford sets out very clearly, everything that we know about man's early past, or rather everything that we think we know, is based on inference. Now many earlier workers, from the fathers of archaeology such as General Pitt-Rivers and Oscar Montelius, down to our own century and Gordon Childe or Walter Taylor, have made contributions to archaeological theory. But many of them have given the impression that they had succeeded in establishing a correct way of proceeding, a set of rules, as it were, by which we could now go ahead and 'do' archaeology, and reconstruct man's past. What Binford has consistently stressed is that we still in the main lack such rules: rules which would allow us to move from our observations of the archaeological record – which of course exists and is observed now, in the present – by reliable processes of inference, to make warranted statements about the past.

Stated so baldly, this crucial point may not come across as a very startling revelation. But in reality it is the fundamental idea of the New Archaeology. It is brilliantly documented in Chapter 2 which, summarizing Binford's recent book, *Bones: Ancient Men and Modern Myths*, sets our earliest human ancestors into a perspective very different from that to which we are accustomed. These points are made here with outstanding clarity and coherence, so that this volume gives an unparalleled insight into the intellectual struggle and debate which constitute the real drama of contemporary archaeology.

Colin Renfrew

Editorial Note

It may be helpful to the reader to know something about how this book came to be written and about our collaborative role in its production. During his visit to Europe from October 1980 to January 1981, Professor Binford spoke about his past and present research to audiences ranging from large-scale public gatherings to intimate groups of professionals. He also taught undergraduate classes and discussed his ideas with graduate students and university teachers, as well as lecturing to large archaeological audiences. On all these occasions the response was extremely enthusiastic. To those of us who are fortunate enough to have been taught by Binford the warm reception he received came as no surprise: he has a great power for making the past come 'alive', for getting to the root of important controversies, and for suggesting very original approaches to methodological and theoretical problems in archaeology.

It was due to the foresight of Colin Renfrew, then Professor of Archaeology at Southampton University (Binford's chief host institution during his visit), that many of the lectures were taped, in the hope that a book based on a sample of the talks might be possible. These tapes were nevertheless far too numerous to be published without extensive editing, a task which pressure of work prevented Binford from undertaking in its entirety. Since we knew him well, were enthusiastic about his work and general approach to archaeology, and also attended most of his lectures in England, we were asked to collaborate in the formidable task of converting tape recordings made on over two dozen separate occasions into a book of interest to the layman or undergraduate student, as well as to professional archaeologists. Our initial duties included taping the sessions, obtaining (or in most cases making) transcripts of these tapes, establishing a coherent format for the book, and piecing together a text from the transcripts. This first, very preliminary draft was sent to the author; he took it with him to South Africa in the summer of 1981, mulled it over, altered several chapters (mainly by expansion), added introductions to the sections, two new chapters, and footnotes, and selected the illustrations. From this greatly improved raw material we then edited the final version. Our main job was to ensure consistency throughout and, where necessary, to simplify as far as possible those passages made somewhat inaccessible by the famous Binford prose style (a problem rarely encountered in his spoken deliveries). This has been a far more time-consuming task than we imagined at the outset, but the pleasure of examining, literally word by word, the latest thoughts of one of the acknowledged leaders in our own field has been its own reward.

For the record, it may be of interest to relate individual chapters to the specific occasions on which the material was presented. Chapter 1 is based on three talks broadcast by the BBC in April 1981 and published in *The Listener* (9, 16, 23 April 1981). Chapter 2 was originally presented as two lectures on Palaeolithic archaeology for undergraduate classes at Southampton University. Chapters 3 and 4 were written specially for this book; the former incorporates observations and ideas arising from Binford's trip to South Africa during the summer of 1981. The transcript of a seminar presented to the Albert Egges van Giffen Institute for Pre- and Protohistory at the University of Amsterdam has been only slightly altered to yield Chapter 5. A lecture to the Department of Prehistory and Archaeology at Sheffield University formed the core of Chapter 6, while Chapter 7 is a composite based on lectures presented to the general public in Sheffield and Southampton and on a talk given to the Prehistoric Society in London. Chapter 8 was given as a seminar at the London School of Economics in a series entitled 'Patterns in History', organized by Ernest Gellner and John Hall, but it also includes sections of the discussion following a lecture delivered in Amsterdam. Finally, Chapter 9 is taken from the tape of an informal lecture to undergraduates at Southampton University.

The resulting book, we feel, demonstrates very well the enormous breadth of interest of the author. There is something here for every archaeological taste –

from the life of our earliest ancestors, through the origins of agriculture, to issues about the development of civilization, or what archaeologists like to call 'complex societies'. Lewis Binford demonstrates moreover that the evidence used to study our past, the archaeological record, is a great deal more complicated than many of us may have imagined. He likens this evidence to an ancient language which has not yet been deciphered. The purpose of this book – in fact of most of Binford's research, past and present – is to find ways to decode that language.

John F. Cherry
Robin Torrence

Author's Acknowledgments

This book is a wide-ranging discussion of our knowledge of the past and of our attempts to learn about it; as such, it represents something of my own experiences during a career as an ethnographer, a student of animal behavior, and an archaeologist. I must therefore acknowledge all the persons who have made my work possible and who have given me encouragement along the way. Specifically, this book owes its existence to the urgings of Colin Renfrew, Robin Torrence and John Cherry. These three people more than any others talked me into recording my European lectures and considering them seriously as the basis for a book; all three have been untiring in their support, encouragement and insistence that this book should be produced. I cannot thank them enough.

While I was in Europe, Colin Renfrew, Clive Gamble and Klavs Randsborg guided me, corrected me, and educated me in the European intellectual climate. For this I am most grateful to these good friends. The European trip also made possible a wonderful midday meal with Denise and François Bordes on New Year's Eve, 1980. It was a fine visit, but sadly it was to be the last time I saw François alive. For this opportunity I am indebted to my European hosts.

As mentioned in the Preface, I refer in this book to a considerable amount of unfinished research, an important part of which was either conducted during, or stimulated by, a marvellous trip to South Africa during the summer of 1981 (the result of an invitation to lecture at the University of Cape Town). During the course of my visit I had the good fortune to make a trip to the Nossob River area in northern South Africa, where for a short time I shared the experiences of naturalists such as Gus and Margie Mills, who are currently studying hyenas. I was also privileged to visit with Dr C. K. Brain, as well as Drs Elizabeth Voigt and Elizabeth Vrba (all of the Transvaal Museum), and was thus able to see the sites of Kromdraai, Sterkfontein and Swartkrans and hear them discussed by these most knowledgeable guides in the world. Richard Klein and the staff of the South African Museum in Cape Town made it possible for me to study faunal collections housed there, including those from the important site at Klasies River mouth (on which I hope to report in the near future). Miss Shaw of the South African Museum was most kind in guiding me through their collections of photographs and ethnographic materials.

The efforts of a large number of people who collectively made possible my African trip are certainly reflected in this book. None, however, should be singled out ahead of John Parkington, who arranged the trip in the first place and made so many things happen for me while I was there; to John I am truly grateful for one of the most exciting experiences of my professional career.

Here in Albuquerque various people have been important in the production of this book. I must mention the staff of the Instructional Media Office at the University of New Mexico, who have become close colleagues during the production of photographic copies of my drawings and who have rendered so many fine prints from my slides and negatives. The Department of Anthropology at the University of New Mexico, as always, has been supportive of my research. In particular, they funded much of the photographic work and supplied an assistant to aid in the preparation of the manuscript and in other concurrent research. Martha Graham and Signa Larralde, my typists, both worked hard and long to produce a good manuscript.

Several people have contributed photographs for use in this book: Charles Amsden, Jim Chisholm, Irven De Vore, Pat Draper, Diane Gifford, Robert Hard, Susan Kent, John Lanham, John Parkington, Edward Santry, Olga Soffer, and Norman Tindale. Credit has been given with all photographs not taken by the author. The work of these people has made this a better book and I thank each of them for their co-operation. Iva Ellen Morris drew the various reconstructions of early man's ways of life (ills. 2, 5 and 16), as well as the imaginative rendering of the 'Garden of Eden' (ill. 128), and I greatly appreciate her help and talent.

Finally, I must emphasize the important role played by Robin Torrence and John Cherry in the production of this book. They oversaw the transcription of the tapes and the initial translation of the spoken word into manuscript. After I reworked these transcripts, they both worked long and hard editing my work and their suggestions about re-organization invariably resulted in a better product. To Robin and John there are no words adequate to express my gratitude.

Lewis R. Binford

Preface

This book represents the reworked transcripts of a series of lectures given in Great Britain and Scandinavia during the fall of 1980 and the first few weeks of 1981.[1] The lectures were designed to achieve a number of objectives, but above all they were intended to shed light on research in progress: that is, they frequently touched on subjects which I was investigating or ideas that I was exploring, but which had not yet been developed to the point of presenting a research paper or monograph. This means that this book, like the lectures, represents not the results of completed research and thought so much as a kind of progress report on various ideas and investigations, as well as opinions regarding other people's work. Everyone must recognize that publication by archaeologists frequently occurs long after the work was actually done; similarly, the stimulation of discussion and exchange of ideas which constitutes the excitement of research commonly goes on among a small 'in-group' of friends and colleagues, and rarely reaches the field at large until much later in those belated reports published upon completion of all the work. Lectures tend to fill the gap between the excitement of on-going research and the dull responsibility of preparing the 'final' report. I hope that by publishing my current thinking and research some of this excitement can be shared, so that others may be stimulated by the airing of unfinished work. I have tried to provide sufficient background information to indicate how I justify the pursuit of certain lines of argument, but I have generally not presented 'conclusions': indeed, in some cases I am not yet certain what conclusions will be forthcoming. While my attitude toward the work of others is, of course, tempered by my experiences and my current interests, I have tried to offer some sort of 'state of the art' assessment with regard to certain areas of research.

A number of years ago I outlined a long-term research program, in which the investigation of faunal remains, the organized use of space, and systems ecology were judged to be the areas most profitable for the development of explanatory theory in archaeology.[2] I have published most of my work on faunal remains (although one substantial piece of research, dealing with criteria for diagnosing scavenging as a food procurement tactic, is yet to appear). Most of the discussion here uses some of the results of these faunally orientated studies, but it focuses on spatial analysis in terms of our understanding of variability both within and between sites. Each of these interests, one near completion and one in the middle of investigation, looks ahead to increased ecological studies yet to come. This position within my long-term research program conditions what I see as interesting and therefore worth discussion.

In addition to being a series of glimpses at and critical assessments of contemporary work, the lectures were weighted differently in some cases in response to my perceptions of the character of the audience. Almost all these lectures were delivered before very varied groups and hence were pitched to different levels of familiarity with archaeology and prehistory. There was an additional slant to take account of what I saw as differences among the professionals present in the audience. I was struck by the diversity that exists among my European colleagues, both in their interests and in their recognition of the relevance of research conducted outside their own particular fields of study. As one might expect, given the fact that Palaeolithic deposits are either very sparse or non-existent in various regions of northern Europe, there was much interest in agricultural and proto-urban archaeology. This bias was not so apparent at gatherings of prehistorians in southern Europe or Africa. Similarly, the archaeologists interested in stone age research were most likely to be working on the remains of Mesolithic sites, i.e. the by-products of fully modern, but pre-agricultural, man. I found that my discussions of the problems of method illustrated by the materials covered in Parts I and II of the present book were considered to be either irrelevant for their work, or of interest only because of a purely academic concern for the Mousterian or the Lower Palaeolithic. I had not expected this sort of reaction, although I would certainly have gotten a similar response from a group of New World archaeologists researching the Archaic or Woodland periods in North America. As a response, I have tried in this book to present the discussions of early man and the Mousterian in terms of *methodology* which I believe is of direct relevance to all archaeologists, regardless of the periods of time with which they may be particularly concerned.

I was surprised too by how many people seemed to be unfamiliar with the ethnographic literature on hunting and gathering societies. Discussions about the archaeological remains of hunter-gatherers seemed to me frequently to be uninformed and based on romantic ideas, rather than on any genuine understanding derived from first-hand accounts. For this reason, I used a great many slides of my experiences with hunter-gatherers, with the intention of illustrating how mobile peoples 'mark' their environment with archaeological remains. This should be particularly evident in Chapter 6, where I have deliberately left the presentation largely at the slide-show level to show how a single people can produce many different kinds of archaeological remains. This reality – although not new to archaeologists – seemed to be poorly appreciated and rarely considered when interpreting the archaeological record. I may be overstating the case, since it is true that most of the archaeologists in the audiences were not concerned with mobile peoples. But my lectures should be seen as a kind of missionary work, pointing to some of the interesting problems of inferential method that arise in dealing with hunters and gatherers.

Many Europeans, particularly the Scandinavians, wanted me to discuss the New Archaeology. Interestingly enough, this was largely thought of not in terms of the issues which I had stressed in publications up through 1969, but instead in terms of the arguments encapsulated in the papers by Fritz and Plog[3] and by Watson, LeBlanc and Redman.[4] My impression was that most European scholars considered these works to be a naive brand of positivism, an attempt to adopt a philosophy for archaeology motivated by a desire to become 'scientific' or by some strange American drive to 'measure things'. I acknowledge that it is very difficult to sell a particular set of tactics if the goal, the teleology, is not clear: until you tell me where we are going, I cannot evaluate your suggestion for getting there. Many of the programmatics of the New Archaeology were perhaps ill-timed in this sense and some of the negative reactions to them were justified.

In response to this reaction, I have tried to organize this book more in terms of arguments from example and to emphasize the nature of the archaeological problems stemming from different realms of research. At the same time, I have tried to link these differences in approach to the need for an interest, common to all archaeologists, in improving our methods for inference. I have not, however, specifically discussed such epistemological issues, only the more practical and tactical ones. If the reader appreciates the latter, then it is inevitable that involvement in epistemological issues will follow. I am as convinced as ever that deep concern for, and experimentation in, epistemological strategies is a key to the growth of archaeological science. The direct call for the adoption of particular positivist tactics was perhaps premature and many archaeologists, in any case, failed to appreciate the basis for such calls. What I hope to illustrate here, through a series of discursive examples, is the need for a real concern with epistemology.

There seem in Europe to be two clearly distinguishable types of archaeologists: the specialists and technicians representing 'science in archaeology',[5] and the 'social philosophers' (structuralists, Marxists, 'morphogenesists', etc.). This book represents something of an attempt to suggest how the two might come together and in so doing carve out a genuine science of archaeology. I do not wish to imply, incidentally, that these two types are exclusive to the Old World – both are certainly present in North America. But the contrast there is more between the 'hard-digging field man' who discusses the strength of the liquor in various Mexican or South Dakotan bars, and the so-called 'theorist' who is more interested in 'what it all means', regardless of whether or not there exist reliable methods for getting answers to such a question. (Thankfully, there is much less *machismo* associated with archaeology in the Old World; both the scientific specialists and the social philosophers are more interested in intellectual issues than are many of the New World 'field men'.)

The 'science in archaeology' approach so common in Great Britain apparently sees the development of methods for inference as primarily dependent upon other sciences. Thus there is an emphasis on zooarchaeology, geology, or some other field working 'in the service of' archaeology. In one sense, this is a sound approach: theories and explanations for observed phenomena developed in other fields can certainly be used as a basis for inference in archaeology. Yet we frequently find ourselves in the situation where the inferences so obtained are perhaps neither useful nor germane to the solution of our problems as archaeologists. The result is that there has been a steady development of little technical subfields treating archaeological remains in their own frameworks, but not necessarily advancing the cause of archaeology itself. In such cases, the archaeological evidence ends up serving the goals of other disciplines – for instance, when breeding diversification in domestic cattle, sheep and goats is studied in purely zoological terms, and the archaeologist then fumbles around for some context in terms of which the work of the zooarchaeologist might be made relevant to his own studies.

It was exactly this conclusion which lead me to the study of fauna and the eventual publication of my books *Nunamiut Ethnoarchaeology*[6] and *Bones.*[7] The support scientist, I found, would never do the research necessary to relate faunal remains to the interpretation of past human societies. At best such scientists might develop techniques for interpreting ancient animal populations,[8] but – alas – the degree to which this is possible without a sophisticated understanding of archaeological formation processes is certainly suspect.[9] Only archaeologists can be expected to do the research necessary for the accomplishment of their own archaeological goals, even if allied sciences may help and may from time to time provide valuable 'gifts'.[10]

I think that most archaeologists have realized that the reliability of an inference about the past is only as good as the knowledge on which the inference is based. We have also known for a very long time that our knowledge about some phenomena is more dependable than about others. Christopher Hawkes[11] implicitly recognized this when he proposed his 'ladder of reliability' in 1954: for those domains where knowledge and understanding were considered relatively secure, inference was considered relatively easy.

This basic link between 'traditional archaeology' and the so-called 'New Archaeology' was nicely illustrated in a lecture I was privileged to attend while in Southampton. The speaker was the distinguished archaeologist M. J. O'Kelly, who has given so much to the excavation and understanding of the important site of Newgrange in Ireland.[12] Professor O'Kelly was quite happy to consider how the great megalithic structure at Newgrange might have been built, what it might have looked like during its period of use, and even what events might have modified the archaeological record into the form observed at the time of excavation. All these inferences were made tenable by his linkage of archaeological observations to principles and laws of causation drawn from the sciences of mechanics, physics, and the related fields of applied engineering. Of interest, however, was his reluctance to consider the nature of the society in which the site had functioned. Why the difference in attitude? The answer must be simply that there are no reliable principles or theories of culture and society to which Professor O'Kelly could appeal in justifying inferences to these domains from the observations he had made. What I am suggesting here is that archaeologists cannot wait for other fields to develop the necessary principles which will permit them to make reliable inferences about the past. They must themselves develop a science of archaeology.

The tactics of the social philosophers represent the opposite extreme.[13] These advocates of various points of view – Marxists, structuralists, materialists, idealists, and so on – believe their own preferred postures render the world understandable and intelligible.[14] They frequently use the archaeological record to advance their points of view by what I call '*post hoc* accommodative arguments': that is, they interpret the past as 'known' in terms consistent with their particular philosophical bias or adopted position. But not infrequently such arguments take the form of syllogistic fallacies. My point is perhaps appropriately illustrated by one of my experiences while in England.

Having accepted an invitation to speak at Cambridge, I presented a short historical introduction to the methodological ideas subsequently published in my book, *Bones*.[15] I then went along to an organized discussion session attended mainly by students of Ian Hodder. This 'discussion' began with two students reading prepared papers in which science, archaeology and my own writings were accused of a long list of deficiencies, misdemeanors, and even intellectual felonies (for instance, I was informed by Hodder that a serious deficiency of my Nunamiut work was the fact that I had not questioned the Eskimos about their attitudes toward dirt![16]). After listening for a long time, it was my turn to respond to the obvious challenge: 'What do you say to that, Professor Binford?' What could I say? The implication was clear: I had been complacent about, even sympathetic with, many of the deficiencies in archaeological reasoning listed. I tried to suggest that perhaps some of the accusations were falsely stated, did not apply to my own work, or were simply untrue and misleading. These protestations were either laughed away as obviously incorrect or an accusing finger was pointed to the fact that I had agreed that several of the criticized positions were faulty.

This incident at Cambridge is an example of a common form of argument used by the social philosophers. First the victim is asked when he is going to stop beating his wife. In reply, he states that in fact he does not beat his wife; however, he does agree with the accusers that one should *not* beat one's wife. Alas, such sterile discussions rarely result in enlightenment or intellectual growth. This whole procedure is a kind of poor man's exercise in the fallacy of the affirmation of the consequence. Nevertheless, it is a common occurrence among the philosophically oriented debaters, as opposed to those seeking the growth of archaeological science.

False syllogisms, then, are common, as are other questionable tactics used by the 'philosophers'. For instance, they frequently advocate the use of a particular observational language which, if used consistently, renders the world understandable in terms of their particular philosophical stance. This practice is of course tautological, but then the tactics of the social philosophers are not scientific. In contrast to their approach, scientific epistemology was initially explored as a means of evaluating ideas by appeal to *objective* descriptions of reality.[17] This book is about how we give meaning to archaeological experience and how in turn we have used and are using such experiences, converted into meaningful statements about the past, both to explore the past and to evaluate our ideas about it. Nevertheless, philosophy without science is simply culture and science without philosophy is sterile convention. We must, therefore, integrate the two approaches, because then, and only then, will we be able to create a productive discipline capable of making contributions to the cumulative growth of knowledge and understanding.

I
Translating the Archaeological Record

The Science of Archaeology

As I was riding on the bus not long ago, an elderly gentleman asked me what I did. I told him I was an archaeologist. He replied: 'That must be wonderful, for the only thing you have to be to succeed is lucky.' It took some time to convince him that his view of archaeology was not quite mine. He had the idea that the archaeologist 'digs up the past', that the successful archaeologist is one who discovers something not seen before, that all archaeologists spend their lives running about trying to make discoveries of this kind. This is a conception of science perhaps appropriate in the 19th century, but, at least in the terms in which I myself view archaeology, it does not describe the nature of archaeology as it is practiced today. In this chapter, I want to explain why I believe archaeologists are more than simply discoverers.

Like many others, the gentleman on the bus was quite mistaken in thinking of the archaeologist 'discovering the past'. *The archaeological record is here with us in the present.* It is out there, under the ground, quite likely to be hit by someone building a new road; it is very much part of our contemporary world and the observations we make about it are in the here and now, contemporary with ourselves. They are not direct observations that remain from the past (as in the case, say, of a historian who uses information from a 15th-century diary which conveys observations actually made by the author in the 15th century). Since observed facts about the archaeological record are contemporary, they do not in themselves inform us about the past at all. The archaeological record is not made up of symbols, words or concepts, but of material things and arrangements of matter. The only way in which we can understand their meaning – if you will, the way in which we can state the archaeological record in words – is by knowing something about how these material things came into being, about how they have been modified, and about how they acquired the characteristics we see today. That understanding is dependent upon a large body of knowledge which links human activities (i.e. *dynamics*) to the consequences of those activities that may be apparent in material things (i.e. *statics*). Indeed, one could think of archaeological facts as a sort of untranslated language, something that we need to 'decode' in order to move from simple statements about matter and its arrangement to statements of behavioral interest about the past.

The challenge that archaeology offers, then, is to take contemporary observations of static material things and, quite literally, translate them into statements about the dynamics of past ways of life and about the conditions in the past which brought into being the things that have survived for us to see. That challenge, most archaeologists feel, is enormous and one not easily met, for it demands of us a better understanding of our own interactions with the material world. After all, we rarely pay much attention to the ways in which our behavior may modify our material surroundings and leave clues about what happens in our daily lives; we simply do not view the world from that perspective. The archaeologist, however, must train himself to do so. He must become concerned with quite mundane matters. How do people dispose of their rubbish? How do they decide that a tool is worn out and whether they need to buy a new one? At what point do they decide that something is no longer useful and may be torn apart to be re-used for some other purpose? Information about decisions of this kind, decisions which modify the form and arrangement of material objects, is critical if archaeologists hope to be able to 'decode' and 'read' the archaeological record in terms of those aspects of the past that interest them.

How can we meet this challenge? Can we begin to accomplish our objectives simply by digging more sites and discovering new things, as the man on the bus implied? My answer must be a resounding 'No'. If (as I suspect) most people will find that surprising, it is because they imagine that archaeologists simply dig sites: they are unaware of all the research that must be done to help decode them. What suggestions can be made, then? Are the methods of history, or of the natural sciences, or of any other disciplines appropriate to the particular problems of archaeology?

The first idea we should reject is that archaeologists are simply strange historians working at a disadvantage: historians, that is, without written records. It has to be recognized how fundamentally different are the types of data used by the two disciplines. Whatever their specific interests in the past may be, historians work with the written record in one form or another – with chronicles, letters, diaries, or any other sort of literary record of the past which was purposefully produced by one person to transmit information to another. Yet, as we all know, letters home may be embellished; diarists in practice often write for some unknown future readership; bureaucratic records are all too susceptible to alteration for personal advantage. The fact that people are not always honest inevitably presents the historian with the problem of understanding the motives that individuals might have had for producing a written record of the past. Now archaeologists, at least at one level, rarely face this particular difficulty. For instance, suppose that during the excavation of a site a hearth were found next to an area filled with rubbish: it would be strange indeed to imagine that someone in the past had deliberately distorted that little piece of the archaeological record for his own purposes, or that he had modified what he threw away as a means of communication with someone in the future. This is not to say, of course, that man doesn't use material things for communication. The clothes or jewelry we wear convey our status or other aspects of ourselves; whether a man is a policeman or a fireman is indicated by the wearing of a uniform that carries very specific information about his job. But, while material things most certainly do communicate coded information, they are rarely coded for the purposes of deceit. The archaeologist works with a very different kind of material than does the historian, at least from the standpoint of the symbolic and communication systems that man employs.

Certain historians have proposed that the best method for finding out about the past is empathy[1] – that is, merely to imagine what actions or circumstances would bring about the conditions observed. For instance, I might find a hearth bounded by stones, with charcoal in the center and broken bones and rocks to the side. So I say to myself: 'I am a man. If I were sitting at a hearth, what might I have been doing that would have resulted in the things that I now see?' At this stage I may well be able to come up with a set of ideas about what the past was like. But getting such ideas is just the first step, involving the use of imagination and our cumulative understanding of the relationship between human behavior and material objects. Far more important is how we *evaluate* these ideas. How do we know that there are not other circumstances that could have happened in the past that might also have produced the patterns we observe in the archaeological record today? Without some methodology for evaluating ideas, we are in the position of having a free hand to generate lots of stories about the past, but not having any means of knowing whether these stories are accurate.

Is the best way to approach the challenge, as some archaeologists have suggested, to follow in the footsteps of others who have gone along the road before us: to adopt, for instance, the methods of the social sciences? The suggestion sounds beguiling. But we should remember that the social sciences were developed to deal with dynamics, with interactions in a social setting. Archaeologists, as I have already emphasized, do not observe social facts; they observe material facts, all of them contemporary, so that the procedures of the social sciences are in a practical sense inappropriate for archaeology. Archaeology must face up to the nature of the data it employs and the uniqueness of the challenge it faces – how to get from the present to the past. What is needed is a science of the archaeological record, one that deals with, rather than ignores, the special problems we encounter in trying to use that record to learn about the past.

If we are not really historians or social scientists, what about the methods of the natural sciences? This is a rather more germane suggestion, for there is no expectation among natural scientists that their observed facts will 'speak for themselves'. Physicists, chemists, biologists, and so on, do not imagine that observed relations between things have meanings which are self-evident. They are continuously engaged in *giving* meaning to such observations and then evaluating how useful those assigned meanings actually are in practice. Surely, this is the position in which the archaeologist finds himself: giving meaning to the (contemporary) archaeological facts he observes and then trying to evaluate how realistic his picture of the past might be. It is for this reason that I have always advocated that archaeology should adopt the methods of the natural sciences.[2] They are the only techniques of which I am aware that can help the archaeologist in his special and peculiar dilemma: the availability only of contemporary observations about material things whose causes are unavailable for observation.

What implications does this conclusion have for the procedures we follow in digging a site? Do we need to worry about what archaeological remains mean, before we actually excavate them? If so, does this bias the results of excavation? Certainly, the archaeologist-as-discoverer must be concerned with such questions. We would not know anything at all about the past, of course, if our energies were entirely devoted to developing a perfect research methodology and we failed to collect any archaeological facts about the past. Yet, on the other hand, if we had a complete archaeological record and no way to give meaning to it, we still would be no nearer to knowing the past. Obviously, the two sides of archaeological research must necessarily develop together, but that is easier said than done. We may do too much digging, without enough research to allow us to interpret the things we observe; or else we may be doing too much methodological research and find when we actually get around to digging a site that the things we need to observe just aren't there. Archaeologists are often heard to say 'Well, *X* is a theory man', or '*Y* is a field man', or to level the criticism that 'So-and-so digs lots of sites very well, but he doesn't interpret them very well.' The message for archaeology is the need for balanced growth between the development of techniques which permit us to make accurate inferences about the past, and the making of archaeological observations which provide us with the materials for interpretation. I don't think you can dig a site very well unless you also know what potential the excavated data might have for making inferences about the past. For example, if I did not know about radiocarbon dating techniques,[3] I would have little reason to save charcoal from an excavation; it is only once I know that the analysis of uncontaminated charcoal samples can give an independent measure of elapsed time that I realize the need for collecting material of this kind and keeping accurate records about it. In short, good excavation techniques depend on an awareness of potential ways of making inferences about the past. But excavation techniques themselves are what continually lead us into more and different kinds of methodological research, because we always find things we do not understand and about which we are curious, things that demand further research before we can use them in making inferences about the past.

Archaeology, then, is an interactive discipline, one that cannot grow without striking a balance between theoretical and practical concerns. Archaeologists need to be continuously self-critical: that is why the field is such a lively one and why archaeologists are forever arguing among themselves about who is right on certain issues. Self-criticism leads to change, but is itself a challenge – one which archaeology perhaps shares only with palaeontology and a few other fields whose ultimate concern is making inferences about the past on the basis of contemporary things. So archaeology is not a field that can study the past *directly*, nor can it be one that merely involves discovery, as the man on the bus suggested. On the contrary, it is a field wholly dependent upon inference to the past from things found in the contemporary world. Archaeological data, unfortunately, do not carry self-evident meanings. How much easier our work would be if they did!

Letting the Present Serve the Past

We are all familiar with the cliché that we study the past in order to learn more about the present. We are less comfortable, perhaps, with the idea that we study the present in order to understand the past. At least, many people seem not quite willing to accept the concept of archaeologists going out to live with the Australian Aborigines[4] or following !Kung Bushmen on their hunting trips.[5] These are not exactly the sorts of activities in which archaeologists are supposed to be engaged. But, alas, many of us are so engaged nearly full-time, at least during some phase of our careers. In fact, there is even a project underway in the United States, in the modern city of Tucson, Arizona, where the rubbish disposal practices of modern urban dwellers are being studied;[6] the archaeologists walk around with the garbage men! I take the fact that such things are now being done as a sign that the field of archaeology is growing and becoming more sophisticated. As a result, it should offer the world more enlightening and provocative notions of our past than we have ever been able to provide before from archaeological facts.

The archaeological record, as I have already noted, is a contemporary phenomenon and observations we make about it are not 'historical' statements. We need sites that preserve for us things from the past; but, equally, we need the theoretical tools to give meaning to these things when they are found. Identifying them accurately and recognizing their contexts in past behavior depends upon a kind of research that cannot be conducted in the archaeological record itself. That is, if we intend to investigate the relationship between statics and dynamics, we must be able to observe both aspects simultaneously; and the only place we *can* observe dynamics is in the modern world, in the here and now.

Let me give an example. One very common class of finds made by archaeologists is stone tools. Since we hope to gain a better understanding of the context in which men make, use and dispose of stone tools, it would naturally be very helpful to see some people using them. This, indeed, was the concern that sent me into the central desert of Australia several years ago, to do fieldwork among a group of people who knew about stone tools and periodically did still use them for various purposes. I hoped to be able to relate information about the actual behavior of these people (the dynamics) to the consequences of that behavior, as seen in the distribution, design and modifications of stone tools (the statics). Some of this work is described briefly in Chapter 7. My aim was to study the relation between statics and dynamics in a modern setting. If understood in great detail, it would give us a kind of Rosetta Stone: a way of 'translating' the static, material stone tools found on an archaeological site into the vibrant life of a group of people who in fact left them there.

The linkages, then, between what we find and the conditions that brought these finds into being can only be studied among living peoples. I myself have worked on this linkage problem with the Nunamiut, a group of Eskimo caribou hunters in Alaska,[7] and with the Navajo, who are sheep herders in the American Southwest;[8] and I have several students working with the !Kung Bushmen in southern Africa. All these pieces of fieldwork are designed to study in a direct way the linkages betweeen the things we find as archaeologists and the various behaviors that resulted in the production, modification and eventual disposal of those things.[9]

Experimental archaeology[10] represents another area of research in which the present is used to serve the past, with the aim of providing insights into the accurate interpretation of the archaeological record. A great deal of this sort of work was pioneered in Great Britain. It involves the experimental re-creation of happenings or processes that we know must have occurred in the past, in order to observe what the archaeological outcome would have been. For instance, if a house burns down[11] and erosion of the remains takes place over a long period, what would be the outcome as seen by archaeologists? In what ways would the original structure and its contents have been modified? Those are questions we can tackle by experiment. Research in this vein allows us to evaluate the degree to which we can accept what we see as directly referable to the past or as something distorted in various ways by intervening processes. Another important role for experimentation is in attempts to re-create the skills of ancient craftsmen: that is, teaching ourselves to make stone tools,[12] pottery or other products of prehistoric technologies and using those skills in different situations to solve problems. Once again, such work can offer genuine insights into the archaeological record. I think it is safe to predict that archaeologists will soon come to employ such experimental methods much more than they have in the past, as they begin to

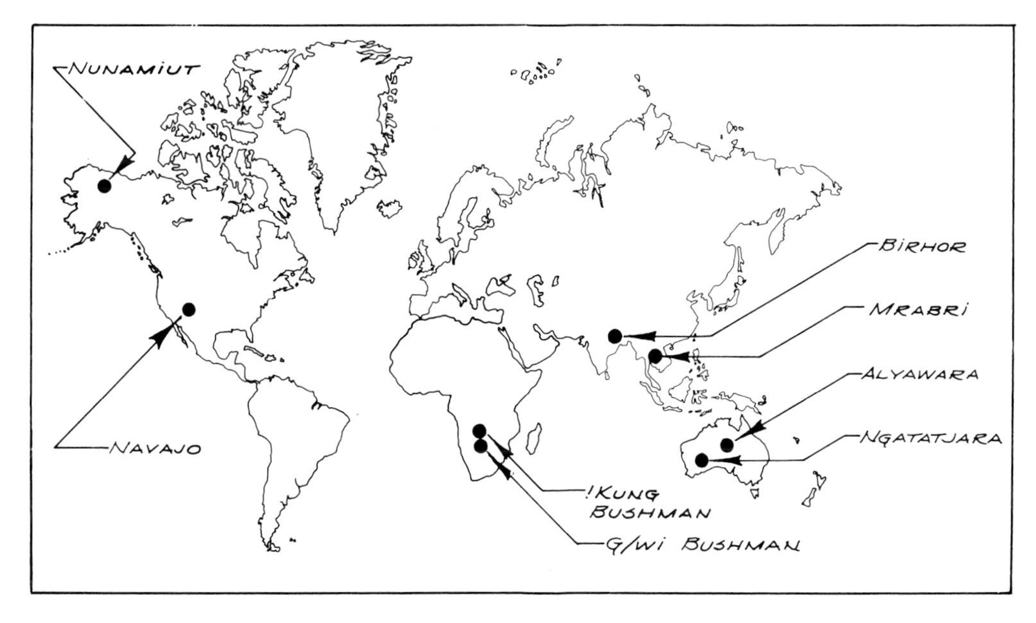

1 Distribution of some contemporary groups mentioned in the text.

realize that merely finding something does little good unless they can give meaning to it.

Historical documents constitute a further major source of information which archaeologists have only just begun to tap. The object of 'ethnoarchaeological' research, of course, is to seek a kind of control on the formation of the archaeological record. By living in a site and observing the various activities of its occupants, the archaeologist hopes to see certain archaeologically observable patterns, knowing what activities brought them into being. Now simply being there and looking is not the only way we can get that kind of control, for there exists a wealth of written documents about man's actions in the past. Often historical records can be used not only to identify former living places, but also to tell us what went on there – what level of craft specialization existed there, for instance, or something of the former social organization of the site. Armed with controls of this sort about the dynamics of the site, we are in a position to excavate the site and relate what we find to reports of the activities and processes that took place long ago. This use of history as a form of experimental control is still in its infancy, but we can surely expect considerable development in this direction.[13] Clearly, the number of people who still make stone tools for hunting and follow a fully mobile lifestyle is decreasing every day. Future generations of archaeologists will be afforded very limited opportunities to go and study stone tool users, as I have done. But so long as we have historical documents which preserve observations, made by people actually present, about the dynamics of places in the past, we have the option of excavating those places and, walking through history, as it were, alongside an historical character, trying to relate what we find in the ground to what he reports as having occurred there.

Naturally, the written word is not the only type of historical document that exists: it is fortunate that, at least for the last century or so, we have had the capability of taking photographs. There exists a wealth of photographs taken at the turn of the century, when there were far more peoples living technologically unsophisticated lives than there are today. How can we take such pictures and convert them into usable archaeological information? My own current research in this area suggests that it is not at all easy. You need to know a number of details such as the focal length of the camera lens, in order to convert an oblique photograph (that is, one taken by a hand-held camera looking out across the landscape) into a map which is in any way analogous to the ones an archaeologist would produce when digging a site. When these technical problems are solved, as I am quite certain they will be, we will be able to make much greater use of the tens of thousands of ethnographic photographs taken in the relatively recent past. Photographs, of course, have a wonderful immediacy: you can see a real person from the past sitting right there in front of you and see what he was actually doing. Consequently, one can relate the spatial relationships of people to hearths, of houses to people, of hearths to houses, all in a behavioral context that is normally difficult to establish, even with the help of the written word. With photographs, one gets a glimpse of past behavior and some sort of 'map' simultaneously, an enormous advantage on which archaeologists will surely capitalize in the future.

These, then, are three important areas – the study of contemporary peoples, the creation of experimental situations where we can control causes in order to study effects, and the use of historical documents of various sorts – which contemporary archaeology has only just begun to develop to any significant degree. As they become more important, the popular image of the archaeologist in a pith helmet discovering a new tomb will give way to that of an eclectic, someone who pokes his nose into almost every domain of human activity with material consequences which might be reflected in the archaeological record.

The Big Questions of Archaeology

What is it that we want to know about the past? It is always difficult to determine whether a suggestion is a rational one, if you don't know what it is that you are trying to accomplish: that is as true of archaeology as of anything else. So what we want to know about the past strongly influences how archaeologists go about conducting excavations and investigating the archaeological record. Unless they have some clear ideas in this respect, it is difficult for them to know how to approach archaeological data or what kind of research to conduct to interpret them. Obviously, then, what we think the past was like affects archaeological research and the development of the field as a whole. It may be useful to discuss briefly not what we know already about the past, but rather what we would *like* to know from the archaeological record: what are some of the Big Questions about man's past that we can hope to answer through archaeological research?

Adopting a typically archaeological approach, let's begin at the beginning! I believe it is extremely important to have some idea of what the behavioral characteristics of our earliest ancestors might have been. We have their bones, of course: fossils of early men, some of them as much as 3 to 6 million years old. But when did the typical *behavior*, unique to you and me as members of the same species, come into being? The answer is that we simply don't know. We have learned when the size of our brain case changed, when our body size changed, how the shape of our pelvis has changed. It is not yet possible, however, to speak with confidence about when man began to use language, when he began to live in small monogamous families, or when he began to share food among adults. And it is these characteristics, after all, which distinguish us from most of the rest of the animal world. How old is such typically human behavior which we all take for granted? What in fact were our earliest ancestors like? These seem to me to be central issues of archaeological research.

Certain archaeologists are currently engaged in a controversy over the question whether already 2 million years ago man was hunting animals, eating meat regularly, sharing food and living in base camps.[14] Such characteristics take on significance when viewed in the context of animal behavior in general: primates other than man, for instance, tend to sleep in trees rather than on the ground and eat where food is to be found rather than where they sleep, as man does. When did a terrestrial way of life involving hunting and food-sharing begin? Was it the hunting of animals, or some other form of behavior, that was critical for the evolution of language? What caused these changes and how should we explain them? Only when we have established *what* actually happened in the past can we begin to ask *why* it happened. And only archaeology, I think, can enlighten us on such central issues. The comparative biological study of the human fossil record cannot by itself answer our questions. The answers will come from the integration of a wide variety of archaeological facts that have survived: not simply information about the anatomy of our ancestors, for example, but also where their skeletal fossils were found in relation to their stone tools and the by-products of their meals. Past arguments about such matters, however, have frequently not been very sound.

For instance, most archaeological textbooks assert that early man was a hunter of animals. The basis of the argument is that sites such as Olduvai Gorge in East 4

Africa, which have produced the earliest hominid fossils and stone tools, have also yielded a profusion of animal bones; and since these bones are in association with stone tools, they probably represent the meals of early man. But this is not necessarily so. The sites where we find these very ancient stone tools are geological deposits created by natural agencies, not by man. Man was simply present in the environment during the time that the natural processes which formed the sites were going on and there is no necessary reason to suppose that all the finds at such sites refer to the same events. A recent, widely publicized set of finds at another East African site consists of hominid footprints preserved in rock about 3 million years old.[15] They were not the only footprints in the deposit: there were also those of elephant, giraffe, guineafowl, even tracks of little worms. Now it would surely be rather absurd to argue that the association of hominid and elephant footprints implies that early man was herding elephants. Yet precisely the same kind of logic is used by archaeologists who would argue from finds of stone tools and giraffe bones in the same deposit that man must have killed the giraffe. In fact, the giraffe may have died there from natural causes, while the stone tool was used and left at the site hundreds of years later, perhaps in the context of cutting plant material. If archaeologists want to understand the past correctly, they will have to solve this problem of separating the various processes and behaviors that lead to the formation of a deposit; these are matters that I discuss in rather more detail in Chapters 2 and 3.

Another interesting controversy in archaeology revolves around the question whether the characteristics we take to be quintessentially human all came into being at once. Or were they *emergent*, in the sense that one characteristic came into being in one context, and another in a different context? Is the evolution of the very essence of man, so to speak, best considered as some kind of 'quantum leap' or rather as a process of accretional growth? Once again, we simply don't know yet. It has been argued, for example, that man's adoption of an upright posture on two legs constituted such a quantum leap, because it freed the hands for use; use of the hands made possible tools; tools made possible language; and language paved the way to many changes in social organization, such as food-sharing and altruistic behavior. That is an evolutionary path about which I am rather doubtful. Personally, I feel we should not underestimate the degree to which planning was necessary in early man's hunting activities (i.e. solving the problem of what to eat during the season of the year when plants are not growing). It is in the context of hunting, perhaps, that information storage and processing began to play a greater role in our own evolution than in that of other primates. My point, however, is that the challenge of investigating the past is to devise ways of discovering whether such statements are correct or not.

Among the most important questions we can hope to examine through archaeological research, then, are when the behavioral characteristics we think distinguish us from other animals came into being and how we can understand their development. A second, related group of problems is one which remains – quite justifiably – a subject of fascination and speculation for many people besides archaeologists. It is concerned with the origins of agriculture and the conditions that led man to settle into ways of life which were much more sedentary than at any time in his mobile hunting and gathering past. Why did man stop moving, settle down and begin to intensify his food production within smaller and smaller pieces of space? That, after all, is what agriculture is really about. Why did it apparently happen in many different places in both the Old and New Worlds? And why did these changes all occur in such different regions within what is, from an archaeological standpoint, a very limited time period of 2,000 years or so? In Chapter 8, I make some suggestions about the direction we might take in seeking answers to these questions. If we could understand even a few of these things, I believe we would be beginning to grasp something of the distinctive operation of our adaptation, our way of life and our particular niche in the animal world. I say this because the adoption of agriculture and sedentism constitutes a most distinctive set of changes: it represents a major re-adaptation of a species without, as far as we can see, major accompanying biological changes. For this second, crucial set of Big Questions for archaeological investigation there is, of course, practically no written historical information to help us.

The third problem area is again one of great general fascination: the origins of civilization. The political systems under which most of us live and the complex urban lives which we nearly all lead are still further removed from the mobile hunting and gathering way of life that clearly provided the context in which our biology was moulded. So what brought about this kind of lifestyle? What made agriculturally based societies move in the direction of increasingly complicated political and bureaucratic types of organization? What caused the tremendous increase in specialization – in crafts, in social roles, in task performance – that characterizes a modern city, or an ancient one, for that matter?

This is necessarily an area where archaeology begins to link up with history, political philosophy and many other branches of the social sciences, for we can still see some of these processes going on in remote parts of the modern world not yet affected by the industrial revolution. The archaeologist, then, can bring his own data in this realm to bear on problems held in common with the other social sciences. I was interested to see that, at each of the three international conferences I happened to attend during 1981, the focus of discussion was the appearance of complex political systems, the possible role of trade in bringing them into being, and the extent to which monopolies over production do, or do not, affect the level of political development (matters on which I give some of my own views in Chapter 9). The point of interest is that these discussions almost exclusively involved *archaeologists*. Such questions have certainly been addressed in the past by historians, by political philosophers, and by many others besides; but archaeology is now beginning to participate in the debate on equal terms with the more historically oriented fields.

Archaeology, therefore, starts in the remote past at the very beginnings of our biological history, a time period for which our ignorance about human behavior is almost total, and it brings us all the way up to the complexities of the modern world, on which archaeological discussions may have some bearing. Such is the span of archaeology! Do archaeologists offer any specifically *archaeological* perspectives that differentiate them from other fields, in dealing with, say, the origins of sedentism or the appearance of complex political systems? I think the answer must inevitably be 'Yes'. Archaeologists start with material objects and, quite naturally, adopt a materialist viewpoint; they often advance arguments of a pragmatic nature in contexts where psychological or motivational forms of argument are much more common. They can be of service, if only by providing a concrete basis for certain high-flown debates in the modern world.

The fascinating Big Questions I have touched on above and which I discuss later in this book depend for their answers on an interaction between observation on the one hand, and research to give meaning to observations on the other. This generates a momentum of its own and that momentum is growing, like the discipline of archaeology as a whole: there are many more archaeologists today than there were fifty years ago. Consequently, there exist many areas of research which are no longer simply pipe-dreams about what archaeology might achieve, but very realistic problems that can be addressed intelligently and that can be solved. In place of vague generalities about the past, we can expect to obtain reliable information. Yet our Big Questions cannot be solved by working on a small scale in our own country or province: they require research spanning huge time periods and broad geographical areas. The archaeological research community is increasingly an international one and the archaeological literature has grown to embrace many languages. Really exciting research *is* in progress. Solutions to our main problems are not far away, and in some cases they are within our grasp.

Part I
WHAT WAS IT LIKE?

What was the past like? How did men once live? How variable were their lifestyles? Such questions are perhaps among those most commonly asked and readily appreciated, by archaeologists and laymen alike. They have also come to be associated in the archaeological literature with one of the aims of archaeology: 'reconstructing the past'. If we are to achieve any part of this aim, however, we must develop rigorous methodology for interpreting archaeological remains. In this first section, I hope to demonstrate the need for interpretive techniques specific to archaeology and to discuss, by way of example, some of the problems involved when we ask what it was like about 1 million years ago, during the period of our early hominid ancestors.

Although the goal of reconstructing the past has frequently been associated with challenges to the field of archaeology made by the American archaeologist Walter Taylor in 1948,[1] his aim was actually very different from what many archaeologists have in mind.[2] Taylor was concerned with the construction of past 'culture contexts', which he considered as a state of mind or 'configuration':

> *I believe that there would have been much less of this uncertainty if the archaeologists had viewed their material in some such light as that proposed in the present study, if they had viewed culture traits as ideas and not as material objects, if they had envisioned cultural behaviour as mediate between ideas and material objects, in short if they had recognized the difference between their own empirical, descriptive groupings and the cultural and culture categories pertinent to the peoples they were studying.[3]*

As this passage indicates, Taylor was not advocating that archaeological remains should be investigated in terms of the mechanical and behavioral processes which brought them into being, both formally and contextually, but instead that they should be considered in the intellectual milieu in which they operated. He clearly had in mind a model of 'mental templates' representing the 'ideas which lay behind the artifacts'.[4]

In the following chapters, I wish to demonstrate that we often seek to know certain facts about the past which have little, if anything, to do with ideas, mental configurations, or even culture in the strict sense. In order to study certain kinds of behavior, there is no need to discover the ideas responsible for the artifacts or for the patterns observed in the archaeological record. Sometimes our questions about what it was like in the past involve finding out the roles which our ancestors played in their environments: the information required will therefore be behavioral and ecological, not ideological. In fact, it is important to point out that archaeologists do not always necessarily attempt to recreate a 'technicolor version' of all aspects of man's early life. A complete reconstruction of the past is a largely unrealistic goal. The attention of scholars who espouse it tends to be biased toward spectacular archaeological sites with extraordinary preservation – little 'Pompeiis' where time has been stopped because of unusual circumstances.[5] By and large, it is these scholars who consider that the nature of the archaeological record limits the types of interpretations and reconstructions which archaeologists can make. This has been particularly true when the goals of 'reconstructionists' are linked with a strict empiricist or inductive epistemology which dictates that we can only generalize about those parts of the past which leave direct traces.

Although Taylor worked in terms of a more or less idealist approach, he did recognize that the reconstruction of the past from archaeological remains was based on inference. He also felt that, if archaeologists were to go beyond what he considered to be sterile descriptions of the archaeological record itself to make interesting statements about the past, they had to make inferences. Taylor named this inferential procedure the 'conjunctive approach' – the linking of empirical observations of the archaeological record to 'phenomena . . . inferred to have been pertinent to the culture and people under investigation.'[6] His was not a totally new idea; previous scholars had also noted that the past is 'created' by archaeologists using observations made in the present and that it is inferred or constructed in terms of the data which archaeologists feel are significant. In contrast, researchers who feel intellectually secure solely with the view that we can only generalize from empirical observations suppose that inferences are to be avoided altogether. Taylor countered the arguments of these empiricists and made an inspiring appeal to archaeologists to go further with their data; but unfortunately he offered no guidelines about how to proceed in practice. He explored neither methods for making accurate inferences, nor for evaluating or verifying them once they had been made.[7]

Nevertheless, archaeologists have always made inferences in order to reconstruct the past, regardless of the quality of the methods used to generate them. In this section, I will review the history of some important research on early man and, in so doing, I will illustrate ways in which some archaeologists, myself included, are now trying to develop methods for making inferences that are more reliable than those proposed previously. If our efforts are successful, someday we may really know something of what it was like in the past.

2

Man the Mighty Hunter?

What sort of creatures were our ancient ancestors who inhabited the African savannah about 2 million years ago? It is only in relatively recent times that we have obtained any concrete knowledge of the beings from whom modern men evolved, where they lived, or even what they looked like. So the methodological challenge of learning about their behavior is itself something new. Archaeologists would be doing well, I think, if their methods could let us know what life was like in such a remote era. The Lower Palaeolithic, in fact, is a sort of testing ground for archaeological methods and techniques: just how far can they inform us about a past so ancient that we can scarcely imagine it realistically on the basis of modern experience? In this chapter I try to give some feeling for the changing intellectual climate in this field of research and suggest a framework for analysis which may prove fruitful.

Man the Bloodthirsty Killer: the Views of Dart[1]

About sixty years ago a South African anatomist, Raymond Dart, was holding practical classes in Pleistocene anatomy. As an exercise, Dart asked his students to search in the local countryside for fossils and broken bones on which they might use their new skills of identification. One young lady brought in information regarding what she thought was an interesting bone. This led shortly thereafter to a major discovery in a limestone quarry near Taung, 130 kilometres north of Kimberley, South Africa. Dart later recalled the chills that ran up and down his spine as he saw for the first time what is now a very famous fossil known as the 'Taung baby', a small juvenile individual of a very ancient form of man. Today we know that its age is probably greater than 2.7 million years, but at the time no one knew how old it might be. In fact, no one had any idea that some of our ancestors might even have looked like that. Right from the start, I think, Dart was convinced that the Taung fossil had an important place on the ancestral tree of man, but his first published anatomical descriptions of the skull led many European anatomists to disagree with the identification and to suggest instead that it was the fossil of a chimpanzee or of some other animal. Dart made a trip to

England and elsewhere in Europe, bringing his little fossil with him for examination, and there arose a major controversy as to whether it was, or was not, in the ancestral line of man.

To Dart it seemed obvious that there was no agreed anatomical basis for making a judgment one way or the other: the fossil skull, with its preserved brain case, was extraordinary, something so different that no clear-cut criteria existed for deciding if it was indeed a fossil man. It was while he was in England that Dart began to change his way of thinking about the problem. The question 'Is this a man?' could not be addressed solely from an anatomical standpoint, because the most important thing about early man was his *behavior* rather than what he looked like. One thing unique to man, he reasoned, was that he is the only primate that eats meat regularly. If we were to find clear evidence of primate predation, that would itself tell us that we were dealing with man (or an ancestor of man) and would allow us – assuming we were lucky enough to find the bones – to discover what the anatomy of early man was like. Similarly, man is unique in making and using fire. So if traces of fire were to be found in association with fossils, we would know man had been present. The same logic applied to man's manufacture of tools. Dart used several other criteria besides, but these three were the most important: they defined man not anatomically, but behaviorally.

This reasoning led Dart towards a kind of research very different from that then current in palaeoanthropology. Previously, anatomists had tried to learn about man's earliest history by the investigation of anatomical facts, archaeologists by studying stone tools. What Dart was saying, effectively, was this. Man is behaviorally unique. What traces would this unique behavior leave behind? Finding bones associated with the behavioral traces of the kind expected ought to provide a way of discovering something about man's physical appearance in the remote past – which was, of course, the issue in dispute. Thus, in the years either side of World War II, Dart studied in great detail the huge quantities of non-primate animal bones from various deposits in southern Africa, particularly the limeworks at Makapansgat. He did so in the hope of determining whether or not the creature responsible for the bone accumulations, if indeed they were the bone refuse of animals that some creature had eaten, might be early man.

History will judge, I believe, that Dart got a little carried away on this quest. In fossil-bearing deposits at another site, for instance, he observed some dark stains, from which he inferred that fire had been present and therefore that man must also have been present. Consequently, the fossil later found at Makapansgat was given the cumbersome name *Australopithecus prometheus*, or 'fire-using southern ape-man'.[2] If (and only if) Dart's interpretation of the stains as hearths were correct, one of his criteria for recognizing human behavior would have been satisfied and would therefore have supported his view that the fossil man-apes from the deposits were ancestors of man.

2 *Our Heritage? Hunters of the Plio-Pleistocene boundary.* 'Mighty hunters' are depicted killing animals and dragging back both food parts and bones (for later use as tools) to a 'home base' in a cave or rock fissure. This scenario implies a strict division of labor: the 'aggressive' males go out after food, while the females and children stay behind waiting for the male providers to return. (Pencil drawing by Iva Ellen Morris.)

His studies of the bones went further than this, however, and led him to the recognition of some interesting new patterns not previously noted: *the bones in these deposits were not present in the frequencies at which they occur in the anatomies of modern animals.*[3] We know without any controversy, of course, how many bones there are in an antelope or lion skeleton, because those animals are still around and we can actually count the numbers of different kinds of bones in their skeletons today. So we have a model, a set of expectations, to use in asking if the archaeological record is the way it ought to be if it was composed of whole, unmodified animal skeletons. When Dart used this reasoning to examine his bone deposits, he found that the patterns observed did not conform to these expectations at all: there were lots of fragments of skulls, mandibles, and lower legs, but markedly fewer ribs, vertebrae and pelves. How could observed patterning of this kind be explained?

Using that most important of human resources – his imagination – Dart supposed that the reason for the differential bone frequencies was that some ancestor of man was hunting and killing animals at a distance from where he lived; that some anatomical parts were left behind at the location of the kill, while others were brought back to be eaten; and, most significant of all, that some bones were carried home to be used as tools. Suddenly, we have a whole new model of the past, a new notion of man! For if Dart's imagined picture to account for what he saw were correct, then man at this period of great antiquity behaved much like you or I. He hunted (sometimes in particularly violent ways), he had a permanent home base, he slept repeatedly in the same place, he carried food back to his sleeping area, he lived in houses of some sort – all behavioral features distinctive of man and quite unlike those of other primates. By combining observation with imagination, a picture had emerged not merely of a very ancient ancestral form of man, but of those ancestors as mighty hunters, 'confirmed killers':[4]

> Man's predecessors . . . seized living quarries by violence, battered them to death, tore apart their broken bodies, dismembered them limb from limb, slaking their ravenous thirst with the hot blood of victims and greedily devouring livid writhing flesh.[5]

There was a further source of variation in this bone material that seemed to support the argument. Dart reasoned that it is only natural that man should experiment with objects near at hand and, if these small-bodied ancestors of ours were indeed predatory killers, then some of the most likely objects to have experimented with would have been the bones of dead prey. That man's first tools should be bone clubs, bludgeons and saws makes sense, Dart thought, because animal bones have natural properties that are directly usable. An antelope's lower jaw can be used without modification as a saw; its dense upper limb bones make nice daggers when broken, since they tend to break with a spiral fracture producing pointed ends. Surely, our ancient human ancestors, those mighty hunters, would have used such bones as tools?

Doubts about Dart

The interpretive picture outlined above appeared in the literature largely during the 1950s,[6] but it did not become widely known at that time. The man mainly responsible for its dissemination and popularization was the writer Robert Ardrey, who adopted Dart's views after a trip to Africa: his first book *African Genesis*, which presented a graphic depiction of our early ancestors as bloodthirsty killers, became a bestseller and was translated into several languages.[7] This model of the distant past also appealed strongly to psychologists such as Konrad Lorenz, whose work on human aggression was influential at about this time.[8] On the other hand many people did seriously question Dart's behavioral model of the past, but it was not until later that anyone actually executed research designed to evaluate it. As I mentioned at the outset, the development of our conception of early man is a contemporary phenomenon, something very much of our own times.

One of the earliest direct challenges to Dart's ideas came – appropriately enough – from physical anthropologists. How, they asked, could this little animal *Australopithecus*, only 90 pounds in weight, have been a mighty hunter capable of accumulating all the bones that Dart had been studying? Why could some other agent not have been responsible? A paper published in 1957[9] suggested that *Australopithecus*, far from being the hunter, was the hunted; that he had provided a useful meal for the African spotted hyena and that the actions of hyenas, not of men, were the cause of the bone accumulations.

Now this was a most interesting proposition that triggered some really profitable research. If it is being argued that the bones were accumulated by hyenas, then it is a simple matter to check whether hyenas do, in fact, do this today. So A. R. Hughes, a colleague of Dart, excavated pits in a hyena layer near the Kruger National Park in South Africa; finding no bones in them, except those of a single tortoise, he concluded that hyenas did *not* accumulate bones and that an explanation of that kind was not a valid objection to Dart's hypothesis.[10] On the other hand, there existed a sizeable literature in palaeontology suggesting that they *did*. Many strata in British Pleistocene sites, for instance, had traditionally been interpreted as hyena layers. Even Roman generals had complained of hyenas digging up the bodies of dead soldiers and eating them.[11] Some of Dart's opponents felt that Hughes's work was insufficient to decide the issue definitively one way or the other. So they began to gather relevant information on the behavior of hyenas and other animals.[12] It became increasingly clear that, under certain conditions (and even then not invariably), hyenas *did* accumulate bones. But spotted hyenas did so more often than brown hyenas. Their behavior varied in different settings (for instance, whether or not they were competing fiercely with lions). Hyenas, leopards and lions each do different kinds of things with bones under different circumstances. Obviously, we needed to know much more about these animals if we were to understand their potential role as the agents contributing to deposits containing evidence of man himself.

The public image of the archaeologist is hardly that of a man who goes into the field to observe hyena behavior. But much of the important work on animal behavior starting in the late 1950s was in fact done by archaeologists. Their own researches had confronted them squarely with the problem: what processes in the past led to the formation of the archaeological deposits we observe today? To be sure, archaeological observations were available; there were patterns in the archaeological material that hinted at the causal regularities that might have brought the record into being; use of the imagination could even suggest what some of these might be. But there existed no method of evaluating these ideas. It was only a couple of decades ago that archaeology in Africa (and elsewhere) began to enter a new and very different era, in which research was oriented towards techniques which might allow ideas about the past to be tested.[13]

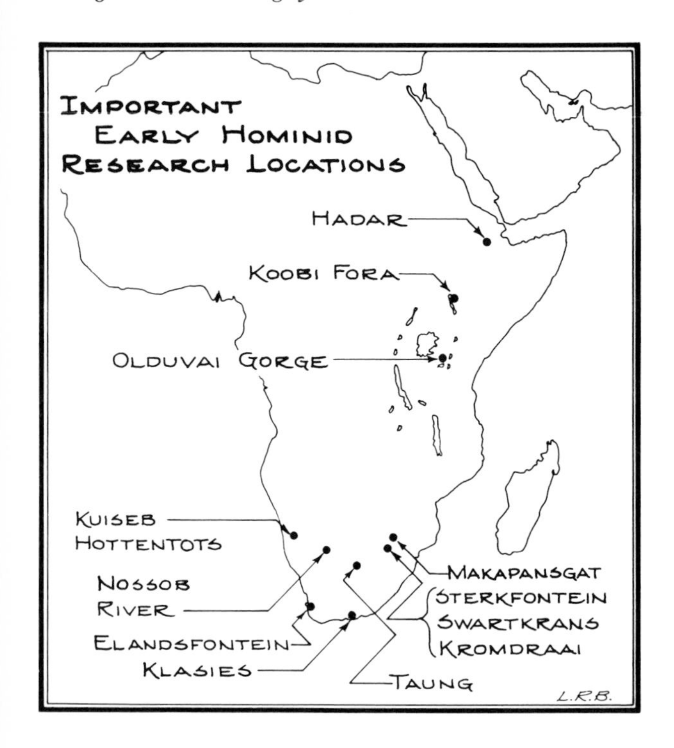

3 Distribution of some important early hominid research locations in Africa.

Leakey's Alternative

At about the same time as the emergence of these methodological interests, another man began to make discoveries that were crucial for our understanding of early hominid behavior. Louis Leakey, despite his immense investment of energy and his great interest in early man, had been unsuccessful in recovering major fossil material in over thirty years of work. He had carried out extensive surveys in Olduvai Gorge in East Africa in the 1930s; he had examined large areas at a major Middle Palaeolithic site at Olorgesailie in the 1940s, using Italian prisoners-of-war to expand his labor force; and after the war, he had reinstituted survey work – always with the great dream of finding some fossils that would inform us in significant ways about the nature of human evolution.

4

The dream was realized in 1959, when Leakey's wife Mary spotted a little facet of bone exposed at the edge of very ancient deposits at Olduvai and recognized it as a man-like creature's tooth arc, resting upside down in the ground.[14] Excavation of the deposit followed almost immediately and revealed the extraordinary fossil skull which Leakey called *Zinjanthropus*. It was clear from the moment it emerged that this skull was that of a creature quite different from those initially described by Dart. The latter were relatively small and gracile, with jaws of moderate size. But the jaw of this specimen was something to behold: the surface area of the third molar tooth was almost as big as an American quarter or a British two pence coin. The jaw muscles must have been enormous, because there was not enough space on the surface of the head to attach them all and an upstanding ridge of bone, known as the sagittal crest, was necessary for further muscle attachments (just as it is on a dog's skull). In these and many other respects, *Zinjanthropus* did not look at all like modern man; yet it seemed clear that he walked upright, had bipedal posture and a large brain case. The Leakeys' discovery of this 'robust Australopithecine' at Olduvai further complicated already complex anatomical arguments. Similar forms had been found earlier in South Africa, but their relative chronology was not certain. Were they ancestral to each other or were they largely contemporary?

Importantly, however, the fossil skull of *Zinjanthropus* lay in a deposit alongside what were unquestionably stone tools. Unlike Dart's bone 'tools', no imagination was required to see tools. Archaeologists already had well-developed criteria for recognizing tools produced by the hand of man from stone, and most people qualified to judge agreed that the stones found in the deposits with the '*Zinj*' skull were indeed tools. So there could be no argument that one, at least, of Dart's criteria had been met.

Here then was an opportunity to see if Dart's picture of 'man the mighty hunter' was correct, for the deposits contained a hominid in association not only

4 A view of Olduvai Gorge at the first fault. (Photo courtesy of Diane Gifford.)

with stone tools, but also with a lot of bones of other creatures. In the first reports to the media in 1959, Leakey announced that the associated bones were those of little birds, birds' eggs, tortoises and baby pigs.[15] The impression received was of early man as essentially vegetarian, but a vegetarian who occasionally ate meat as opportunity afforded. If he happened to run into a bird's nest, he stole the eggs; if he chanced to step on a lizard, then he probably ate it; if he came upon a pig which had recently given birth, he would probably steal the young ones. As Washburn and Howell commented:

> The extraordinary new discovery at Olduvai Gorge has clarified some . . . important questions concerning australopithecine behavior. It affords clear-cut evidence that these primitive hominids were to some extent carnivorous and predacious, augmenting their basically vegetal diet with meat, particularly from small animals and the young of some larger species. It is very unlikely that the early and small-bodied Australopithecines did much killing, whereas the later and larger forms, which probably replaced them could cope with small and/or immature mammals. There is no evidence to suggest such creatures were capable of preying on the large herbivorous mammals so characteristic of the African Pleistocene.[16]

This interpretation, however, was based only on the results from an excavated area about 4 metres by 6 metres! In view of the enormous interest in the findings, the National Geographic Society decided to provide substantial financial support on a long-term basis for Leakey's work at Olduvai Gorge. A much larger floor area was opened up around the initial tiny excavation at this location (known as FLK22).[17] The preservation was astonishing; even small rodents, insects and insect-casts were recoverable. But the most surprising aspect, in view of Leakey's earlier remarks, was the number and variety of species represented within such a limited space. In one area were the bones of an okapi (a Pleistocene form of giraffe), in another the fragmentary remains of Pleistocene pig, horse and a variety of African antelope. Remains of exotic animals also turned up: catfish skulls, rodents, chameleons, turtle bones. In fact, by the time the excavations were over the inventory of larger mammals included many different species. It was rather reminiscent of one of those wonderful Victorian pictures of man with all the animals in the Garden of Eden. 128

So it began to appear that the data from these excavations actually supported Dart's original view of early man. Certainly, a scenario involving hunters good enough to handle horse, large antelope, okapi and other animals seemed incompatible with Leakey's first notions of a timid vegetarian who sucked birds' eggs and apologized for stepping on lizards!

The Olduvai material seemed reasonably clear cut. Most researchers were prepared to believe that, in the associations between tools and bones, they were seeing 'living sites' generated by the actions of ancient hominids. For instance, at the FLK NN3 site it seemed fairly certain that Leakey was dealing with an ancient land surface that had not been greatly disturbed: the intact remains of a number of land tortoises were found on the floor with their bones roughly in correct anatomical position. Near the tortoises were the *in situ* vertebrae and ribs of a single African antelope with stone tools scattered around it. Although some sites were not viewed as quite so simple as this, many locations with bones and stones in association were accepted as living sites. Given that the contents of these sites were attributable to the actions of hominids, then the picture of man the hunter was not contradicted by the seemingly self-evident finds. For instance, at the site called FLK, Mary Leakey[18] excavated a level containing the remains of a *Dinotherium*. This strange Pleistocene animal had teeth as huge as elephant tusks protruding from its lower jaw like a front-end loader, which it used to root through the marshes for plant foods. One of these great beasts lay there at FLK partially disarticulated, and close by were found quite definite stone tools. Opposition to the idea of early man as a mighty hunter was, understandably, quieted.

Unfortunately, Louis Leakey died in 1972 while raising funds for yet further excavation; his work has been carried on by his wife Mary and son Richard in other places. Leakey's evidence from Olduvai, however, serves as the basis for the most common, current views of the nature of early hominid behavior, the views to be seen in virtually all today's textbooks. Admittedly, no traces of fire were ever found in any of the Oldowan (i.e. earliest Olduvai) deposits thus far studied, nor did levels with stone tools contain obvious examples of the kinds of bone tools Dart envisaged: so the lack of evidence for two of Dart's criteria offered a basis for questioning his arguments in those respects. But the story of the stone tools and fauna appeared to many unequivocal.

The new orthodoxy is nicely represented in the many writings of Glynn Isaac, one of the leading contemporary Africanists.[19] The picture of the past which he paints is vividly expressed in the following passage: 5

If an observer could be transported back through time . . . what would he see? . . . Far across the plains, a group of four or five men approach . . . As the men approach the observer becomes aware of other primates below him. A group of creatures have been reclining on the sand in the shade of a tree while some youngsters play around them. As the men approach these creatures rise and it becomes apparent that they are bipedal. They seem to be female, and they whoop excitedly as some of the young run out to meet the arriving party. . . .

The object being carried is the carcass of an impala and the group congregates around this in high excitement. There is some pushing and shoving and flashes of temper and threat. Then one of the largest males takes two objects from a heap at the foot of the tree. There are sharp clacking sounds as he squats down and bangs these together repeatedly. The other creatures scramble around picking up the small sharp chips that have been detached from the stones. When there is a small scatter of flakes on the ground at his feet, the stone worker drops the two chunks, sorts through the fragments and selects two or three pieces. Turning back to the carcass the leading male starts to make incisions . . . each adult male finishes up with a segment of the carcass, and withdraws to a corner of the clearing, with one or two females and juveniles congregating around him. They sit chewing and cutting the meat with morsels changing hands at intervals . . . One of the males gets up, stretches his arms, scratches under his arm pits and then sits down. He leans against the tree, gives a loud belch and pats his belly . . .[20]

Drawing on the generally accepted understanding of the relevant Pleistocene deposits, Isaac has argued that already about 2 million years ago man was a hunter who brought back the products of the hunt to his sleeping places to share among both males and females (for he lived in family groups with division of

5 *Our Heritage? Sociable altruists of the Plio-Pleistocene boundary.* A tightly-knit 'band' of early hominids is depicted. Food sharing among adults is indicated by the pair at the right; instruction in tool making is suggested by the adults and child seated at the left. The group responds with curiosity to a pair of males returning from the food quest. What are they bringing back to their 'home base' – plant foods or meat from hunted or scavenged animals? (Pen and pencil drawing by Iva Ellen Morris.)

6 The Koobi Fora hippopotamus site (FxJj3) under excavation by Glynn Isaac. (Photo courtesy of Diane Gifford.)

labor by sex). The claim, in short, is that several kinds of essentially human characteristics were present as a behavioral repertoire at a surprisingly early stage in hominid evolution. We may justifiably ask how the vivid picture presented by Isaac was inferred from deposits of this remote era. 6

Brain's Approach

The discoveries at Olduvai Gorge effectively silenced many members of the scientific community who had previously been unhappy about Dart's conception of the nature of our ancient ancestors. An uneasy quiet in this controversy about the 'mighty hunter' concept reigned for some years. But today, as a result of fresh excavations in Africa and methodological research there and elsewhere in the world, a very different kind of interpretive approach is beginning to emerge, one which in my opinion should provide the basis for a far more realistic examination of this early material. Much of the impetus for it may be traced to the innovative work begun in the mid-1960s by the South African C. K. Brain.[21]

7 C. K. Brain (right) studying bones excavated from Swartkrans, August 1981.

Brain's early work had been in South African deposits similar in some ways to those which Dart used as the basis for his arguments about the use of bone tools and the hunting of animals by the Australopithecines. I have not mentioned so far that there were other important sites in South Africa yielding faunal assemblages in association with Australopithecine remains. One of the leaders in the investigations at the site of Sterkfontein and others in the same area was R. Broom; with G. Schepers he offered the opinion that the bone accumulations were probably the work of hyenas rather than the living places or home bases of very 'predacious' early men. In fact, the view developing among many eminent researchers[22] prior to Leakey's discovery of tools on the *Zinj* floor was that the materials in South African sites were perhaps attributable to other animals or the result of scavenging behavior by our early ancestors. Leakey's finds seemed to be inconsistent with such ideas.

The initial problem to which Brain addressed himself was how the deposits Dart studied for so many years had come into being: what *formation processes* were involved? Remains of ancient hominids had been found sporadically within dense pockets of animal bone. Brain believed, quite rightly, that understanding the conditions that brought such deposits into being would put the interpretation of what was in them on much firmer ground. His earliest observations in this regard, however, were largely incidental to the problem itself. He had noticed an interesting feature of the landscape around a number of the South African sites with which he was very familiar. It was a classic savannah environment with low scrub merging gradually with desert formations; but the trees, instead of being stunted and scattered as is normally the case, were clumped and often quite large. 8 The cause, he found, was geological. Solution of the deep limestone deposits in the region had produced chambers in the rock which acted as natural catchments, with deep pools resulting from the percolation of groundwater or from surface run-off. It was this water resource, of course, that the big trees were able to tap in what is otherwise a very dry environment. So Brain and others began to wonder whether the beds investigated by Dart represented not caves or rock shelters that one could walk into, but deep trap-like fissures into which bones had been washed and living animals had occasionally fallen.

While in the early stages of his investigation, Brain linked this observation with a second one: that leopards tend to drag their prey up into trees when harassed by other predators.[23] Such behavior, in fact, together with the tendency for leopards to use rock shelters and fissures as lairs (especially when a female has young), was acknowledged even by Dart as a possible agent contributing to these deposits.[24] But was information of this sort sufficient to create a convincing picture of the past in terms of formation processes? Clearly not. Brain needed

8 A view across the excavations at Swartkrans, looking toward Sterkfontein, August 1981. Note the trees growing beside limestone fissures on the left.

9 C. K. Brain excavating at Swartkrans, August 1981.

more detailed and relevant observations from natural history before he could advance interpretive arguments, so the next obvious step was to learn something about leopard behavior. What he discovered was that most of the carnivorous predators of Africa can easily out-compete a leopard in a direct confrontation: the leopard has adapted to this by dragging its prey up into a tree, in order to be relatively safe from competitors (particularly hyenas). The prey is draped over a branch with its legs dangling down on either side. As the leopard begins to consume the prey along the central axis of the back, various parts start to fall to the ground. Among all the predators of Africa, apparently, leopards are unique in behaving in this way.

Comparative study of bones left on the surface below the trees and around the fissures as a result of leopard behavior produced some useful results. To cite only one example, the skull bones characteristically showed many depressed fractures and puncture wounds. Contrary to the impression given by Tarzan movies, the big cats, whenever possible, kill by closing their mouths over that of their prey and by keeping them closed until suffocation occurs; that way, the prey is almost hypnotized and lies still without flailing its legs (something dangerous for the predators who are likely to have their stomachs ripped open). This behavior results in a systematic pattern of skull punctures which can be matched with the spacing between a leopard's canine teeth.[25] Armed with various modern anatom-

10 Reconstructed scene of a leopard eating an early hominid in a tree above a limestone fissure. (Pen drawing by Mary Coombes reproduced with permission from *South African Museum Bulletin* No. 9, 1968.)

ical observations of this kind, Brain re-examined the Swartkrans material and [9] was able to show that there too the skull fractures were probably the result not of club blows by man (as Dart had thought), but of death by suffocation in the way just described. In the bones from Makapansgat, likewise, the contrast between intact lower limb bones and largely absent vertebrae could be related to the typical pattern of consumption by leopards. In fact, the breakage patterns were essentially indistinguishable from the ones Brain was finding in his studies of contemporary leopard behavior. [10]

Here, then, was a most provocative situation. The geological context produced clumps of trees, offering shade and protection in an otherwise open landscape; such environments formed the natural habitat for the consumption of food by one of the major predators; and such food consumption resulted in the accumulation of bones at the very edge of natural fissures. This combination of circumstances convinced Brain that these same processes and conditions, operating over millions of years, had contributed to the formation of the palaeontological deposits then being excavated in South Africa.

11 *Schematic summary of the formation sequence of the South African early hominid sites: Early stages.*

The initial step (A) is the formation of an underground cavern by the solution of the dolomitic limestone under the water table. Erosion over long periods results in the down-cutting of the rivers and lowering of the water table, so that the solution chamber eventually becomes a cavern or hole in the limestone, high and dry above the water table.

At this point (B), the percolation of groundwater initiates the formation of travertines within the cavern, while the percolation fissures leading in and out are enlarged by solution and mechanical erosion. Further caverns may be in the process of forming within the zone of lowered groundwater below the original one, which becomes a conductor or groundwater to them. Large blocks fallen from the roof modify the internal shape of the original cavern and channel water percolation through it.

Nevertheless, Brain did not stop with the study of leopards. He studied the African porcupine, which was known to accumulate bones in its lairs. He also examined the roosting behavior of owls which had certainly contributed considerable quantities of bones from small creatures to the deposits in the limestone sites. He researched the behavior of hyenas and (unlike Dart) realized that the actions of this interesting animal could account for many characteristics of the faunal assemblages from the early 'ape-man' sites. All these studies of animal behaviour were coupled with continuing excavation and investigation of the important site of Swartkrans.

The insights stemming from Brain's methodological research have now made it possible to develop a picture of the processes by which some of the South African deposits were formed. Ills. 11 and 12 present a generalized illustration of how their contents were conditioned by a sequence of events taking place in the context

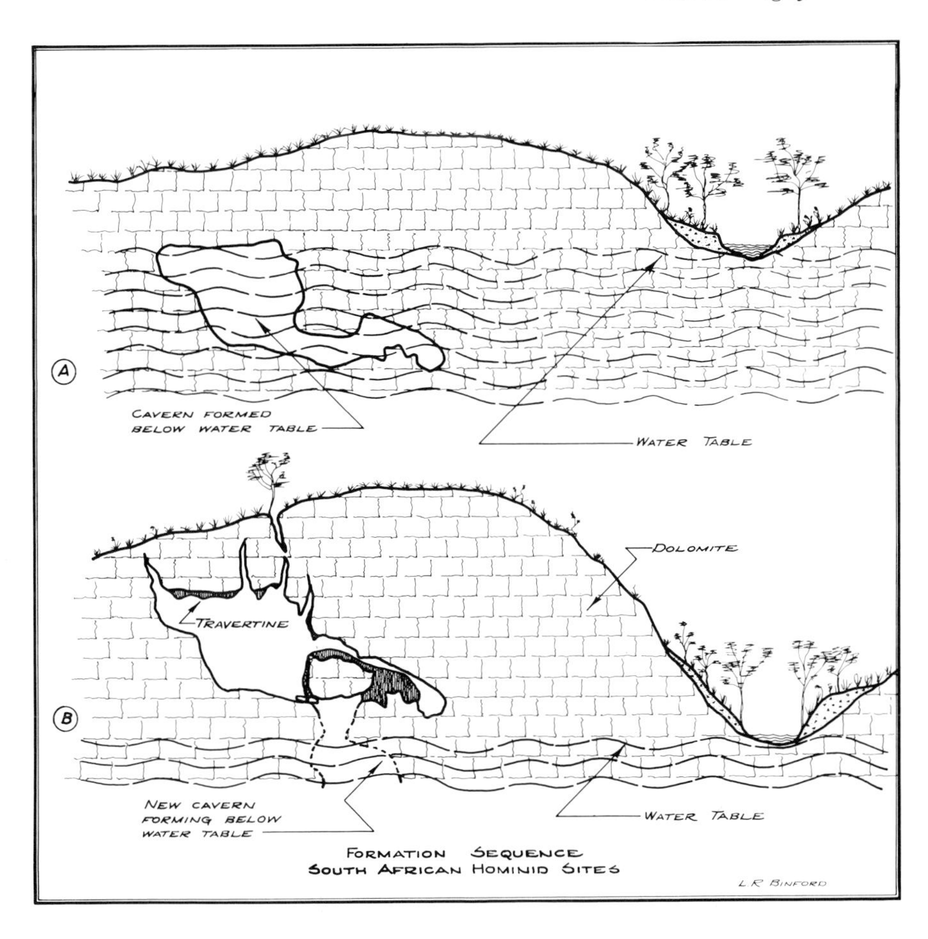

of geological processes. In reality, of course, the situation is very much more complex. But the major point should be clear: these deposits are the result of a large number of processes, which can be related to a large number of agents acting under changing conditions. While evidence of hominid behavior and actual hominid remains may be present, *their associations are referable to dynamics at the ecosystem level of organization* (rather than to the specific behavior of a single species, as Dart assumed). Brain's work on formation processes, then, represents the development of methods for inference – that is, the investigation of properties which permit the 'diagnosis' of a deposit and the accurate attribution of its components to the agents and processes responsible for their occurrence.

At this juncture it is reasonable to speculate. If the cave and fissure deposits of South Africa are accumulations formed by many different and varied processes which operated in the past environment, might the same not also be true of the

12 *Schematic summary of the formation sequence of the South African early hominid sites: Later stages.* Small fissures develop (1), linking the surface to the cavern below. Trees grow around these sinkholes, whose openings provide opportunities for a wide variety of animals: owls and bats roost within, while primates (including hominids) sleeping at the entrance attract hunting leopards and scavenging hyenas. The specific interactions among these animals largely determines the content of the very gradually accumulating deposits (Member I) washed down into the cavern.

In time, the fissures become larger through erosion (2), allowing an increased volume of surface water run-off to begin to flush out the cavern and carve drainage channels through the previously accumulated deposit. The opening of such channels accelerates the erosion of the surface and leads to considerable changes in the size and shape of the fissures and their immediately adjacent areas.

Major periods of erosion result in some openings becoming clogged with fallen rock and soil, while others might become enlarged – particularly where the fissures intersect the plane of the surface at an angle, producing small rock shelters or cave-like entrances (3). These modifications at the surface affect the appropriateness of the place for use by differing combinations of animals, including the hominids. For instance, once less agile animals like the hyena can gain access to the protected cave mouths, primates would find less security there as sleeping locations; leopards, in turn, would encounter fewer primate prey during their nocturnal visits and more formidable competitors. Under such conditions, the major contributors to the deposits in the cavern below (Member II) are the hyena and perhaps other carnivores (although at Swartkrans sporadic finds of hominid fossils and tools in the Member II deposits indicate that members of the family *Hominidae* occasionally used the gallery entrance).

Finally, the deposit becomes relatively stable (4), although further erosion and deposition of more recent age may in practice result in a complex stratigraphic intermingling.

---

open sites of East Africa? If they too are palimpsests of this sort, how would we recognize the fact? And how could we set about doing research, analogous to Brain's work on caves, as the first steps in gaining a new understanding of the East African material? If the associations between artifacts and bones are not necessarily clear cut and the bones are not a 'self-evident' witness to the nature of early man's diet, then maybe the behavior of the early hominids was quite different from the orthodox reconstructions proposed by researchers in East Africa.

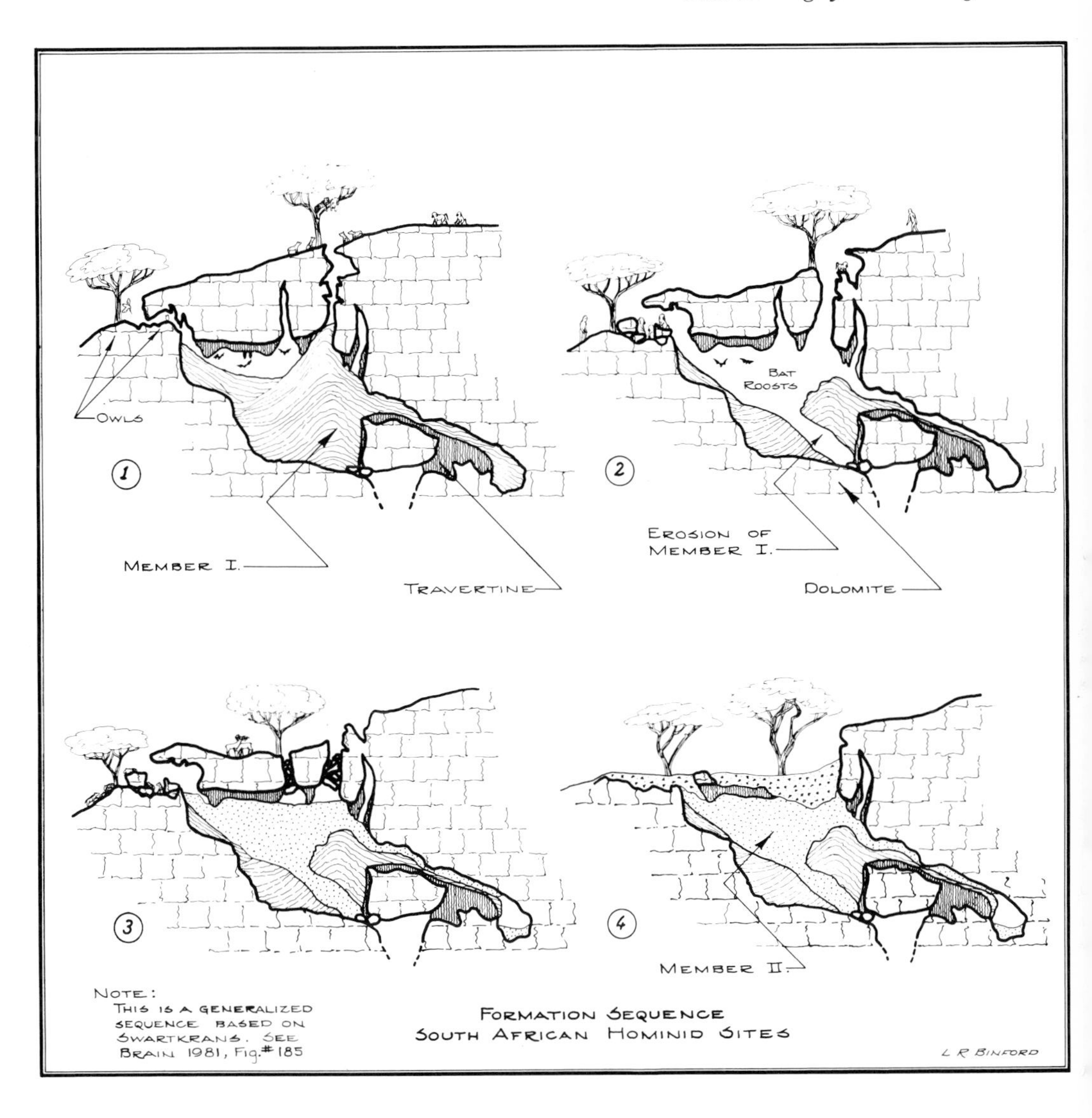

Help from Contemporary Studies

It will be recalled that Dart had observed that the different parts of ungulate skeletons were not present in the Makapansgat population in direct proportion to the frequency with which they occurred in the anatomy of living animals. He reasoned that the bias in anatomical parts was to be understood in terms of selection of parts for use as tools and food by the Australopithecines. Brain had noted that his leopard feeding data showed that certain parts tended to be eaten

13 A view of a large tree at the mouth of a limestone fissure at Swartkrans, 1981: what early man might have seen from within his sleeping area.

and destroyed, others to survive the leopard and even the scavenging hyenas. Although these observations were thought-provoking, most of Brain's samples were small and he was not convinced that he understood the causes of the phenomenon noted by Dart. To gain some further understanding, he started an ethnoarchaeological project with a group of contemporary Hottentot pastoralists living in Namibia.[26] These people keep herds of goats which they kill and eat right in the villages in which they live. Since they do not trade meat in or out of their settlements, all the bones should be there – at least in principle. So Brain was keen to see whether the goat bones recovered in such a setting occurred in the 'correct' proportions. But in fact the Hottentots keep large numbers of dogs which, being unfettered, have free access to all the garbage in the village – and, as we all know, dogs are pretty good with bones! In his collection of several thousand bones from more than one village, Brain found a tremendous bias in the relative frequencies of anatomical parts – a bias in favor of mandibles and the distal ends of most bones, and against vertebrae, ribs and proximal ends. Since there were scavenging animals in the past too, it hardly seemed surprising that there should be a great deal of similarity in the bone frequencies in the Hottentot villages and in the Makapansgat deposits associated with *Australopithecus*.

All the foregoing evidence, some of it drawn from controlled observations in the modern world, made Brain fairly certain that Pleistocene leopards and other animals, not man, were important agents responsible for these deposits. According to this new interpretation, *Australopithecus* had not necessarily lived where his bones were found: he was merely eaten there! The sites were not living places, but various natural traps and sleeping places.

It can be exciting when two people, literally half a world apart and each unaware of what the other is doing, find themselves thinking along very similar lines. At the time Brain was studying leopards and Hottentot goat bones, I neither knew him nor had any idea of what he was doing. Yet it turned out that some ethnoarchaeological studies of my own, merely incidental to ethnographic work I was doing with the Navajo Indians of New Mexico, were moving in much the same direction.[27].

During fieldwork I had noticed in a casual way that the frequencies of bones in the rubbish dumps of the Navajo winter camp at which I was a visitor seemed to be very different from those at summer sites. Being well aware of all the problems of interpretation posed by variations in anatomical part frequencies among the Lower Pleistocene remains discussed above, I decided to start a small student project to study whether my initial impression about bone frequencies was correct and – if it was – what caused the differences. Working in a remote area of the Navajo reservation, we had no problem getting access to suitable material: indeed, the Indians laughingly encouraged the insane professor and his students to come and clean up their front yards! We collected the bones from sites for which we had information about the people who had lived there, about the duration of occupation, about seasonality, and so on. I had imagined that the Navajo simply killed and ate sheep and goats from time to time and that the pattern would be a straightforward reflection of this behavior. But our study revealed that there were vast differences in the relative anatomical part frequencies on Navajo winter and summer sites.

Once we saw the differences, we began to consider what caused them. These sites were in a high desert area with severe winters in which there is often deep snowcover in January and night-time temperatures regularly drop as low as 0°F (–18°C). Consequently, many of the lambs born the previous spring, together

14 A Navajo woman preparing to butcher a sheep. (Photo courtesy of J. Chisholm.)

with a good number of the old animals, simply freeze to death in winter: these the Navajo either eat themselves or (if they are only skinny little lambs) feed directly to their dogs. So winter sites produce an archaeological faunal record with a biased age frequency. On summer sites, it is fat sheep in prime condition, chosen for their good health, that are selectively consumed. In both situations, dogs had free access to the garbage and, obviously, the bones of the old ewes offered them more of a challenge than the soft bones of the little yearlings. Our laboratory studies of bone density in relation to growth allowed us to generate graphs showing how changes with age in the hardness of each bone in the body affected their probability of survival. We could demonstrate easily that markedly differential frequencies would result from subjecting all the bones equally to the same agents of attrition. So it seemed to us that what determined the variable frequencies of anatomical parts *within* the Navajo sites was the bone densities of animals of different ages, while the differences *between* sites lay in differences in the age structure of the animals whose bones were being gnawed or eaten by dogs.

The logical next step was to see whether such a simple model based on bone density could help us understand variation in the frequencies of anatomical parts at archaeological sites such as Makapansgat. Most of the animals there were antelopes, many of them as small or even smaller than sheep, although with a rather different birth sequence. But the same processes ought to be relevant, if we were indeed dealing at Makapansgat with the work of a predator, such as a leopard, which preferentially kills very young and very old animals; and we did in fact find a very good match between the frequencies of bones in the modern Navajo sites and bone survival at Makapansgat. Here was further support for Brain's prior conclusion – that the differential occurrence of ungulate bones was simply a reflection of their differential potential for surviving attrition by carnivore gnawing or stream-bed abrasion, rather than the result of Australopithecine hunting activities.

Both Brain and I were studying dynamic processes in the modern world as the basis for the development of methods for making inferences about static remains from the distant past. We were both very much aware that archaeologists must be able to identify the agents responsible for a deposit before they can begin to interpret it. In my fieldwork with the caribou-hunting Nunamiut Eskimo in northern Alaska[28] (see Chapter 6), I saw a further possibility of obtaining *controlled* comparative information from the modern world relevant to the contrast between animal and human hunters in their treatment of bones. For example, I had the opportunity to observe thirty-six wolf kills and to get back later to twenty-four of them in order to make an inventory of the bones that remained (the other kill sites were destroyed in the interim by grizzly bears or by the melting of the

15 Students engaged in a sheep butchering experiment designed to investigate how the properties of bone vary with age; Albuquerque, 1973.

lake ice). I also investigated a number of wolf dens and recorded the composition, breakage and gnawing patterns of the faunal assemblages there.[29] A little later it came to my attention that the British scholar Andrew Hill[30] was doing exactly the same type of study on the open kill sites of lions and hyenas in Uganda and southern Ethiopia and he had been successful in gathering a large and interesting body of data. Hill had no information on dens, however, and my own was not a sufficient basis for generalizing about what animals do to bones when they drag them back to their sleeping areas. Fortunately, this lacuna could be filled to some degree, for the archaeologist Richard Klein[31] had detailed records of the large faunal assemblage from his excavation of a hyena den in South Africa.

When all this material was put together and compared – Hill's predator kill sites, Klein's hyena layer, my own wolf dens and kill sites – a very repetitive pattern emerged. Wolves, hyenas and the large cats, it seems, behave very much alike and produce extremely similar bone assemblages, even in quite different settings. The chief difference lies in the frequency with which each species introduces bones into layers at their sleeping places: lions don't seem to do it, hyenas do it all the time, while wolves behave like packrats in bringing back everything they can. Amongst all the species, what varied was not so much the *types* of bones resulting from predatory behavior, as the *quantities* in which they occurred. So by combining various kinds of information, it was possible to obtain a realistic picture of the nature of assemblages which can occur as the outcome of predatory animal behavior.

Back to the Pleistocene

How can this kind of information help the archaeologist reconstruct human behavior over 2 million years ago? My reasoning goes in the following way. Where we have archaeological or palaeontological contexts in which many factors may have contributed to the formation of a deposit, we need to find ways of removing the known or recognizable elements that are not of direct interest, in order to see if anything 'unknown' is left that might be related to man's activities. Chemical qualitative analysis follows just the same strategy, of course. You are given some compound in a test tube and asked to say what the unknown substance is: the classic procedure is to extract and identify all the known elements in the compound until you are left with an unknown (but relatively pure) residue which is sufficiently unambiguous to be identified from the textbook. Archaeologists unfortunately have no such textbook, but their analytical tactics can still be similar – moving from known to unknown conditions by isolating the residues.

I took as 'known', then, the structure of bone assemblages produced in various settings by animal predators and scavengers; and as 'unknown' the bone deposits excavated by the Leakeys at Olduvai Gorge. Using mathematical and statistical techniques, I considered to what degree the finds from Olduvai Gorge could be accounted for in terms of the results of predator behavior and how much was 'left over'. This proved to be an exciting analysis. My expectation had been that all the variability in the Oldowan faunal material would be attributable to the activities of predators and scavengers, that *Zinjanthropus* was there because he got eaten by some other animal. But when I actually looked at my results, I consistently found that in sites with relatively high tool frequencies there was a recognizable amount of residual material which could *not* be explained by what we know about African carnivores. Mandibles and minor skull parts occurred at marginally higher frequencies, but the really big differences lay in the regular excess of lower limb bones (for instance, metatarsals and distal ends of the tibia). What could our ancestors have been doing? After all, there is not much meat to speak of on such bones, only the bone marrow in them is of any food value.

This bit of information in itself is suggestive. The African predators and scavengers compete for *meat*, while bone marrow is mainly consumed only by juvenile animals, especially of the canids and hyenas, gnawing on bones. Now in any intimate set of relations between animals a very common adaptation is for one species to live off the by-products of another – herds of antelope have an escort of dung beetles, for instance. A species carving out a new niche for itself almost never competes directly with others already present, but investigates the edges of the energy system, as it were, to find a way of using the entropy of other animals. Might this account for the residual bone frequencies? The food item most commonly left unconsumed at predator kill sites, even after scavengers like hyenas have left, is the marrow trapped in bone reservoirs; and this would have been something early man could readily have consumed without competing directly with all the other predators in the environment. I have always been a little uneasy about the supposed *machismo* of little 90-pound Australopithecines confronting 350-pound African lionesses!

The interesting thing about these faunal analyses is not simply that the (conceptual) removal of material which can be understood in terms of animal behavior regularly left clear residual patterns, but that such patterns were themselves very similar from case to case. I detected a repeated residual pattern that made some sense in terms of scavenging behavior; yet its magnitude was also largely proportional to the quantity of stone tools in each deposit – something that in no way could have been a result of my analyses of the bones themselves. Despite much discussion, the fact remains that the earliest Oldowan tools are simply smashed rocks which could probably have served only as hammer-stones, clubs or choppers. The flakes struck off them were not in general utilized, for in the lowest deposits cutting tools are rare, while morphologically sophisticated tools (such as scrapers) are entirely absent.

These observations must be set in the context of the stratigraphic sequence at Olduvai. The various excavations there are in geological deposits spanning an extremely long period of about 1.2 million years, from the lowest levels dated about 1.8 million years ago to the upper excavated deposits of Bed II dated around 600,000 years ago. Contrary to what one might assume, it is the *lowest* and *oldest* beds that are the best preserved. The early levels represent activity beside a lake whose margins gradually receded; the upper levels are much more disturbed by local hydrological processes, which have given rise to slope-wash deposits full of gravels and rolled materials. As one moves up through the beds at Olduvai in the same location, there is a sequential change from lake-edge sediments to braided stream-channel deposits. That same sequence exhibits related changes in the faunal assemblages, from lots of bones and relatively few teeth in the bottom levels, to lots of teeth and few bones in the upper levels. Tooth enamel, of course, is effectively the hardest part of an animal's body and is the most resistant to mechanical destruction or to solution by soil acids. So the regular directional change in the tooth-to-bone ratio in the Olduvai deposits from bottom to top warns us not to treat the rate of bone attrition or transport by water as something constant through time.

Where water transport occurs – as seems to be the case in the upper levels at Olduvai – some mechanical sorting of tools by size can be expected to affect the frequencies at which they appear: the more violent the stream-flow, the more it will wash away small pieces of stone, leaving only big ones. Knowing what we do about the geological contexts, we would predict lots of small flake-tools in the lower *in situ* deposits and lots of large heavy tools in the uppermost ones. *But the reverse is true!* Erosional processes, then, cannot be the main agent responsible for the changing composition of the stone tool assemblages. So there are grounds for suspecting that what we are monitoring in the increased use of cutting-edge tools is a dim reflection of some really important behavioral changes amongst hominid populations over this enormous span of time.

This suspicion is buttressed by a further intriguing correlation. As the relative frequency of flakes and flake tools goes up, so too does the frequency of animals of large body size: the upper levels contain relatively large numbers of hippopotamus, giraffe, elephant and rhinoceros (all generally represented by teeth). Of course, this is essentially what we would expect from the erosional patterns I have just mentioned. Small animals would be washed away altogether, giving a bias in favor of the teeth of larger animals. But if in the lower levels we have the record of man scavenging mainly for bone marrow around the fringes of predator kills and other animal death-sites, and if there is indeed a shift through time towards increased use of cutting tools, then it is at least reasonable to imagine that man was gradually beginning to compete as a scavenger for *meat* (rather than bone marrow). And if that were so, he would surely tend to focus his activities increas-

16 *Our Heritage? Eclectic foragers of the Plio-Pleistocene boundary.* A foraging group of males, females and children encounter a relatively fresh carcass of a dead animal near a water source and begin to scavenge, while others approach to join in the feeding. Various animals, also frequent users of the same place, are indicated. This scenario implies nothing about home bases, division of labor, the taking of food back to sleeping areas, or even food sharing. (Pen and pencil drawing by Iva Ellen Morris.)

ingly on larger animals. When a lion eats a Grant's gazelle, there is nothing left over. But with an elephant carcass, even after the Malibu storks have finished and all the hyenas in the region have bloated themselves and left, something edible still remains for the really persistent scavenger, if he gets there soon enough. Simply on a statistical basis, meat scavengers will tend to be more successful more of the time, if they concentrate on animals of large body size. 16

How much of this picture is correct we do not yet know. Still, it is worth stressing that around two dozen floors, spanning 1.2 million years and increasingly disturbed as they get more recent, constitute much of what we have to work with in modelling the behavior of our earliest ancestors in the Pleistocene. Yet patterning does exist in the data. Some of it at present remains merely suggestive. The repeated pattern of residual bone frequencies in the lower levels, however, I feel more sure about: this is evidence of man eating a little bit of bone marrow, a food source that must have represented an infinitesimally small component in his total diet. The signs seem clear. Earliest man, far from appearing as a mighty hunter of beasts, seems to have been the most marginal of scavengers.

3

Life and Death at the Waterhole

Where did Early Man Eat and Sleep?

We have seen in Chapter 2 how Brain's studies of certain processes operating in the world today have gradually created a body of knowledge and understanding which makes it possible to interpret the South African cave deposits from the perspective of the dynamics of their formation. Such an interpretation, in turn, gives us some idea of the role which early man played in the ecosystems reflected in these deposits. For instance, it seems that hominids sought out protected sleeping places during the cooler months, in much the same way as baboons do today.[1] Equally interesting is the general lack of evidence that food was brought back to these sleeping areas and eaten there; most food consumption at such places was by predators, particularly leopards, which preyed on the sleeping primates.

17

17 Baboons at Gilgil in Kenya sitting on a protected rock ledge. Protected rock crevices and shelters such as this are often used as sleeping areas (cf. Brain 1981, 271–3). (Photo by Barbara Smuts, courtesy of Anthro-Photo, Cambridge, Massachusetts.)

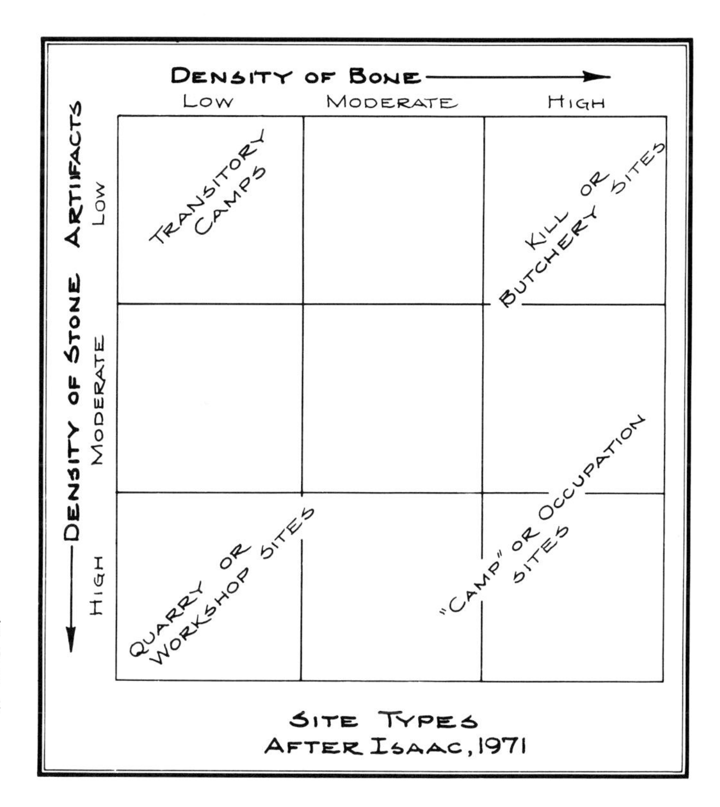

18 Matrix for classifying site function using Isaac's dimensions of artifact and faunal densities. (After Isaac 1971, fig. 10a, p. 285.)

Now, the South African sites discussed in Chapter 2 are roughly contemporary with the famous 'floors' at Olduvai Gorge, and with Site 5 at Koobi Fora,[2] another important research location in East Africa. Archaeologists working in East Africa insist that the hominids there were living in home bases to which they brought food to be shared and consumed within small family groups. The South African deposits, by contrast, document the fact that for one form of hominid, at least, the activities of sleeping and food consumption had not yet been linked together spatially at this time. So there is an apparent inconsistency in the conclusions drawn from the South and East African evidence. What, then, is the basis for the opinion of East African researchers that at this remote period, over 1 million years ago, hominids were behaving in a typically human manner, in so far as sleeping and eating in the same places were concerned?

3

The answer to this question leads us to recognize that a series of conventions and '*post hoc* arguments'[3] have been used by archaeologists working in East Africa to warrant their opinion that the so-called 'living floors' were in fact home bases. Glynn Isaac's observation that 'The habit of creating concentrated patches of food refuse and abandoned artifacts is amongst the basic features of behavior that distinguish the human animal from other primates'[4] amounts to an operational definition of an occupation site as a place where man works with tools, consumes food and sleeps. As a result, the association of stone tools with animal bones has become accepted by convention as indicating a home base: a site where man lived, worked and slept. Some scholars, as outlined by Isaac (ill. 18), have gone even further to suggest that relative differences in the densities of bone and artifact distributions can be accepted as evidence for different types of sites. A high density of bones and a low density of tools, for example, is held to define a kill or butchery site, whereas high densities of both lithic and faunal remains are expected to occur at living sites. Further attempts by Isaac and his co-workers to refine these conventions set out in 1971 have in general led them to the same opinion as before:[5] sites are thought to be home bases, places to which food was brought by hominids to be shared among members of the group. Several justifications are commonly offered for this belief: (1) bones and stone artifacts are said to co-exist in 'anomalously high concentrations'; (2) the pattern of damage to the bones is believed to be a result of hominid behavior; and (3) the compositions of bone present are said to be at least 'not incompatible' with the inference that hominids accumulated the bone.[6]

It is perhaps a little ironic that such reasoning involves what are essentially the very criteria used by Dart to justify his claim that hominids were the agents responsible for creating the accumulations of bones in the South African caves! It seems to me that – as with Dart's arguments – we would be ill-advised to use the conventions advocated by Isaac and his colleagues for interpreting the archaeological record, until we know rather more about the processes responsible for the production of these deposits in East Africa. In my opinion, the most helpful clue to the solution of this problem is the one I have already mentioned, namely, that the South African evidence appears to be inconsistent with the idea that the early hominids ate and slept at the same sites. This is precisely what the East African archaeologists *assume* from the outset to have been the case, so that it is inevitable that they should interpret the concentrations of bones and artifacts as occupation sites or the remains of home bases. How might we begin the task of investigating properties of the contemporary world (what are sometimes called 'actualistic studies') to help us make accurate diagnoses of the behavioral characteristics of our early ancestors? How do we find out, in fact, what it was like in those times so long ago?

Learning from Modern Waterholes

Just as with Brain's studies of the processes leading to the formation of cave deposits, we must begin the study of ecosystem dynamics by focusing our attention on waterholes, stream channels or lake margins in otherwise relatively dry land-

19 Dry bed of the Nossob River in the southern Kalahari Desert (see ill. 3 for exact location.)

scapes; for it is in environmental settings of this sort that the East African open sites conventionally interpreted as home bases once existed. It is difficult for most of us to visualize in detail the relevant classic savannah and interior grassland environments of Africa, characterized by dense concentrations of game animals. The scene is a vast landscape punctuated by clusters of trees and shrubs, often in dry river channels or around waterholes. For one unaccustomed to seeing wildlife in great abundance, the environment has a tempo which is breathtakingly dramatic.

My own first experience of such an environment in Africa[7] began one morning when I entered an area rich in game and walked along a dry river bed. Around each turn in the valley there came into view groups of ungulates clustered near waterholes. Lying in the shade of great trees near one water source might be groups of blue wildebeests: ten, twenty-five, even forty individuals would not be uncommon. As we approached, a great bull would rise to its feet, shake itself and, engulfed in dust, lower its head slightly to gaze in our direction. Ostriches ran across our path. The ubiquitous springboks would stare at us but go on feeding, slowly wandering along the valley towards shade or an area of tawny grass. The valley, with its water sources, was truly the domain of the ungulates.

19 20 21

The only clue to violence in the landscape was the occasional vulture perched in the tree tops or soaring above us, eventually to land and add its number to a

20 Blue wildebeest bull and gemsbok near a water source.

feathered group taking a meal around a dead animal. When one looks around the environment in a little more detail, carcasses or parts of them are easily spotted: silent indications of violent death are constant features of the land surfaces around the waterholes.

If one remains in the area for some time, however, the ostensibly placid rhythm of the land is seen to be anything but subtle. The ungulates certainly rule the water sources at high noon; but as the sun begins to kiss the western horizon, they begin gradually but deliberately to move back towards the valley margins and climb the dunes out of the valley. The abandonment of the daytime domain of these animals is striking, as they disperse out into the vast rolling landscape away from the water and disappear. In the slanting light of sunset, the predators, lords of the night, move into the valley to occupy the waterholes and exercise dominion over the land used by ungulates during the day. 22

Generally, the hyenas are the first to arrive, approaching the waterholes slowly and passing old carcasses of ungulates killed previously by predators and of other animals which died less violently near water. The hyenas may gnaw on these relatively dry bones, but eventually go in to drink, for they almost always take water before hunting. The actual search for food may not begin in earnest until much later in the night, so it is not uncommon for the hyenas to remain in the 23

21 Springbok feeding in the Nossob River Valley.

immediate area of the water source, gnawing bones, moving body parts around, and engaging in various social activities. After dark some calling (the characteristic 'whooping') may occur; later on, the hyenas leave rather deliberately to make a kill and secure fresh meat. Lions and leopards, too, often visit the water sources during the night, since they also need water during the active hours of hunting and pursuit of game. The roars of the lion are commonly heard late in the evening between ten o'clock and two o'clock, when they may travel great distances visiting waterholes along the way before stalking and attacking prey. 24

Between about two o'clock and four-thirty in the morning, activity seems to subside: at least, the sounds of predators dwindle away and the night becomes still. Just before sunrise, lions' roars increase; predators tend to be moving along well-travelled routes which frequently take them through or past water. As the full rays of the sun flood the landscape, the vultures are already soaring, searching for the previous night's carnage. Gradually, as the warmth of the sun returns to the valleys, the ungulates reappear, moving back to the water sources. The cycle begins again. 25

Primates, ourselves included, are creatures of the daylight. Our eyes are daytime organs and we are ill-adapted to killing, foraging or even protecting ourselves at night. One wonders how a creature so poorly fitted for activity in the

22 *(Above)* Spotted hyena approaching a waterhole just before sunset. Note wildebeest in the background moving out of the valley away from the waterhole. (Photo courtesy of John Parkington.)

23 Carcass of a blue wildebeest which died near a water source.

24 Bones from several carcasses which were dragged together by hyenas on the night of 14 July 1981. Parts of eland, wildebeest and gemsbok are present.

25 *(Below)* Gemsbok near water source in mid-morning.

dark could safely maintain a sleeping place immediately adjacent to a water source in the sort of African landscape I have just described. It is unsurprising that the modern hunter-gatherers who live in relatively remote African environments generally do not locate their camps immediately adjacent to water sources; they use fire to discourage predators and, of course, have the option to employ relatively effective weapons against them if necessary. The place I would *never* choose to establish a camp in the African savannah is next to a water source! Nevertheless, archaeologists tell us that our hominid ancestors habitually located home bases in exactly these places. At this point, it becomes relevant to ask whether the three criteria used by the East African researchers (see above) really permit the reliable recognition of home-base occupation sites.

26

Let us begin thinking about the problem by accepting the stone artifacts at face value – that is, as objects produced and used by hominids. What is of interest is the degree to which the behavioral context in which these tools were used involved precisely the same setting as that in which the associated bone was deposited. My observations at African water sources illustrate several points relevant to this problem: (1) natural deaths are common near these water sources; (2) predator kills also occur there; (3) hyenas gnawing on relatively dry bone in the vicinity

26 Contemporary Bushman camp at /Gausha pan, Namibia, 1976. This camp is located nearly 1.5 kilometers from the nearest water source. (Photo courtesy of the South African Museum, Cape Town.)

27 Eland bones gnawed and broken by hyenas at a waterhole. These bones were scavenged from a dry carcass such as the one in ill. 23. (Photo courtesy of John Landham.)

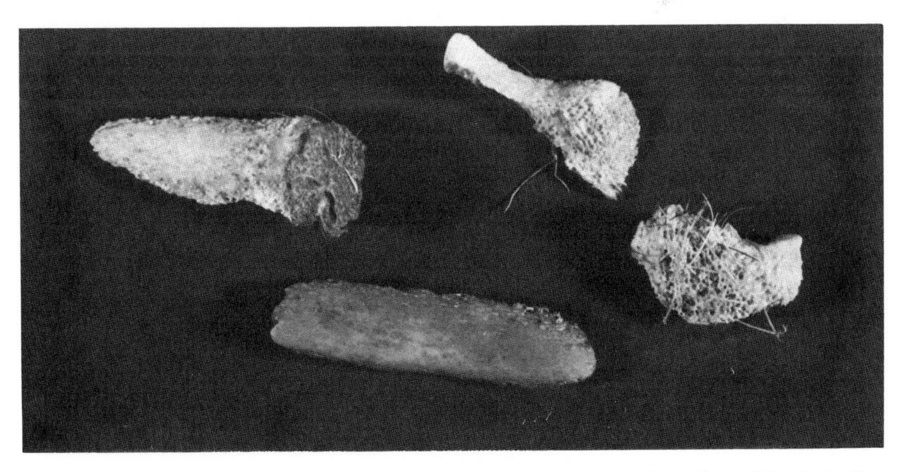

28 Fragments of bone collected by the author from the faeces of one lion. Much similar, small bone from both defecation and regurgitation could accumulate around the daytime lounging spot of lions.

of the water sources may drag together bones from several different carcasses; and (4) considerable quantities of bone may accumulate as much as 100 meters from the water. These facts mean that *considerable quantities of bone can be expected to occur around water sources.* The actual amounts probably vary with the rate of burial and with the reliability and accessibility of water sources in the region. Furthermore, lions often drag prey into the shade for consumption, nor is it unusual for them to concentrate in relatively large groups under trees by water during the day. Consequently, small bone fragments, regurgitated or passed in their feces, can contribute considerably to a deposit, particularly if they accumulate over a number of years before burial.[8] Such observations are thought-provoking and it clearly seems possible that bones can be expected to occur around water sources, even though hominids may have played no active part in the process of accumulation. But we need to seek additional evidence that 'natural' bone deposits of this sort in fact occurred in the past.

The Archaeology of an Ancient Waterhole

While in southern Africa recently, I had the opportunity to visit the truly spectacular site at Elandsfontein, which probably dates to the period between 200,000 and 400,000 years ago.[9] The interpretation of this site is anything but secure, but it is the structure of the associations observed there with which I am principally concerned here. Most scholars agree that the deposits were built up in the environmental context of a spring and the associated water sources of a variable internal drainage. Today, the site consists of a series of sand dunes which are actively moving, although there is good reason to believe that their destabilization is a relatively recent phenomenon.

As the sands blow and shift about, a truly remarkable assemblage of fossil animal bones is being uncovered. In some places, there may be what are certainly the remains of the carcass of a single ancient animal, whose bones have been slightly scattered in just the same way as a modern carcass might be dispersed by scavengers or as part of natural decay processes. In some cases, a hand ax or even several tools associated with a recognizable carcass can be observed; in the vast majority of cases, however, no obvious evidence of man is present. For example, during an afternoon spent walking over the major exposures, I noted only one recognizable concentration of bones (probably those of a single animal) in which there was any evidence that long bones had been broken open for their marrow by hammering or impact; one solitary manuport (i.e. a stone carried to the location by man) was the only associated item. In certain spots, there are bone groups seemingly concentrated into particular clusters by some agent in the past, whether animal or natural, but the conditions under which these aggregates formed is not

29 Bones exposed by wind on the surface of the Elandsfontein site. (See ill. 3 for location of the site.)

30 Hand ax exposed on the surface of the Elandsfontein site.

well understood. Elsewhere, there is evidence for the former existence of carnivore lairs; hyenas, in particular, are represented by coprolites (fossilized feces), while concentrations of small bone splinters and gnawed fragments like those found around spotted and brown hyena dens are also present.

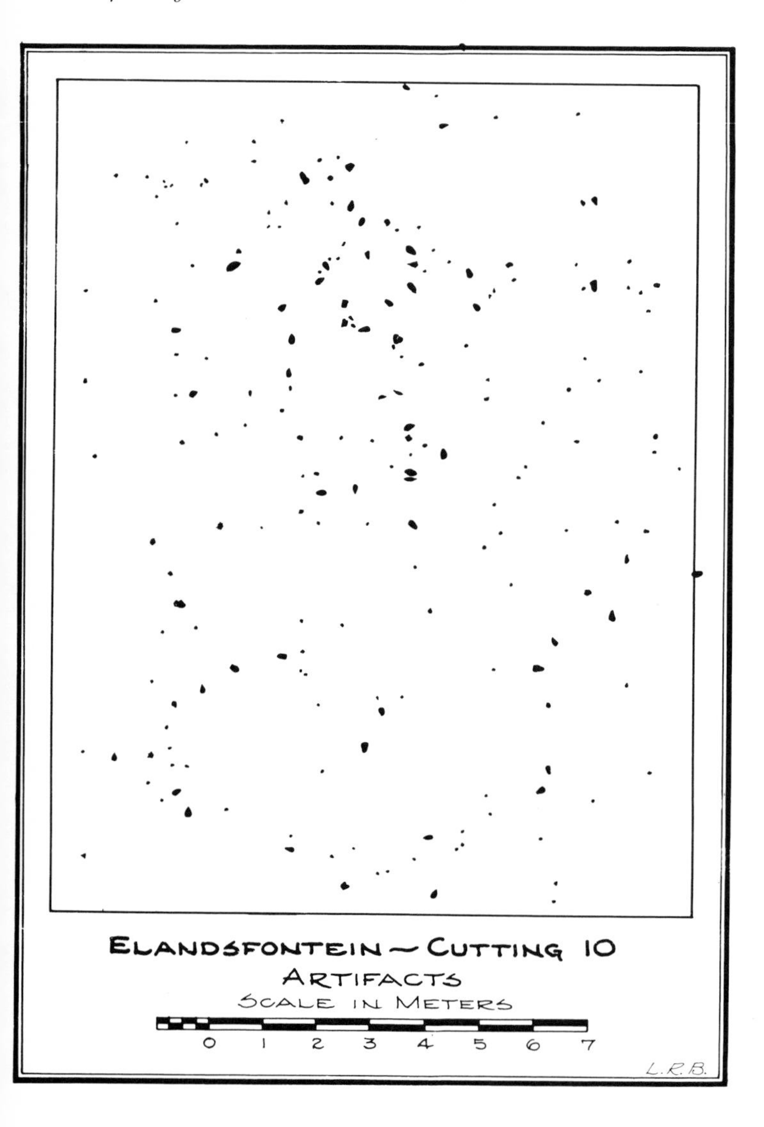

31 Plot showing the distribution of artifacts at 'Cutting 10', Elandsfontein site. (Information obtained from Singer and Wymer 1968.)

Besides the variety of patterns mentioned so far, there are certain locations which yield substantial concentrations of both bones and artifacts.[10] There is evidence from one excavated example, 'Cutting 10', that a number of different agents contributed to the deposit. Yet viewed from the perspective of the interpretive conventions of the East African archaeologists, the association between tools and bones would lead directly to the conclusion that this was a living site, the base camp of some of our Pleistocene ancestors. This may indeed be true. But the presence of concentrations of tools at a single small location, surrounded in all

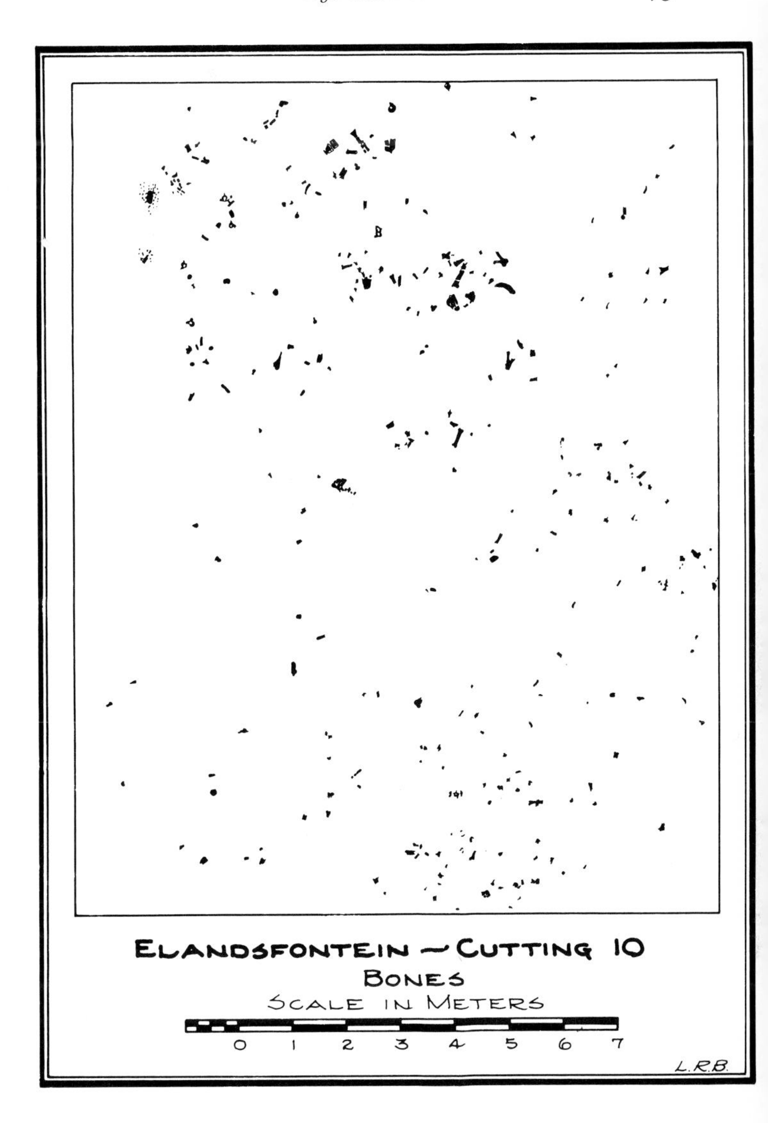

32 Distribution plot of bones at 'Cutting 10', Elandsfontein site. (Information obtained from Singer and Wymer 1968.)

directions by large and variable distributions of animal bones, does not support the idea that the association between tools and bones in this case is unique. In fact, it is hard to imagine any part of the site where tools could have been deposited, but which would not also have been a place where there were substantial quantities of animal bone.

The Elandsfontein site can be seen as a kind of palaeontological 'cautionary tale': as such, it would repay extensive research to determine the range of variability in faunal patterning in a setting where ancient bones tend to be well preserved. The next step would be to establish whether there is any particular form of patterning in terms of the mix of animal species and in the anatomical parts represented which co-vary with recognizable tools. If co-variant patterning could be demonstrated in faunal assemblages from favorable sites such as Elandsfontein, it would teach us something in general about the make-up of bone samples recovered with tools; and that would allow us to separate analytically the associations seen on early man sites.

If nothing else, this site illustrates the simple point that *many* different patterns of faunal assemblage composition can be expected adjacent to water sources, in the past as much as today. It also makes it clear that, since evidence of man or hominids is relatively rare at Elandsfontein compared to the abundance of well-preserved fauna, it is not at all unreasonable to expect that, at the few locations where tools do occur, substantial quantities of bone will also be found. So if bones and water sources 'go together', regardless of the presence or absence of man, it remains for us to discuss the particular conditions under which tools might also be deposited by hominids in such places.

Developing a Plausible Argument

Ever since I began studying the archaeology of early man, I have been puzzled by several repeatedly observed facts of Middle Pleistocene archaeology: (1) many sites of the Acheulean period (Lower Palaeolithic) yield large quantities of stone tools;[11] (2) in most cases these tools appear to be relatively unmodified by use; (3) the use of caves and rock shelters during the Middle Pleistocene seems to be rare, and the earliest known examples tend to be in temperate environmental settings; and (4) most of the locations which archaeologists have called 'sites' are directly associated with water sources.

Now most authors agree that sites of this period with large aggregations of tools can reasonably be considered to be palimpsests of tool distributions accumulating in the course of many separate occupational episodes. If so, however, it is rather difficult to imagine the circumstances under which the substantial scatters of tools lying on the surface were seemingly ignored. The implication must be that, despite the abundance of stone materials already present at the site, its occupants continued to introduce more and to discard them after what must have been quite minimal use. Such a situation to me seems incompatible with the notion of a group which needed to use tools at the site where it lived.[12] After all, which is the more likely – that the occupants of the site would first search its immediate area for appropriate tools and/or raw materials, or that, ignoring the litter of relatively unused tools discarded previously, they would travel to other places where fresh raw material could be obtained and return with tools and/or raw materials?

Sites characterized by the four traits mentioned above[13] in fact seem to represent the endpoints of very short episodes in which planning was involved. Something like the following probably took place. Hominids leave a sleeping place and begin foraging for food in the environment. They make tools suitable for the scavenging tactic being executed and carry them with them until successful; the most likely setting for success would be around water sources where carcasses are apt to be concentrated. Having used the tools for removing edible parts from scavenged carcasses, they discard them and either eat on the spot or return certain parts to a living and sleeping site, or to the nearest waterhole, where consumption might take place. Taking scavenged food back to living sites was probably a characteristic of hominid behavior by the Upper Acheulean and on into the Middle Stone Age of Africa (or the Mousterian in Europe).[14] However, the extent to which this was also the case during the earlier time ranges is precisely what we are trying to determine. The high frequency of finished tools, the lack of evidence that they were used much, and the concentration of tools near water sources where scavengeable carcasses could be found are all conditions that are consistent with the view that these places were locations for the procurement and consumption of scavenged meat and bone marrow, rather than occupation sites where hominids lived in home bases and shared the products of their own hunting activities.[15]

The scenario presented above may appear plausible. It may even account for more facts than the interpretation of such locations as 'living sites'. *But plausibility does not render the interpretation true or accurate*; it simply emphasizes the utility of investigating such possibilities. In advancing these arguments, we are in the same intellectual position as Brain, when he questioned Dart's interpretations and was able to posit reasonable alternative scenarios: the fact that his new ideas made sense did not make them 'true'. Plausibility simply demonstrates that a given line of research is a rational endeavor. Research stemming from such arguments of plausibility ought to result, one hopes, in the production of reliable methods for inference. In studying past human behavior, we must develop criteria which go beyond simple conventions, such as the 'meaning' attached to the coincidence of high densities of artifacts and bone remains.

Current Research

Research on early man sites in East Africa at the present time rather reminds me of my own work in the period between 1966 and 1969 on the 'Mousterian problem', to be discussed in Chapters 4 and 5. The numerous research reports produced by the team members investigating the important sites in the Koobi Fora area[16] indicate that one person is looking for butchering marks and bone breakage patterns; another is studying the steps involved in stone tool manufacture, refitting flakes and tools to establish the sequence of core reduction; yet a third, presumably, is studying the spatial patterning among these bones and tools; and I am sure still others will investigate the materials from these sites in terms of further observational domains. Each new study of this type results in the generation of more facts from the site, but *they are all statements about the archaeological record alone.* In the absence of robust methods for inference, all that can be accomplished is the gathering of more and more facts, whose significance in terms of past behavior is unknown. These facts are commonly interpreted using the method of 'multiple working hypotheses' – put baldly, we recognize that things might have been this way or that way and we exercise judgment as to which appears the more plausible.[17] Only in rare cases have established methods for justifying the inferences advanced been achieved. One such exception is Lawrence Keeley's[18] recognition that flake tools had been used to cut meat as well as some type of plant material: here an established method for measuring tool use, independently tested and rooted in physically founded arguments of necessity, stands behind the inference.

One wonders, indeed, what middle-range research[19] would justify the interpretations which will surely be drawn from newly-acquired facts about spatial patterning, cut marks on bones, frequencies of species, etc. Many archaeological researchers seem not to have accepted fully that studies of the archaeological record provide the stimulus for research in the modern world which, in turn, one hopes can render our archaeological observations into accurate statements about the past. Large numbers of archaeologists still try to make discoveries which are thought to carry self-evident implications for the past. That the past unfolds for those who make careful observations is a cheering thought: unfortunately it is wrong. Research in East Africa must begin to ask the next important question: 'What does it mean?'

Part II WHAT DOES IT MEAN?

In Part I we considered the situation in which a particular curiosity about what behavior or events in the past were like led to attempts to monitor the relevant behaviour in the archaeological record. This section, by contrast, deals with problems which arise from the accumulation of detailed observations and which are therefore only recognizable after *intensive investigations of the archaeological record itself have taken place. When the archaeologist has conducted studies resulting in the recognition of interesting patterns in the archaeological record, the question that then arises is how to understand what such patterns mean. In other words, what happened in the past to bring into being the forms of patterning that archaeologists have observed?*

Most of us realize that we do not simply invent methods for studying the archaeological record and then use these procedures as a completely objective way of searching for patterning. Quite the contrary: we develop procedures for studying the archaeological record because we think they permit us to make relevant observations about those properties of the past we seek to elucidate. Typically, archaeologists have invented procedures for classifying the things they find and have used various conventions for giving meaning to the classes so recognized. These taxonomies or classifications then guide their observations concerning the distributions of things, in terms of time and space. Similarly, archaeologists have expectations about the character of the patterns which should result from their studies, for they set out with certain ideas about what these classifications measure.

I have used the term 'convention' above, since it is argued here that the 'theory' with which archaeology normally operates has assumed a set of conventions for giving meaning to observations from the archaeological record. These conventions ensure that no empirical materials could come into conflict with prior assumptions. It must be emphasized – given that all statements about the past are inferences – that there is simply no way to reason from a set of assumptions to a conclusion which conflicts with those assumptions. As Popper noted: 'For neither a deductive nor an inductive inference can ever proceed from consistent premises to a conclusion that formally contradicts the premises from which we started.'[1]

Archaeologists frequently make assumptions about the way the archaeological record was conditioned in its formal and distributional properties. For instance, it is commonly assumed that cultures were internally homogeneous and were strongly integrated, by virtue of their participants' ideas and values. In this view, the expectations for patterning in the archaeological record are quite clear: '. . . the types and their proportions are stable and constant within a single culture during a given period in a given region, at least within certain limits.'[2] *In simple terms, we should find that sites are more similar, the closer they were to one another in both time and space. If the real world differs from these expectations, what happens is that endless 'auxiliary hypotheses' are generated to accommodate the observations to the theory.*

Thus the tactic followed by conventional archaeologists is to offer additional arguments which, 'if true', would bring theory and reality back into correspondence. Popper[3] *has dubbed this strategy 'immunizing' a theory from testing. Archaeologists have been committed to such a strategy: their attempts to immunize their prior assumptions in this way have become their reconstructed histories of the past. If, for instance, they fail to observe similarities through depositional sequences, their theory of cultural transmission is 'protected' from these facts by postulating a migration of new people into the area. This hypothetical migration, in turn, becomes a built-in part of the 'true' reconstruction of the past which archaeologists are supposed to be seeking. 'A nice adaptation of conditions will make almost any hypothesis agree with the phenomena. This will please the imagination but does not advance our knowledge.'*[4]

Archaeologists are particularly prone to this type of philosophical and methodological trap, since all statements about the past must be inferences and the methods which tend to justify their inferences consequently cannot be tested by experiment with archaeological data. Put another way, we can never use the inferred past to test the assumptions we make in generating such inferences. It is not surprising, therefore, that most archaeologists unquestioningly accept their methods for making inferences and argue about data, rather than the validity of such methods themselves. Only rarely can we gain sufficient perspective to 'get the message' that our methods for inference may be faulty. When this does happen, however, there can begin the methodological search for some better understanding of the dynamic conditions which brought into being the forms of archaeological patterning we have documented. Once we can answer the question 'What does it mean?', we can begin provocative research aimed at learning 'what it was like'.

4
The Challenge of the Mousterian

Businessmen and politicians sometimes give their opponents the derogatory label 'Neanderthal'. For most of us, the name conjures up the picture of a stocky, somewhat hairy individual with a receding forehead, large features and a fur skin draped around the waist. This creature is generally depicted staring blankly at a bewildering world from the cave-mouth, surrounded by the garbage from carnivorous meals. Neanderthal man's public image is of a rude, dumb, uncultured animal motivated by the most basic human drives for food, sex and creature comfort. In contrast, the archaeological textbooks tend to give Neanderthalers an innovative role in human history. It is frequently pointed out that they were the first of our ancestors to use pigments,[1] to bury their dead[2] and perhaps to practice some type of ritual focused on cave bears.[3] In the days when we tended to view the past as a saga of man's emergence from the realm of beasts into the human domain, the Neanderthalers were usually depicted as the creatures which exhibited the first glimmerings of our modern interest in aesthetics (i.e. art and religion), behaviors far removed from the dominant basic concerns characteristic of our bestial ancestors. In the more recent literature, particularly that produced by our biologically oriented colleagues, the Neanderthalers are considered to be a racial variant of fully modern man; they are not uncommonly assumed to be similar to us in behavioral terms, since the origins of such very human behaviors as speech with true language are thought to have occurred prior to their appearance. Given this last perspective, speculations regarding our evolutionary history are therefore commonly focused on eras preceding the Middle Palaeolithic of the Neanderthalers.

While it is true that there have been differing views regarding the behavior of Neanderthalers (a 'What was it like?' question), it was not in fact this diversity of opinion which stimulated the controversy and research which I will discuss in this chapter. Here I want to consider the problem of the Mousterian (the archaeological name for the period associated with Neanderthal man, about 125,000 to 30,000 years ago), a problem which arose out of strictly archaeological, methodological concerns. It represents a different kind of discussion from that presented in Part I. For instance, the controversies examined in Chapters 2 and 3, regarding whether early man was a hunter and whether he lived in base camps and shared food, concerned the contents of the archaeological sites in question and whether they were exclusively attributable to the behavior of early hominids. Once this hurdle could be negotiated, there was little else of methodological concern relevant to these issues. The challenge for early man studies was quite simply: how do we know the past? The debate which centered around Neanderthal man had different historical roots, since it arose out of archaeological research *per se*. In addition, the discussion has been based on dissimilar units. With early man the focus was on the behavioral interpretation of the associations recorded among many kinds of things at individual sites; the Mousterian problem, however, arose in the context of controversy regarding the meaning of variability observed within a single class of items recovered at many sites. Furthermore, it arose because increasingly complex patterning among the formal taxonomic units used by archaeologists was recognized for the Middle Palaeolithic.

The 'Relic and Monument' Period

From the very beginning of archaeology, two basic questions have remained fundamental: (1) how do we describe in formal terms the variability in things remaining from the past and (2) how is the observed variability distributed chronologically and geographically? In the early days of archaeological work many things, relatively speaking, were collected, but the context of the finds was not well documented. Archaeologists could classify and recognize similarities and differences among artifacts and constructions – that is, organizations of matter which were clearly referable to the hand of man. These things were known as 'relics and monuments': a hand ax, a bronze spear, Stonehenge, the spectacular passage grave of Newgrange in Ireland, and so on. As archaeologists worked to discover the distributions of the various classes of finds, they found that certain properties of these materials yielded distributional results, while others, at any given stage of research, seemed to show less recognizable patterning. For instance, in the early, seminal work of C. J. Thomsen in Denmark it became clear that the type of raw material from which tools were manufactured exhibited significant chronological patterning; hence, the Ages of Stone, Bronze and Iron were born.[4] In Palaeolithic research it began to emerge that the design of tools within a single category of raw material was meaningful both in a chronological and geographical sense. Hand axes seemed to occur only in certain types of geological deposits and in association with certain types of fauna. On the other hand, retouched pieces, such as those recovered from Solutré in France, occurred in very different geological and faunal contexts.

The attributes which seemed to exhibit chronological and/or geographical patterns were isolated as indexes to ages and areas. The model for this type of

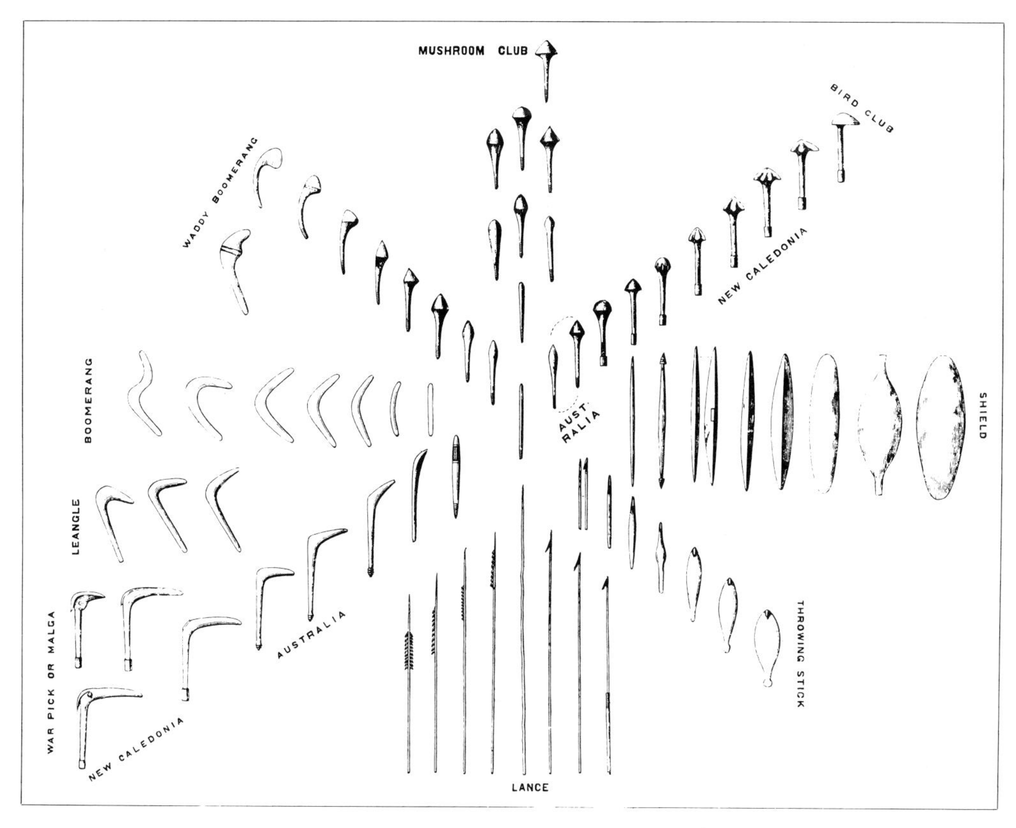

33 General Pitt-Rivers' proposed reconstruction of evolutionary lines of development from the simple stick to more complex tool types: a characteristic 19th and early 20th century view of the past. (Reproduced with permission from Myres 1906, pl. III.)

approach was the obvious success achieved in geology and palaeontology, where index fossils could be shown to be diagnostic of different ages and eras in the earth's history. Linked with the belief that taxonomic study involved the discovery of natural order in archaeological data was the idea that man's past was characterized by progress. The idea of progress is perhaps most clearly stated in the writings of General Pitt-Rivers, one of the 'fathers' of archaeology, at least in the English-speaking countries:

> The task before us is to follow . . . the succession of ideas by which the mind of man has developed, from the simple to the complex, and from the homogeneous to the heterogeneous; to work out step by step . . . the law of contiguity by which the mind has passed from simple . . . states of consciousness to the association of ideas, and so on to broader generalizations.[5]

At first for most archaeologists the sequence of man's development towards civilization was also a logical, progressive, evolutionary sequence from simple to complex. It was a playing out of a logical succession in which one piece of knowledge conditioned the next, and so on. General Pitt-Rivers epitomizes this approach.[6] In ill. 33, for example, we see the origin of a variety of industrial 'phyla' in a simple unmodified stick. Under one set of initial modifications we can monitor a progression leading to the Australian shield, while under another set of initial conditions a second sequence leads to the war club and so forth. When viewed in this manner, mankind was seen as progressing through a series of interdependent stages of progress. Since the sequence was thought to be dependent on serial order, all mankind should have proceeded through the same series of stages. Variability in the modern world was seen as representing various degrees of arrested development, such that some contemporary peoples had become stabilized in stages which had been passed through by other peoples at a much earlier period. This view of cultural evolution justified the common practice of fleshing out prehistory by drawing heavily on descriptions of contemporary primitive societies. For example, in order to recreate Neanderthal man's way of life, the Australian Aborigines were frequently used as a model. I quote from a wonderful little book written from a classical, cultural evolutionary perspective based on the assumption of progress (*Everyday Life in the Old Stone Age*, published in 1922):

> We must search for some primitive people living under similar conditions, and at about the same stage of civilization as the Mousterians, and see if we can draw some useful comparisons. The aborigines of Australia are such a people.[7]

Within the intellectual climate in which the idea of progress dominated, there were several other important points of view which were sometimes maintained independently and at other times were merged in various ways into a kind of generalized vitalism. The concept of emergent process saw the evolution of man as resulting from the realization of his potential, assumed to be an essential quality or intrinsic 'spark' which grew and developed in slightly different ways under differing biological or physical environments. For instance, in accepting the (fake) jaw[8] found at Piltdown in England in 1908 as evidence that our very early ancestors possessed a larger brain than *Pithecanthropus* (which at that time was thought to have been younger in age), Henry Fairfield Osborn and others were lead to the following type of conclusion:

> If *Pithecanthropus* is truly of mid-stone age, as now appears, it must be regarded as a surviving primitive type of Dawn Man sequestered in the forests of Java. . . . This survival of a primitive type of man shut off from competition with more vigorous types is by no means a unique occurrence, because we still find

many very primitive types of humanity living in remote and isolated parts of the earth, such as the Tasmanian natives.[9]

In line with this view, the linkage of evolutionism with a kind of racism was also not uncommon; and other elitist ideas besides were mustered to explain the differential achievements of man. For instance, the 'great man theory' (which sees progress occurring by virtue of the behaviors of especially gifted individuals) was common in the past and is still very much a part of archaeology, as is well illustrated in comments made by François Bordes as recently as 1969:

. . . intelligence and creative intellect ought not to be confused. The latter is rare, even today, and it appears that one can deduce from the history of diverse civilizations that the proportion of creative intellects is, cultural conditions and the pressures of environment being constant, a function of the total number of individuals. Then it is possible that generations among Palaeolithic peoples which were not very numerous have come and gone, within the same group, between the appearance of creative intellects. Progress then has been slow even though the populations may have been intelligent and have put to good use the data already acquired.[10]

This view is also accepted by Grahame Clark who wrote in 1979 that 'the course of history has been shaped less by popular heresies than by the original thinking of outstanding men.'[11]

In the early days of prehistoric archaeology, regardless of the exact theory which one preferred for explaining how things came to be, few questioned the progressive view of man's past. Given such a perspective, the goal of archaeology was, logically enough, the discovery of the actual sequence of progressive change. In 1893 Otis Mason, addressing the founding fathers of American archaeology, said: 'The most profitable inquiry [of archaeology] is the search for the origin of epoch-making ideas in order to comprehend the history of civilization.'[12] Much the same aim and understanding of archaeological goals was stated by N. C. Nelson half a century later: '. . . our science is called upon to demonstrate the time and place of origin of all the principal inventions and to trace their spread over the world.'[13]

By the first quarter of the 20th century Palaeolithic archaeologists considered many of these goals to have been achieved. The Old Stone Age was conceived in stages. The earliest period, that of the 'Drift', represented by open-air sites located along river beds, was characterized by heavy core tools, the hand axes which had been discovered by Boucher de Perthes to reveal man's great antiquity. The next state of cultural development was the Mousterian period or the era of 'cave men', typified by tools made on flakes and most commonly retouched on only one side. The Mousterian was followed by the Aurignacian, Solutrean, and 34

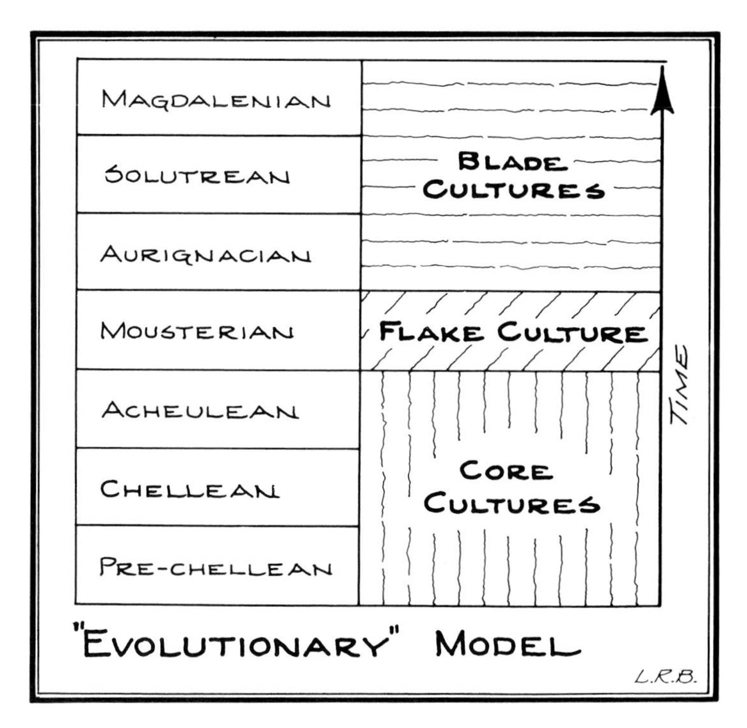

34 Model of cultural evolution as conceived by prehistorians during the late nineteenth and early 20th centuries. The names of periods are listed on the left, the major tool types correlated with them on the right.

Magdalenian periods during which men lived both in caves and in the open, made stone tools on blades but also used bone, antler and ivory, and practiced art and ritual.[14]

The 'Artifact and Assemblage' Period[15]

If early Palaeolithic archaeology can be characterized by its concern with how relics and monuments indicated the relative achievements of mankind, the subsequent 'artifact and assemblage' period saw increased concern for the classification of artifacts and the description of assemblages, defined as aggregates of associated artifacts thought to be contemporary. The character of assemblages, in turn, was thought to be referable to identifiable ethnic peoples. The spirit of this view can perhaps best be summarized by this famous statement written by V. Gordon Childe in 1929 for the introduction to his book, *The Danube in Prehistory*:

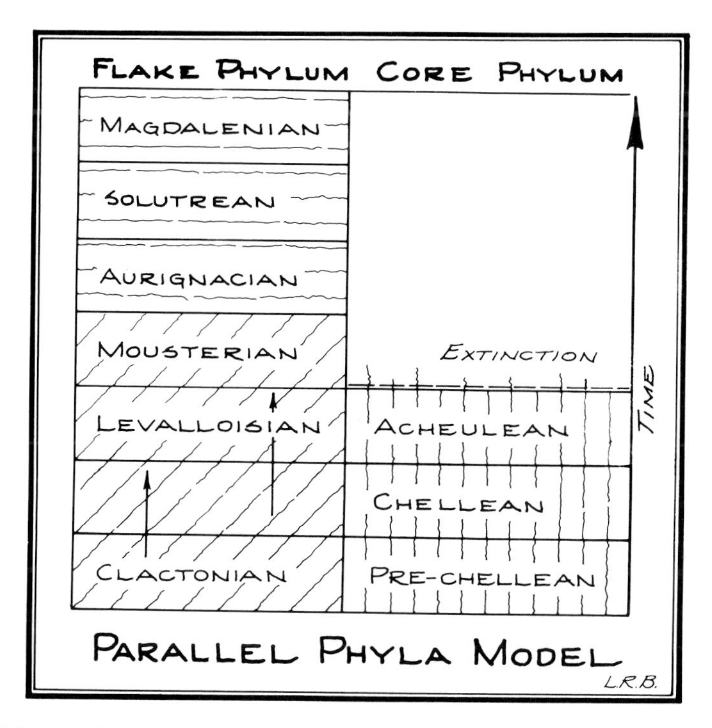

35 Model of *parallel phyla* as popularized by prehistorians after *c.* 1930. Different cultural groups, represented by particular types of stone tools, were thought in some cases to be contemporary, rather than to follow each other in a strictly evolutionary sequence (as in ill. 34).

> We find certain types of remains – pots, implements, ornaments, burial sites, house forms – constantly recurring together. Such a complex of regularly associated traits we shall term a 'cultural group' or just a 'culture'. We assume that such a complex is the material expression of what would today be called a 'people'.[16]

The idea of ethnic history, of course, was not new and had been debated since at least the turn of the century in contexts younger than the Old Stone Age.[17] In Europe there were several theoretical positions regarding the role of *pure races*, versus what today we would call *hybrid vigor*, in stimulating progress. Similarly, there were considerable differences of opinion regarding the inventiveness of man. Some scholars thought that man was extremely conservative and innovations were rare, while others considered that since man reacted to the same stimuli in similar ways, one could expect many inventions to be made independently at different times and places. In general, those who believed in pure race as the mediator of cultural progress saw man as uninventive and hence expected to find cultural traditions to be highly stable and to have great time depth. On the other hand, those who took a more liberal view saw man as relatively creative and envisaged culture as being subject to change from within as well as from diffusion of ideas from outside; hence they felt it was difficult to trace cultures back in terms of pure lines.

These arguments, combined with the generalized growth of various historical schools of interpretation, had little significant impact on Palaeolithic research because the study of the Old Stone Age seemed to demonstrate progress according to stages of cultural growth. In other words, the empirical materials seemed to be in tune with the older evolutionary ideas: arguments against evolutionism seemed irrelevant for students of the Palaeolithic. This was all changed, however, when in the early 1930s the Abbé Breuil[18] advanced his views that parallel phyla (or, in more modern terms, major cultural traditions) existed contemporaneously during the vast time spans of the Old Stone Age. The impact of Breuil's ideas is well illustrated by a statement made in 1938 by Dorothy Garrod:

> In the old system, the Palaeolithic cultures appeared as a straightforward succession with clear-cut horizontal divisions as in a diagrammatic geological section. For the pioneers of prehistory these cultures developed logically one from the other in an orderly upward movement, and it was assumed that they represented world-wide stages in the history of human progress. Today prehistory has suffered the fate of so many of the component parts of the orderly universe of the nineteenth century. New knowledge has given a twist to the kaleidoscope, and the pieces are still falling about before our bewildered eyes. The main outline of the new pattern is, however, already beginning to appear. We can distinguish in the Old Stone Age three cultural elements of primary importance. These are manifested in the so-called hand-axe industries, flake industries, and blade industries, and we know that the first two, at any rate, run side by side as far back as we can see, and we are beginning to realize that the origins of the third may have to be sought much farther back than we had suspected. Only a moment of reflection is needed to see that we have here the old divisions of Lower, Middle and Upper Palaeolithic, but with a new axis; we must be careful, however, not to make these divisions too rigid. In fact, these culture streams do not run parallel and independent; such a view of human history would be absurdly artificial. They are perpetually meeting and influencing each other, and sometimes they come together to produce a new facies.[19]

This statement by one of Britain's most eminent prehistorians demonstrates nicely just how revolutionary Breuil's ideas were. It is interesting that, while there was certainly opposition to this radical reinterpretation of our past, 'parallel cultural phyla' became the orthodox view rather rapidly. Furthermore Breuil elaborated his notion of the past by suggesting that the independent cultural traditions exhibited somewhat contrasting distributions with respect to time and environment:

> . . . we find biface industries alternating with flake industries. The flakes come before and after the peaks of cold and the bifaces in the interglacial periods. It seems reasonable to deduce that this alternation was due to the movements of human groups which as the glacial conditions came on, followed the animals they hunted to the south and west.[20]

It did not take long before an equation was made between these contrasting traditions and the belief then current that different forms of ancient men were contemporary:

> It will appear that during the earlier part of Pleistocene times . . . two different races occupied the area. At first industries belonging to a flake tool culture (Cromerian) appear, but later in the west the Chello-Acheulian culture, spreading up from Africa and belonging to the core-tool civilization swept the board . . . with the coming of the last glacial maximum the coup-de-poing makers retired from the scene and cultures belonging to the flake-tool civilization occupied the whole area.[21]

The view that there was a 'flake-tool tradition' manufactured by *neoanthropic* forms (hominids ancestral to modern man) contemporary with a 'core-tool tradition' produced by a *palaeoanthropic* form (which did not contribute to our immediate ancestry) was popular in the 1930s and 1940s and was still widely discussed during the 1950s.[22]

In 1936 D. Peyrony extended the reasoning about parallel phyla to the Upper Palaeolithic. He argued that what had previously been designated Aurignacian in the scheme of de Mortillet was more appropriately viewed as two different cultural traditions, the Aurignacian proper and the Perigordian.[23] His argument was widely accepted and remains the basis for much of the classification of French Upper Palaeolithic artifacts.[24]

The Tree of Life

Following a reorientation in the way a science views its subject, there is usually a change in the methods and approaches used in classifying or ordering observations. In the case of Palaeolithic studies, the work of François Bordes has been 36 instrumental in this regard.[25] Bordes developed both the most widely adopted system for classifying stone tools, as well as the techniques used for describing assemblages quantitatively. His quantitative summaries of the forms of stone

36 François Bordes on a trip to Australia, 1974.

tools found together in excavated levels became the primary units of comparison, and from this work came assemblage-based systematics of the archaeological record. In addition, Bordes argued that the *techniques* used in the manufacture of stone tools should be treated independently of the actual *forms* of tool design. The latter attribute was manifested in such traits as relationships between the orientation of the original flakes, the shapes of the working edges and the orientation of the working edges relative to the form of the flake on which the tools were produced. In opposition to design traits, the techniques used in the production of flakes were argued by Bordes to be conditioned by the character of the raw materials available in different places and therefore of little utility for reconstructing culture histories, for detecting the emergence of distinct peoples, or for studying social interaction among separate cultural groups of distinct peoples.[26]

With these points in mind, Bordes energetically set about the study of previously excavated materials and also began a series of long-term excavations[27] which were to change considerably our views of the past. Using his standard list of types, he could classify all the tools recovered from a recognized archaeological level. The frequencies of the various tool types could then be summarized by means by a cumulative graph.[28] When the shapes of these graphs for sites of the Middle Palaeolithic Mousterian period were compared, Bordes recognized what seemed to be a repetitive pattern: there appeared to be just four basic forms of

37

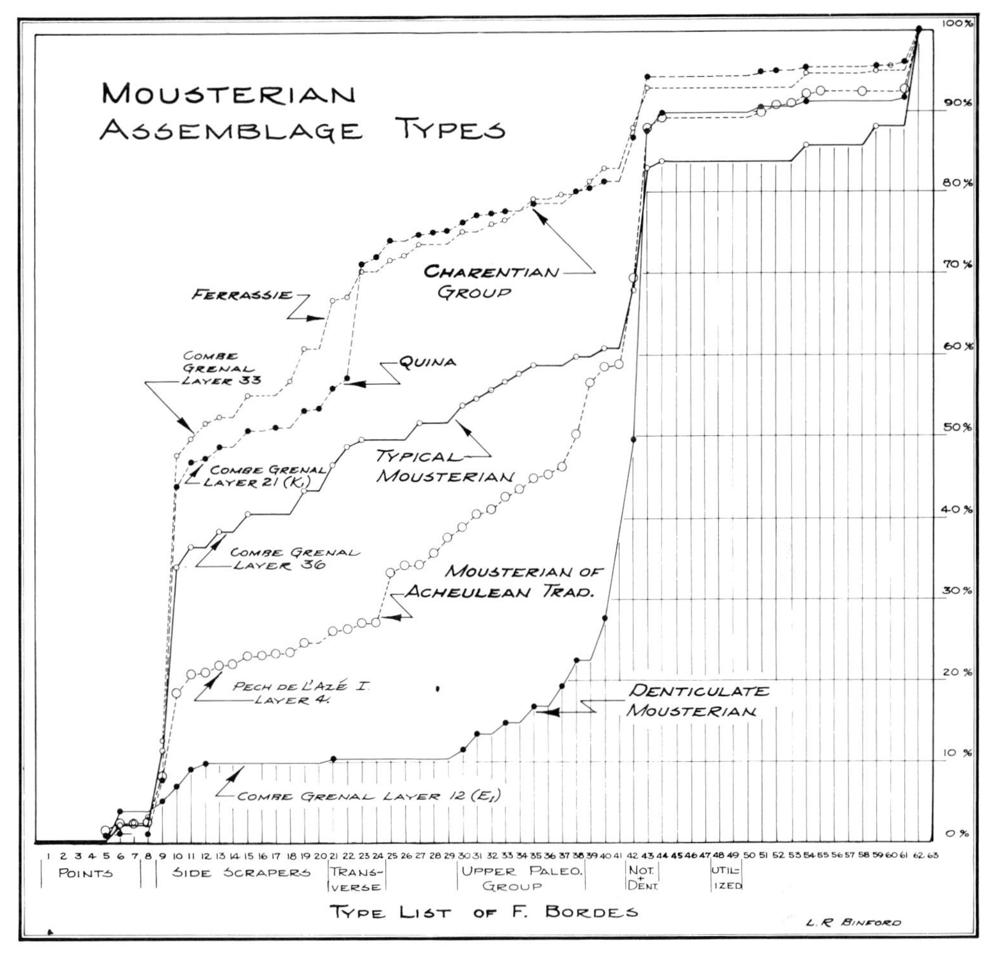

37 Graphic definition of Bordes' Mousterian assemblage types. The tool types are listed along the horizontal axis. A plot of the cumulative percentages of each tool type within an assemblage generally conforms to one of the four major shape categories. The controversy that resulted from these data was about the *meaning* of the four distinctive curves.

graph represented by many examples, with only a few judged to be ambiguous or intermediate cases. The four types of Mousterian recognized by Bordes can be summarized as follows:

1 *Mousterian of Acheulean Tradition*

This assemblage is generally recognized by the presence of hand axes, moderate numbers of side scrapers, many denticulates and notches, and a distinctively high frequency of backed knives. The distinctive shape of the graph is a low curve.

2 *Typical Mousterian*
This type generally forms a diagonal graph (because most of the tool types are present in roughly equal proportions). It differs from the Mousterian of Acheulean tradition primarily in the rarity of hand axes and the lower frequencies of backed knives and other tool types analogous to common Upper Palaeolithic types.

3 *Denticulate Mousterian*
The distribution of this type normally comprises a low, concave graph, because there are few scrapers but many notches and denticulates. Hand axes are rare to absent; scrapers are poorly made; and backed knives are rare.

4 *Charentian Group*
A final group of assemblages is recognizable by a high, convex graph dominated by scrapers. Denticulates and notches are infrequent, while hand axes and backed knives are rare to absent. Bordes recognizes two subtypes of the Charentian: (a) a *Quina* type in which the scrapers are typically transverse in form and the Levallois technique is rare to absent; and (b) the *Ferrassie* type characterized by scrapers produced on the sides of flakes and by the frequent presence of the Levallois technique.

In current terminology I would label Bordes' early studies as 'pattern recognition work', because he defined and refined in an ordered manner the properties of things which he could systematically observe. He then made many observations about the archaeological record and recognized structure in the data.

What shocked some archaeologists at the time was the nature of the patterning which began to emerge from the application of *La Méthode Bordes*[29]. An observation made previously (and both verified and clarified by the application of Bordes' methods) was that the stratigraphic sequence of changes in the forms of stone tool assemblages was not necessarily directional, nor did it appear to represent either gradual or transformational patterns of change. This had been observed for the Mousterian by Peyrony,[30] but was forcefully demonstrated by Bordes, particularly through his excavations at the now famous site of Combe Grenal.[31] Using his techniques Bordes showed the existence of three characteristics of the data which were

38

1 *Alternating Industries.* Throughout a long stratigraphic sequence with successive levels of beds, one type of Mousterian, for instance Typical, might be followed in time by Denticulate, but then a still later level would yield a Typical Mousterian assemblage again. In this pattern the types of Mousterian assemblage maintain their distinct identity through time, but alternate with one another in various ways through particular sequences.

2 *Parallel Phyla.* Seen from the perspective of the region as a whole, however, the different types of Mousterian preserved their identity through long spans

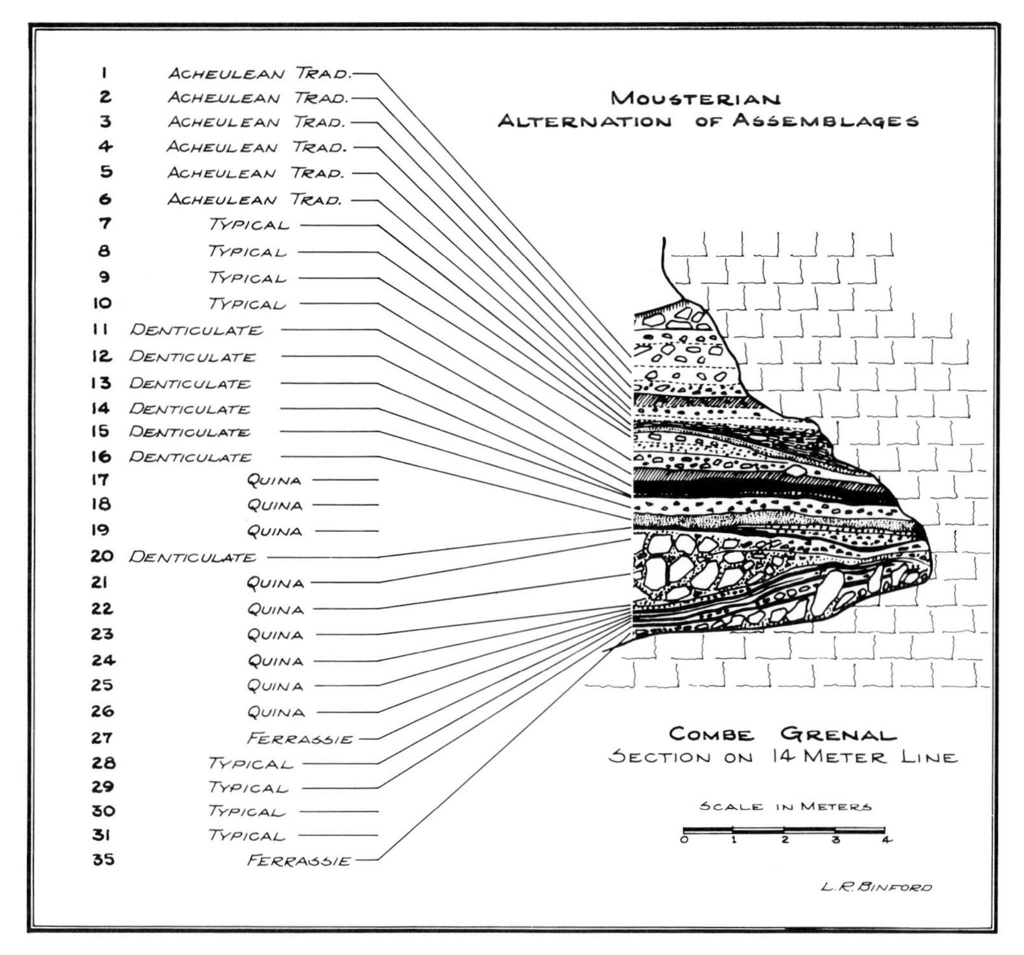

38 Archaeological section from the Mousterian site of Combe Grenal in France, illustrating alternating assemblages.

of time and they co-existed as recognizable cultures.[32] The implication was that when they were absent in the sequences of one site, they would be represented in the patterns seen at some other contemporary site.

3 *Tenacious Cultures.* The patterning uncovered by Bordes could be further described as indicative of tenacious cultures: that is, forms of behavioral organization represented relatively unchanged in the archaeological record over long periods of time. These different assemblage types were also unaffected by contact with other equally distinct cultures which were present in the same general area.

The general view of the past produced by the use of Bordes' methods supported the picture proposed by Peyrony and argued by the Abbé Breuil, namely that there were different cultural lines which extended far back into antiquity.[33] These lines or phyla maintained their formal integrity much as biological species do and therefore were not capable of hybridizing readily with different 'species'. The distribution of these cultural species ebbed and flowed back and forth across geographic space, resulting in archaeological deposits in the form of assemblages which might alternate with others and which might come and go in the same region through time. The concept of assemblages as representing cultural species has recently been characterized as the *organic* view of the past:

> Culture history can be regarded and accounted for in essential *organic* terms. This notion more specifically entailed two unspoken assumptions. The first was that a direct parallelism exists between the cultural and organic worlds of such a kind that we can expect to find a one to one correlation between archaeological and natural stratigraphy. The second was that any given cultural complex, like any given paleontological complex, should be more or less invariant in the manner in which it expresses itself. This last means that the cultural entities recognized in archaeological systematics are to be regarded as natural categories, which – in the manner, say of organic species – are inherently discontinuous and do not modify their form from one context to the next. It follows that a specific tradition should give rise to but one characteristic type of industry in any specific block of time and space in the archaeological record.[34]

So, in spite of his major refinements of method resulting in the demonstration of patterning in the archaeological record with a level of accuracy never before achieved, Bordes' innovations were nevertheless integrated within an older view of culture and the past compatible with a biological model: the tree of life, as A. L. Kroeber aptly called it.

The Present: A Conflict of Views

It was the crisp patterning, developed and demonstrated with Bordes' refined techniques of observation and description, that really forced myself and others to recognize that the view of the past to which the archaeological record was being accommodated by our French colleagues was in conflict with the general notion of culture developed by Americanist scholars through the study of modern, native peoples in the New World. This difference has been described by Americans as a contrast between the *organic view*, illustrated by the tree of life, and the *cultural view*, represented by the tree of culture. The cultural view had been derived by researchers studying the spatial distribution of traits and complexes among known

39

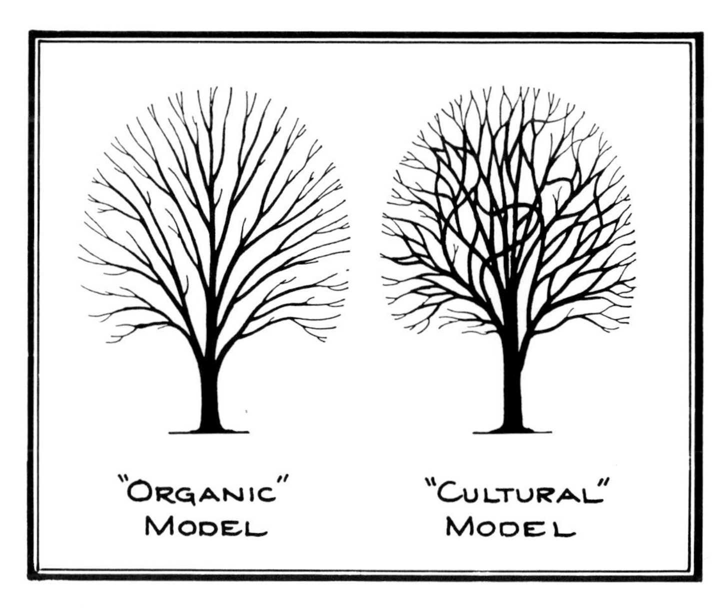

39 Comparison of *organic* and *cultural* views of the past in terms of the 'Tree of Life'. (Based on Kroeber 1948, fig. 18.)

ethnic and social groups across vast regions of North America. One result of this work, for instance, was the finding of a strong correlation between the distribution of distinctive cultural forms and kinds of environment,[35] but archaeologists working with the materials studied according to Bordes' methods have generally denied that such correlations might have occurred in their data.[36] In addition, American anthropologists have found it difficult to distinguish regional boundaries between social or ethnic groups.[37] Variability among such socially defined units tended to be graded across many groups, rendering the recognition of ethnically distinct groups a nearly impossible task. In marked contrast, ethnic distinctiveness was considered by those holding the organic view to be characteristic of past peoples. In summary, there was a direct opposition between the views of culture underlying Bordes' techniques of archaeological analysis and those based on observations of the distributions of things produced by ethnic groups in the modern world.

At this point a critical question had to be faced: was the past so different from conditions documented in the modern world, or were there characteristics of the way we look at the past which created an image in our minds different from what we saw in the modern world? It was of vital importance to know what meaning had been assigned to the observations made on the archaeological record when using Bordes' procedures for description. In short, what was Bordes' taxonomy actually measuring and what was really indicated by the contrasts in assemblage composition seen at different sites? In 1966, together with Sally Binford, I suggested conditions which – if they had obtained in the past – might have led to some of the forms of patterning observed by Bordes.[38] Our work at that time was based on the realization that this inconsistency between views of the past demanded research designed to investigate the way the archaeological record was formed and to identify the kinds of variability that are derived from different forms of systems dynamics. These issues are pursued further in the next chapter.

The history of research in the case of the Mousterian is very different from the disputes about early man (Chapter 2), in which research quickly became orientated towards understanding the archaeological record in terms of the conditions which brought it into being. The Mousterian problem was less clearly about method, since the techniques used by Bordes were accepted by most as being very sophisticated and were therefore seen as *the* methodology. The patterns revealed through the use of Bordes' approach were considered to be empirical and hence not subject to question. The conflict did not lead to a scramble for methods which could be used in support of one's interpretations of the past. The meaning to be given to the patterning seemed to follow from the data in a self-evident fashion. There were tenacious cultures and alternating industries: how could this be disputed? As more and more archaeological patterning was demonstrated at a higher and more rigorous level of documentation, it gradually became apparent that the patterning illustrated over and over conflicted with one view of the nature of cultural variability. Only when the archaeological record was made to 'speak' through the improved descriptive procedures of Bordes did the previously hidden conflict between the views of culture guiding the methods of Bordes on the one hand, and the concepts derived from descriptions of American Indian material culture on the other, become apparent. The recognition of fundamental differences in assumptions about the archaeological record, as well as about culture itself, was therefore prompted by the emergence of the Mousterian problem.

While the discussion about early man has a certain theatricality involving frequent argument and 'playing to the wings', research on the Mousterian problem has been relatively quiet. Nevertheless, it too is likely to have a substantial impact on archaeology in general: for with the Mousterian controversy we are engaged in questioning our basic ideas, those related to the very nature of culture.

5
An Archaeological Odyssey

Discovering the Past

Those of us who began our careers in archaeology in the late 1950s and early 1960s were trained in rather traditional ways. Most of our teachers had spent their careers trying to solve chronological problems by studying changes in artifact forms and various types of sequential arrangements of material, largely without the aid of stratigraphical information. So the minimal methodological training that I and my age grade received involved learning how to compare assemblages and arrange them in series, in the hope that such series somehow reflected time. Seriation was emphasized over stratigraphy, because there was a myth abroad at that time – at least in eastern North America – that there were few or no stratified deposits.[1] Archaeological methodology was almost exclusively concerned with questions of chronology.

What changed all that and led some of us to start making noises in the late 1950s was the invention and application of radiocarbon dating. Many of us thought that C14 would solve, once and for all, most of the traditional problems of chronology to which our teachers had devoted so much effort. And if those problems were at least partially solved, then it would become possible to use archaeological remains in a more economical fashion.[2] That is, if chipped stone tools and pottery and the other artifacts archaeologists study had so far been used only to solve a chronological problem which could now be solved simply by analyzing lumps of charcoal, what was to be done with all the artifacts? There must be *other* kinds of information to be extracted.[3] The breakthrough in radiocarbon dating was not the only factor involved: other dating techniques (such as dendrochronology), a renewed interest in geology, and the late recognition that there *did* in fact exist good stratified sites in North America were also important. But our response to all these changes was to begin to look for ways of getting new information about the past and about subjects other than chronology itself.

In retrospect, I think that much of the work in those early days followed a strongly inductive strategy. We reasoned that if we wanted to know about the past in new ways, we would have to work out new ways of looking: as the invention of the microscope had shown, if a new way of looking is found, then lots of new facts will be seen and, in principle, those new facts should refer to new kinds of phenomena. That, at any rate, was our early idea. So I began to work, for example, on mortuary practices.[4] Similarly, although it now sounds amazing, there was little experimental work by Americans with chipped stone tools at that time; John Witthoft was really the only American archaeologist in my predecessor generation who had done any experimentation on the manufacture of stone tools.[5] I started to try thinking of lithic assemblages in terms of reduction sequences, examining the by-products all the way from raw material to the production of finished tools.[6] Stimulated by Witthoft's work I began to play around with techniques for the analysis of lithic waste.[7] But all these approaches were a search for new ways of looking, for ways of isolating new kinds of facts from the same old material. At that point we never thought to ask 'How do we give meaning to what we see?'; we looked only to see new things. We were optimistic that we would somehow 'know' their meaning.

It was in that context that I began to write about sampling in archaeology[8] and about the potential applications of probability and statistics to the excavation and analysis of archaeological materials. But far more important, as it turned out, were two new kinds of problems that I became involved in. The first of these was the question of the origins of agriculture,[9] an old problem that archaeologists had already discussed for years. This was essentially a question of explanation: how and why did it happen? In Chapter 8 I will discuss this type of problem as well as my current thinking about how it could be solved.

The other problem was something rather different: it concerned the meaning to be given to variability in the archaeological record and, specifically, to the variability isolated in the European Mousterian industries by François Bordes (Chapter 4). This was something I became very familiar with in the early 1960s and argued about long and hard before anything was ever published, because it seemed to me that this was an altogether new kind of problem. The argument was *not* about the nature of the archaeological record. Most of us knew the archaeological facts, the sites themselves and what had been found in them; we trusted Bordes and had no argument with his typology. What we were arguing about was something quite different – the *meaning* of the patterning demonstrated to exist in the archaeological record. Before the Mousterian problem arose, this kind of difficulty had not been faced squarely (or certainly not in my own studies of burials, chipped stone, and so on). As a student, I can now see, most of the arguments I had learned were about the conventional interpretation of archaeological finds. Someone might say, for instance, 'I've found a site at *X* and a site at *Y*, both of the same date, so I think there ought to be another one somewhere in the middle at *Z*'; then someone else would say 'No, I don't think there's one at *Z*'. Almost all the conversations and arguments in which I had participated were of this kind, concerned with the *character* of the archaeological record. The

Mousterian argument, at least as I conceived of it, was something very different.

Yet even though I recognized this distinction, I still tried to work towards a solution of the problem through discovery techniques. As I knew that further excavation could not solve the problem, I thought it might be possible to solve it by analyzing in a different way the material that already existed. So I began to explore what I now refer to as 'pattern recognition techniques', using multivariate techniques which help us to isolate and recognize patterns that in one way or another are inherent in the data of the archaeological record.[10] I was pleased with the strategies for pattern recognition we began to apply early in the 1960s, not only to Mousterian finds but to many other areas besides: Bob Whallon, Henry Wright and several others were all using and exploring these approaches for a wide variety of archaeological material.[11] But the basic argument, of course, did not go away. It just got more intense. 40

40 Bordes' initial response to the *functional* argument for explaining assemblage variability in the Mousterian. The procedure followed by the Binfords is simple: pour stone tools into one end of a computer and Neanderthal man walks out at the other end! (Cartoon drawn by Pierre Laurent on the inside cover of an offprint by de Sonneville-Bordes 1966).

The Facts do not Speak for Themselves

In 1967 I received funds[12] to go to Europe for a year to work more closely with Bordes in Bordeaux. My program for research was the following. If we could not study the chipped stone directly, perhaps we could study faunal remains and the horizontal distributions, on excavated archaeological floors,[13] of both fauna and chipped stone. Then it might be possible to relate variability in the lithics to these other properties of the archaeological sites in question, properties that had not so far been studied systematically. Different kinds of activity, I reasoned, must have combined in different ways to produce these assemblages, so there should be some sort of correlation between at least some activities and some of the by-products of food consumption (e.g. animal bones); equally, there should exist some form of relationship between some, if not all, of the tools related to the procurement, processing and consumption of animals. I worked for a year in France, identifying and plotting all the stone tools and animal bones by anatomical part and by breakage pattern.

41, 42

Then began the first of a whole series of disillusionments. When the sites were excavated, it turned out, each stone tool had been plotted using three-dimensional spatial co-ordinates, so that they could be plotted horizontally and vertically in order to reconstruct their distribution on past ground surfaces; the bones, on the other hand, had been collected only by level. The quality of the data was high, but not high enough to allow me to analyze one type of information in the same units I was using to analyze another one. It was possible to run cross-correlations between whole faunal assemblages and whole lithic assemblages, but not to look for distributional correlations between bone and stone within levels. Nevertheless, I performed one correlation study after another – so many, in fact, that I needed a great steel trunk in order to carry all the papers back to the United States. I could tell you cross-correlations between any pair of Mousterian tool-types, between tools and bones, between bones and the drip-lines in cave sites, between

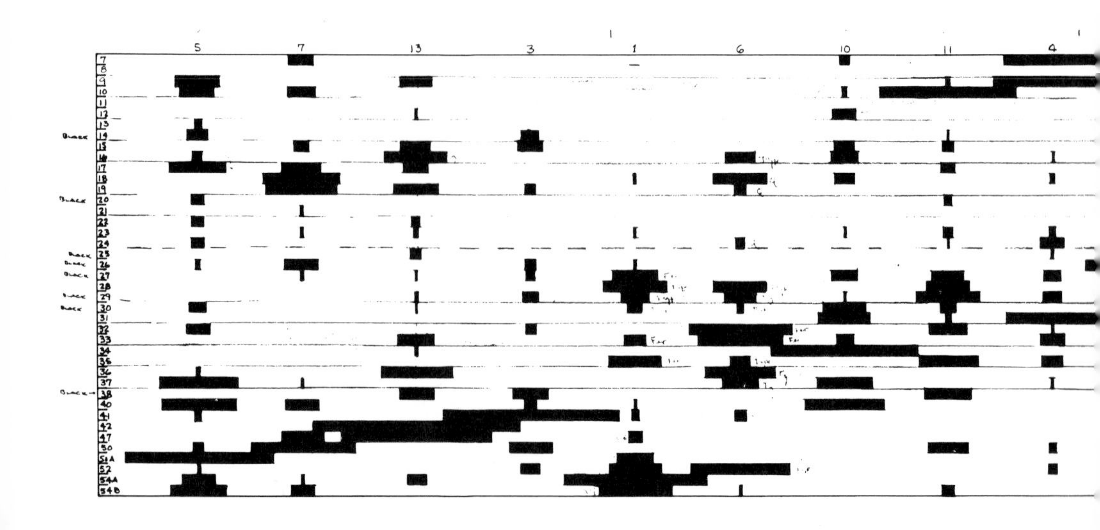

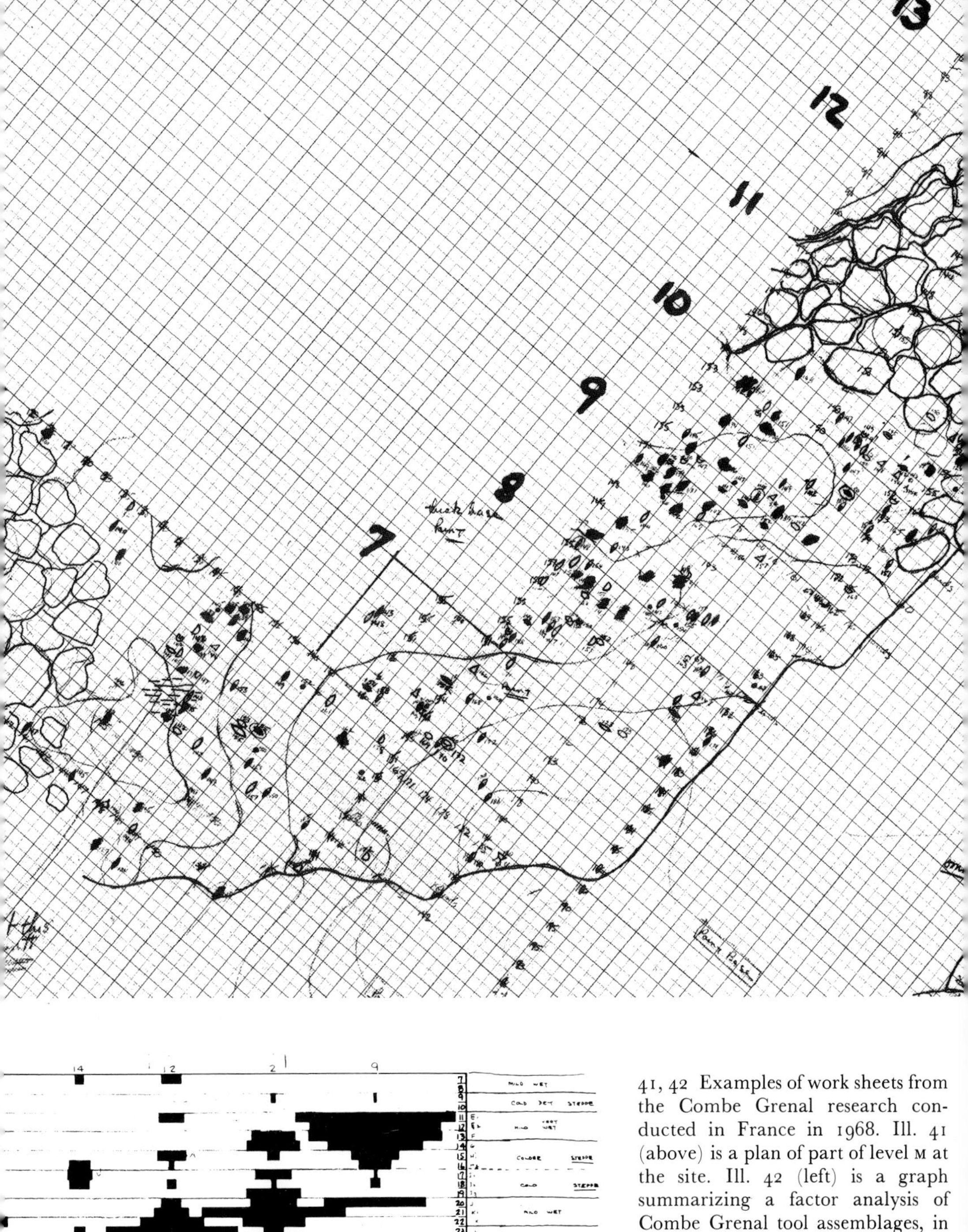

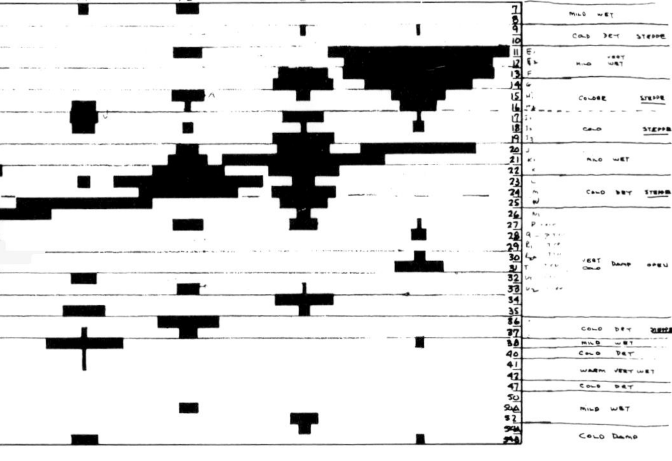

41, 42 Examples of work sheets from the Combe Grenal research conducted in France in 1968. Ill. 41 (above) is a plan of part of level M at the site. Ill. 42 (left) is a graph summarizing a factor analysis of Combe Grenal tool assemblages, in relation to independent measures of environmental change.

almost any type of data you care to name. What I found, of course, was many new facts that nobody had seen before. But none of these new facts spoke for themselves, just as the initial facts had not. By generating more and more facts and by detecting more and more patterns, I had simply increased the scope of the problem without reaching any solutions. None of the correlations carried sufficient information to tell us why they were that way: they simply stood as increasingly complex patterns of static association in the archaeological record.

It is important to realize that it was with such a *wealth* – not a *dearth* – of information that it gradually began to dawn on me that none of the approaches I had followed possessed any explanatory potential. None of them was likely to tell me what meaning should most appropriately be associated with any of those facts. My metal trunk was so big and heavy that I decided to return home by boat and that five-day trip from Le Havre to New York gave me an opportunity for some disconsolate self-reflection. The whole project was obviously a total failure. What had I done wrong? What had I not done that I should have done? Could it really be that archaeologists simply cannot learn anything about the past? Where was I missing the real problem?

I still have at home a little notebook in which I made a logical outline of my thoughts, starting from some really fundamental concepts: a sort of *Lecture to Myself*. (Many of those thoughts have been incorporated into Chapter I.) The first heading says 'What *is* the archaeological record?'. Underneath I wrote 'The archaeological record is static', and there follows a long series of jottings to the effect that (excluding earthworms) there is nothing dynamic in the archaeological record itself. Now what we are interested in about the past is dynamics: what people did, how they lived, whether they competed or collaborated. Here, then, is the basic and fundamental problem, one not unique to the Mousterian period but endemic to archaeology – how can we make inferences from statics to dynamics? Lower down, my outline says 'The archaeological record is contemporary; it exists with me today and any observation I make about it is a contemporary observation'. Yet of course it is the *past* that interests us as archaeologists. Thinking about that, it seemed to me that archaeologists must be among the world's biggest optimists. Unless we know the necessary and determinant linkages between dynamic causes and static consequences, how can we ever justify an inference from one to the other? The dynamic aspect of the past is long gone.

The Contemporary World Offers a Solution?

By the time we steamed into New York City, just before the New Year of 1969, some of the answers to these problems were suggested, at least in my thoughts. I prepared a research proposal to go to the Arctic in the spring of 1969 to live

43 Young Nunamiut Eskimo girl wearing her parka with a wolverine ruff and a colorful cloth over-cover; Anaktuvuk Pass, Alaska, 1971.

with a group of Eskimo hunters. My reasons for going there were little more specific at that stage than that it could hardly fail to be a good educational experience. If I was ever to be able to make accurate inferences from archaeological facts, I was convinced that I had to understand the dynamics of living systems and study their static consequences.

The Eskimos were my choice, however, for several good reasons. In the first place, in Bordeaux I had studied reindeer bones from Mousterian sites to the point where I thought I never wanted to see another one, but here was an opportunity to study a living group of people who were still hunting the very same animal that I had studied archaeologically. Secondly, it was possible to study a group who were still almost entirely dependent on hunted foodstuffs, something which is no longer very easy to observe in the modern world. Thirdly, their environmental setting was Arctic and thus not dissimilar from that of the French occupation sites I had studied (which contained little arboreal pollen

43, 44

45

46

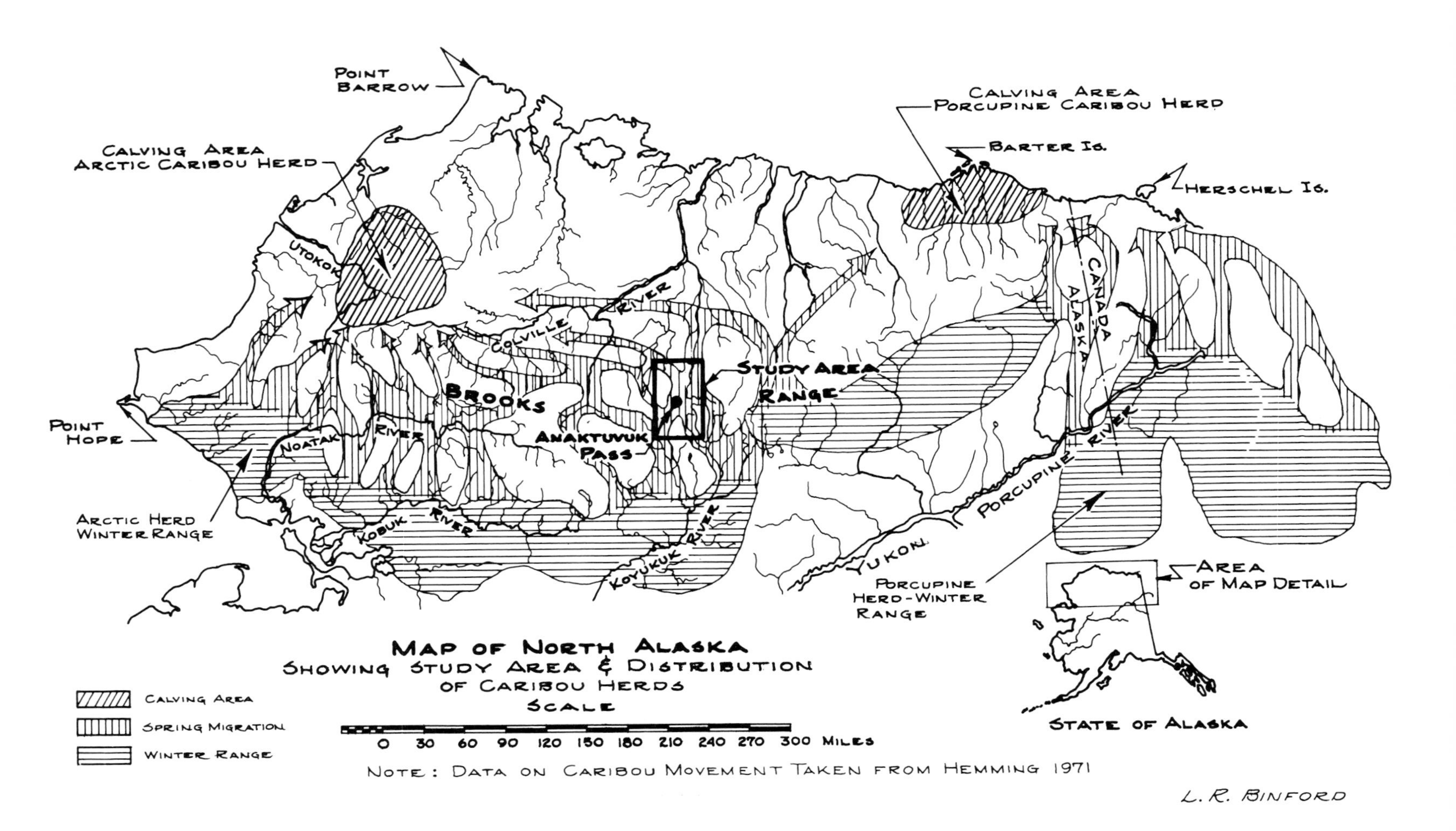

44 Map of north Alaska showing the location of Anaktuvuk Pass in relation to the distribution of caribou herds.

45 Zacharias Hugo skinning a caribou in Anaktuvuk Pass during the spring migration. (Photo courtesy of Robert Rausch.)

46 *(Below)* View toward the southeast across Anaktuvuk Valley from just north of the Eskimo village of Anaktuvuk Pass, Alaska, Spring 1971.

indicative of a wooded landscape). In short, I was led to the inescapable conclusion that there existed no way to develop archaeological methods of inference, except via the study of contemporary living peoples, or by controlled experiments under laboratory conditions, or by doing archaeology in situations whose dynamic component is historically documented. 'Ethnoarchaeology', 'experimental archaeology', and 'historic sites archaeology' seemed to me to be the only chances we have for the development and perfection of methods of inference dealing with humanly-generated artifactual material. Work in experimental physics, after all, had resulted in the techniques of radiocarbon dating – techniques that are not strictly speaking archaeological, but which are of great value to archaeologists. So, too, these three approaches were not developed specifically for the purpose of developing an inferential framework for archaeology, but could certainly be useful in that way.

47 Crew from the 1969 field season at Tulugak Lake, Alaska. Left to right: Richard Workman, Charles Amsden, Don Campbell and Lewis Binford.

48 Dan Witter collecting bones from Eskimo meat caches during the 1972 field season.

I spent several seasons, in the period from 1969 to 1973, doing ethnoarchaeology in the Arctic (Chapters 6 and 7), many of the results of which are now published in my book *Nunamiut Ethnoarchaeology*.[14] Much of this research was concerned with animal exploitation and faunal analysis, but I also wanted to return more directly to the problems of interpreting lithic assemblages; so in 1974 I travelled to Australia[15] to work with some aboriginal people who were still manufacturing stone tools for their own use (Chapter 7). One spin-off of this work was the re-kindling of my earlier interest in the origins of agriculture (Chapter 8). That fieldwork experience of living with hunters and gatherers had convinced me that, if we wanted to get good models and explanations for agricultural origins, we had to understand accurately the range of variability – ecological, economic, social – in the organization of hunting and gathering peoples; it was on this range of variability, after all, that some kinds of selective forces operated to bring into being new kinds of production involving agriculture and domesticated animals. This led me to begin in 1971 a long-term project to accumulate comparative ethnohistorical and ethnological information on the world's hunters and gatherers,

47

48

concentrating in particular on how they vary in their organization with environmental factors.

So there have been three main themes in my research throughout the 1970s: (1) methodological studies of animal bone assemblages (Chapter 2); (2) the spatial organization of activity debris and the structure of archaeological sites (Chapters 3, 6, and 7); and (3) comparative studies of hunters and gatherers on a worldwide basis. All three relate back directly to the two problems mentioned earlier – the origins of agriculture and the question of variability in the Mousterian. Interest in the early time periods has developed out of my faunal studies.

Nonsense and the New Archaeology

Those who are familiar with the archaeological literature of the past fifteen years will perhaps have noticed something odd in the chronology of the research program I have just outlined. One of the landmarks in the development of the so-called 'New Archaeology' was the publication in 1968 of the volume of essays entitled *New Perspectives in Archaeology*. It made quite an impact and generated a lot of discussion in the early 1970s. Most of the ideas and work by my colleagues and students that appeared in it came into being earlier in the 1960s and certainly before I left for France to work on the Mousterian. The publication of the book was roughly coincident with the major switch in my own work towards methodologically oriented research: just as it appeared in print I took a right-angle turn and went off on another tack. All the time I was away doing fieldwork or analyzing the results, I tended to avoid many of the arguments that were common in the archaeological literature of the 1970s. I stood on the sidelines and watched some of the themes and arguments I or my colleagues had introduced picked up and sometimes taken in directions I really did not think they ought to go.[16] So it is perhaps not inappropriate to consider briefly how I viewed the relationship between my own research program and some of the things that happened to the New Archaeology in the USA during the 1970s.

It was in a paper published in 1967 that I began to discuss the logic of the philosophy of science in relation to archaeological research.[17] At that time, I was simply trying to make a negative point, an argument *against* particular viewpoints that were then current about the interpretation of the archaeological record. My claim was that when one looks at a body of archaeological data and says 'This is what it means in historical terms', an inference is already being made. The only appropriate strategy I could see for evaluating an idea which one already had was to deduce consequences of it for further empirical conditions that might exist in the world. It was assumed, however, that some set of ideas about the past was already in existence.

What happened was that certain archaeologists followed this line of reasoning by doing a little reading in the literature of logical positivism and then claimed that we should all do research following deductive principles. I do not understand this suggestion, and I never have! I think the way we do research is that we look at data, we recognize patterns, and we have flashes of insight, or bright ideas, or simply revive worn old notions that have been around for years; but wherever ideas come from, we try to give meaning to what we see. We should do so by using the form of logic which concentrates on the implications of our ideas for the real world. This is the important place for deductive reasoning. It has to be stressed, however, that this is not to say that it is in this way that ideas are obtained in the first place, nor that a deductive form of logic is to be used when talking about observations *per se*, rather than the evaluation of ideas. As an example of the sort of confusion that exists, I might cite a research proposal I evaluated for the National Science Foundation in the early 1970s. The authors of the proposal proclaimed that they followed the 'logico-deductive method' of doing archaeological research. They intended to survey the such-and-such river valley. Their hypothesis was that camps existed along the levees and deduced from it that there must therefore be artifacts to be found on the levees. The proposed field program was intended to test this hypothesis. Obviously, this is complete nonsense; it is a proposition about the character of the archaeological record which, if correct, would tell us only about the author's good judgment.[18] Suppose (to give an analogy) I hypothesize that this book is 6 inches wide and it does indeed turn out, when we take a ruler and measure it, that it is 6 inches wide. The fact that I was right has no intellectual implications whatsoever, except for my ability to judge the width of books accurately. Deductive reasoning is only important if evaluating some intellectual implications derived or deduced from a body of ideas, an argument. Empirical propositions, such as the examples I have just given, never have such implications.

This, then, is one aspect of the New Archaeology that is somewhat confusing and the way in which the question was presented and argued in much of the American archaeological literature has, I feel, been counter-productive. I would be the last to deny the importance of deductive reasoning. But while I probably have to shoulder some of the blame for the poor arguments about deduction and hypothesis testing that were so prevalent in the 1970s, I should like to think that I'm not entirely responsible.

Some comment is also called for on the confusing and slightly disagreeable sociological aspects of American archaeology in the aftermath of the upheavals of the 1960s. I suppose I must take some blame for these also, since – as Albert Spaulding once commented – I'm the oldest new archaeologist in town. In the early 1960s I scored some successes in arguing with my colleagues and fellow archaeologists. It was our 'opponents', not we, who coined the term 'New

Archaeology'; Robert Braidwood went so far as to call it a religion. The result was that many other young archaeologists, modelling themselves on some of the successes of the 1960s, felt they had to define a still newer kind of archaeology: Behavioral Archaeology, Social Archaeology, Astroarchaeology, and so forth. Much time and energy has been spent in recent years arguing about these new 'fields'. Personally, I have tried to avoid such debates, for they do not concern serious proposals within a scientific discipline, but rather a form of sociological posturing within the organization of American archaeology. They have confused the archaeological literature, especially for those who are not themselves involved in archaeology in America. So this is an aspect of the New Archaeology from which I should like to dissociate myself.

Ultimate Concerns

In a nutshell, then, this is the path my research has taken over the last two decades, a path often divergent from that of the New Archaeology itself. It reflects what I believe should be the priorities in the development of the field of archaeology. I believe very strongly that we need a robust methodology for making inferences and that so far we do not generally have one. Archaeology has not been a science: it grew up with a rag-bag series of conventions which most archaeologists, at one time or another, have used for 'interpreting' their finds. Most such conventions have never been tested and we simply do not know whether they are valid and useful. Just around the corner are other methods which I think will allow us to make much more accurate and interesting statements about the past. Such methodological research is obviously crucial, but we should not forget about the more substantive problems of archaeology – for instance, the origins of agriculture, or how cultural variability is to be explained, or what causes differences in stylistic and ethnic phenomena. All these aspects must grow together, because methodological research cannot be done in isolation, but within the context of problems for which, in the long term, some solution is hoped. In my own case those ultimate concerns have been to explain the origins of agriculture and variability in the Mousterian. So in a sense, while of course I have been involved in many different facets of archaeology over the last twenty years, I have really worked on no other problems in my entire career.

6
Hunters in a Landscape

A Stationary View of a Dynamic Landscape

Excavated sites are the archaeologist's bread and butter. His view of the past is necessarily restricted to these discrete, isolated points in the landscape. It is a stationary view, whereas past behavior – especially that of hunters and gatherers – was highly mobile. Each site, therefore, presents a limited, biased picture of a whole range of activities, depending upon its unique position within a regional system of behavior. One could imagine, for example, that the different Mousterian stone tool assemblages described by Bordes (Chapter 4) are simply tiny segments of the way of life of a hunting and gathering group. There is the further complication that if the pattern of activities during the Mousterian was not precisely the same at different times and in different places, then consecutive levels at each site would represent slightly varying 'snapshots' of the past.

These simple ideas, together with my conception of how people behaved during the Palaeolithic, formed the basis of my challenge to Bordes' interpretation of the patterns to be seen in Mousterian assemblages. He thought that differences between them reflected the ethnic identities of the various groups which had made them. My own approach, on the other hand, revolved around the idea that at each site Mousterian man's use of both space and technology had been a specific response to unique circumstances. In other words, I was envisaging a cultural system in which different activities took place at separate locations. Furthermore, I imagined that the tool technology was flexible enough to cope with situational variations in demand placed upon it, so that if necessary, for example, the same activities could be carried out at several sites with different tools.

At the time I was questioning existing notions of archaeological variability in the Palaeolithic in this way, ethnographic accounts of how hunters and gatherers use their landscape suggested that my view was at least plausible; but there were no detailed investigations of the links between the way locations (i.e. sites) were utilized and the adaptive organization of the system as a whole. Similarly, variations in the role of technology in response to site-specific circumstances had not been studied. It was largely to pursue these issues that I went to Alaska to observe the Nunamiut Eskimo (see Chapter 5). During my ethnoarchaeological research there, I attempted to view the dynamics of the settlement pattern throughout the seasonal cycle of movement from an archaeological (i.e. a site-orientated) perspective. Although this research confirmed my most general assumptions about site formation, my observations clearly indicated that archaeologists currently lack appropriate methods for detecting in their data the immensely complicated patterns of landscape use exhibited by hunters and gatherers such as the Nunamiut.

In order to illustrate the nature of such interpretive problems, I will describe some of the sites which I recorded during my research among the Nunamiut 44 Eskimo in Anaktuvuk Pass, Alaska. I will begin with land use and settlement patterns at the regional scale and go on to describe how certain levels of behavior must be understood in terms of whole groups of sites or in terms of activities within individual locations. The examples which follow should demonstrate some of the sources of variability which characterize the archaeology of mobile peoples.

The Scale of Land Use

The use of space by the Nunamiut on an enormous scale demonstrates that archaeologists need to recalibrate their perspective of hunters and gatherers from the 5 foot square excavation unit at a single site to an area of more than 300,000 square kilometers. If we discount certain exceptional cases in the equatorial zones, such an enormous area represents the scale of the domain over which a typical hunter-gatherer group, composed of perhaps only thirty to forty people, monitors its environment. Rarely does the band exploit all this land at any one time, but it requires the entire region to be available in order to provide a secure set of options. In order to understand how a small band of people makes use of such a large amount of space, it might be helpful if I first examine the spatial unit utilized by a group during one season and then demonstrate how variation in this unit over a long period of time eventually leads to the exploitation of an immense region.

49 As a baseline we can take the area in which one group of Nunamiut Eskimo established settlements or base camps throughout the seasonal cycle of a single calendar year. This *residential core area* usually extends up to about 5,400 square kilometers, although the land which is exploited by means of trips out from the main camps may cover an area as great as 25,000 square kilometers. The Eskimo, it must be emphasized, are by no means atypical in terms of their use of space: 1 the residential core area used by one G/wi Bushman family over a period of eleven months shows that other hunter-gatherer groups also exploit vast regions.[1]

The archaeology created by a small band of people moving throughout their territory in this way must be immensely complex, if the Nunamiut case is repre-

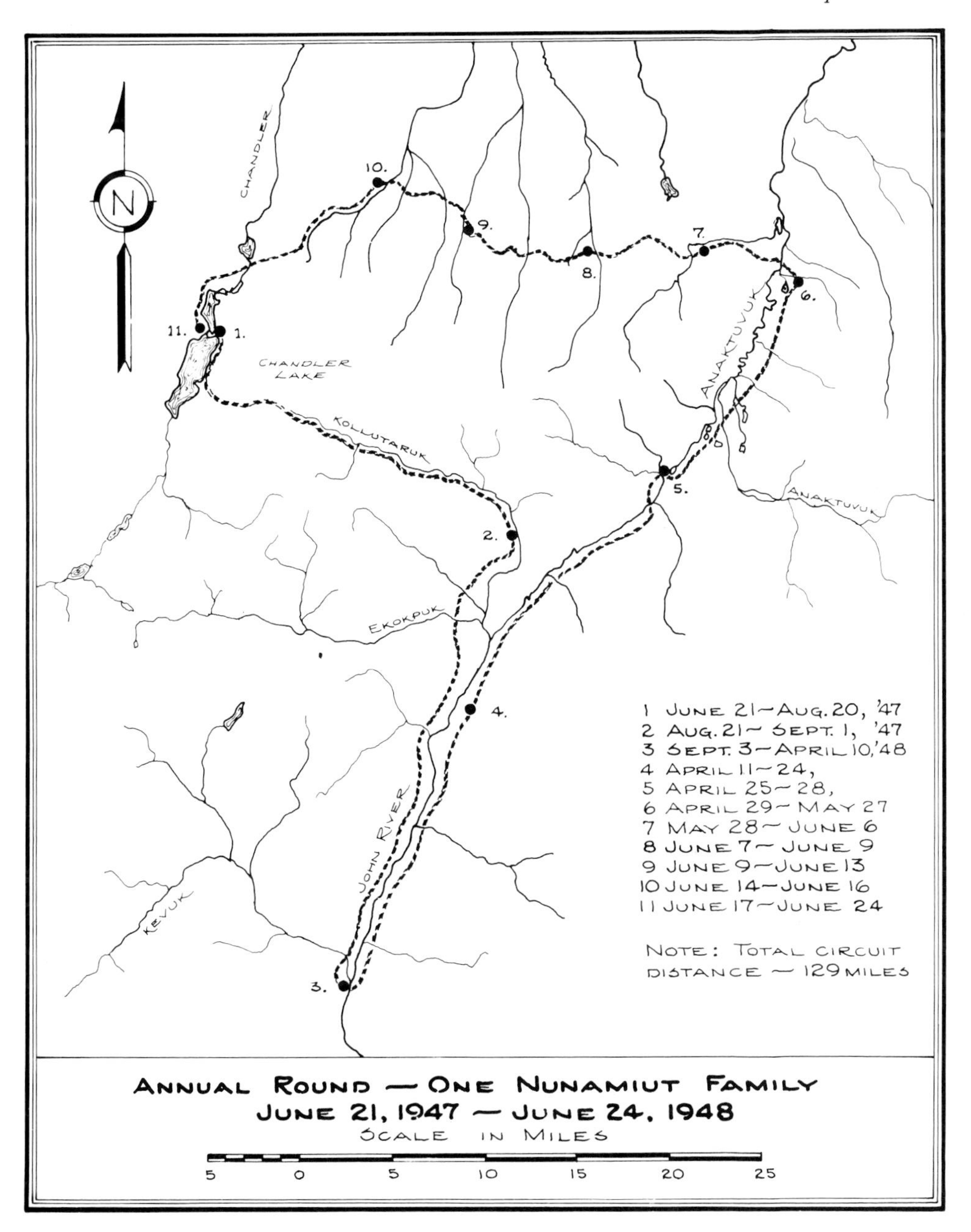

49 Location of the sites occupied by one Nunamiut family during an annual round of settlement in 1947–8.

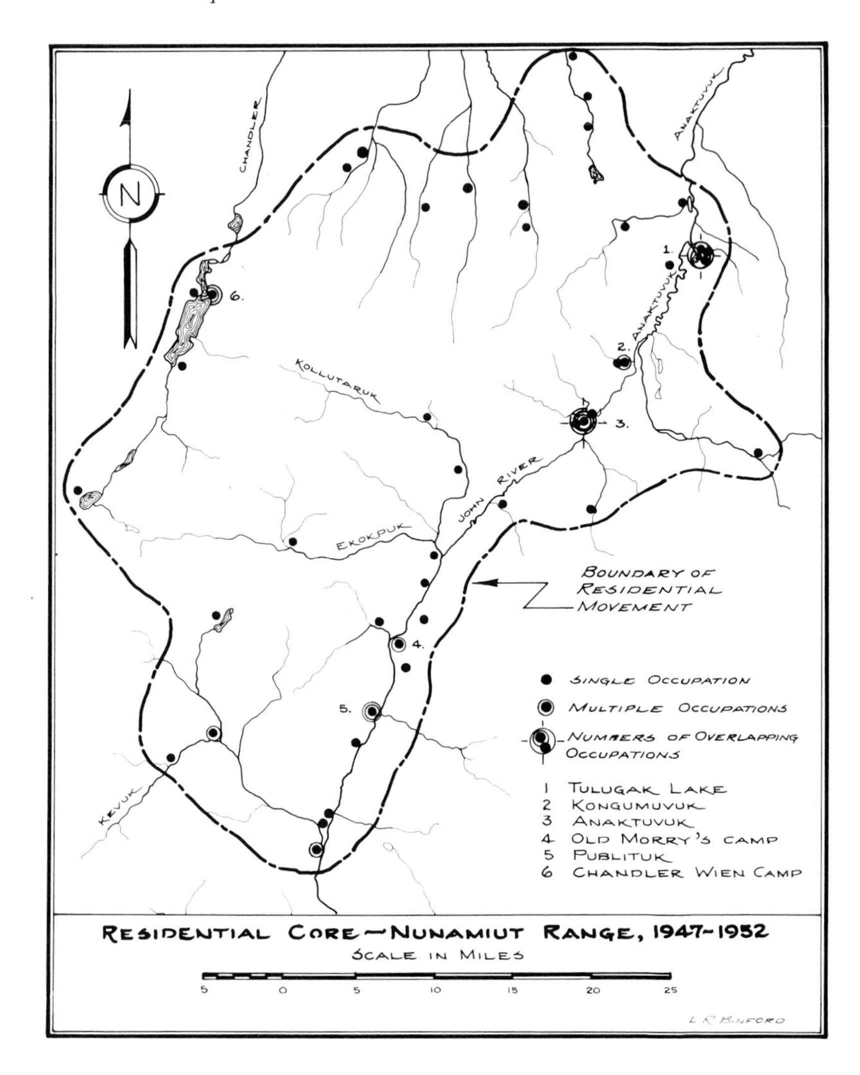

sentative. The locations of the residential sites created by five Eskimo families during a period of five years are shown in ill. 50. The first point to note is the size of the residential core occupied by such a small group of people. Surprisingly enough, these five Nunamiut families covered about as much space as is repre-
51 sented by the entire Dordogne area in France, where the classic Mousterian sites are located. Given the large scale on which hunting and gathering groups typically operate, Bordes' argument (Chapter 4) that differences in the composition of the toolkits deposited at various levels in these sites represent four distinct cultural groups is hard to sustain. The problem is that archaeologists have been approaching their research on Palaeolithic sites from a modern sedentary

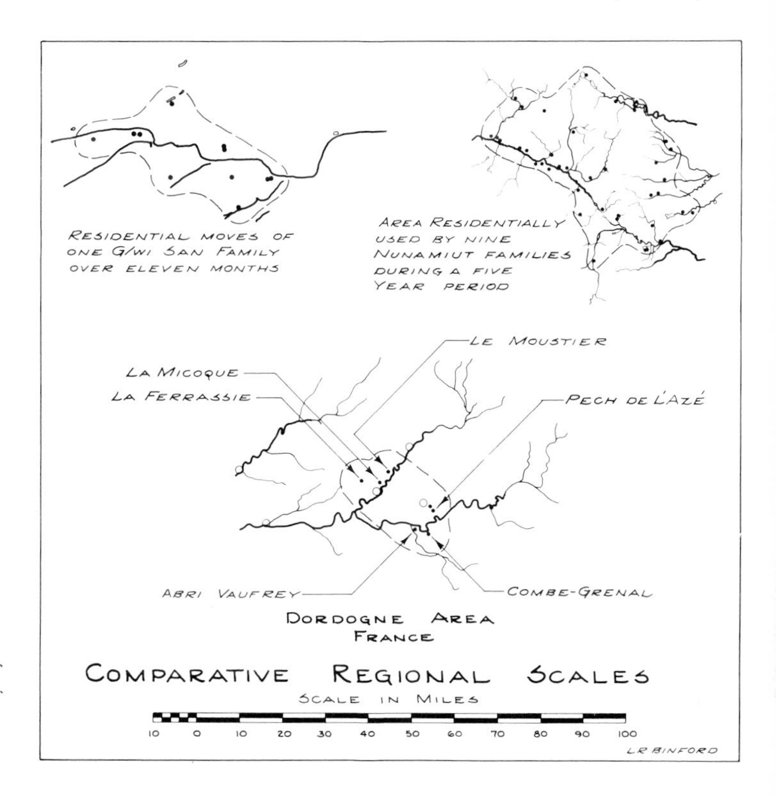

50 *(Opposite)* Location of the residential sites occupied by five Nunamiut families over a period of five years. The distribution of these sites is equivalent to the *residential core area* of this Eskimo group during this period.

51 Comparisons of the sizes of the residential core areas among the Nunamiut Eskimo and the G/wi Bushmen with the area in which the 'classic' Mousterian archaeological sites of the Dordogne region of France are found (see Chapter 4).

view of the world. Since the hunting and gathering peoples which we are trying to study probably did not share that view, we must try to bring our perspective closer to reality.

A second important observation emerges from ill. 50. Not only is the number of sites considerably greater than those used by one family over one year, but the archaeology also becomes very complicated, chiefly because certain locations in the territory were occupied repeatedly from year to year whereas others were not. The pattern of re-use at these sites has to a large degree determined their size, in terms of the distributions of artifacts and features; consequently, locations occupied repeatedly are considerably larger than those used only a few times. This means that variability in the amount of space occupied by a site, a property normally recorded by archaeologists, would not be due to differences in the size or social organization of the group who resided there, but would merely reflect the degree of repetitiveness in the way the landscape was used by the same mobile band.[2] The reasoning used by Richard MacNeish[3] and other archaeologists whereby differences in the size of sites are equated with various scales of group organization (such as 'micro-bands' and 'macro-bands') is therefore likely to be faulty. Judging from my observations of the modern Nunamiut, it is obvious that we can no longer make simple equations between variability in site size and nature of the group which resided there, until we know more about all the other factors which contribute to the spread of debris at a site. In other words, archaeologists have to know about the *formation processes* of the archaeological record – that is, the way sites come into being.

Lifetime Cycles of Land Use

The land-use pattern of the Nunamiut illustrates yet another factor which affects the archaeological record. Rather surprisingly, many hunters and gatherers do not reside exclusively in one territory, but – contrary to the assumptions of most archaeologists – exploit a series of discrete areas, occupying each one until the environment becomes degraded. Often after a period of years, the firewood or animal resources become depleted and, at the point of diminishing returns, the group simply moves to a completely different territory, where the resources have been allowed to regenerate. Among the Nunamiut, for example, the length of stay in any one residential core area is approximately ten years.

On the basis of interviews with old Eskimo men, I have constructed an idealized model showing the way the Nunamiut expect to exploit a region during one 52 person's lifetime.[4] The basis of the model is a cyclical pattern of land use. The residential core area that the group occupies when a person is born is known as that person's *birth territory*. If the band had recently moved there, he or she would expect to live in that area for about ten years before moving to another completely separate residential core area which had not been occupied for about fifty years. This second area would be known as the *becoming territory*, if you were male, and the *courting territory*, if female (because girls are married about the age of sixteen whereas males wait until they are around twenty-eight years old). As a male within this area, one would begin to learn to hunt and would travel extensively, becoming intimately acquainted with the environment. After another ten years, it would be time to move again; now a male would enter his courting territory, while his sisters would be having their first babies. When a male finally marries, he will generally go to live in the territory of his wife's family for several years.

Six to eight years later, when a male is likely to be at his peak and most effective as a hunter, he will enter a further completely different area. In his final territory, a successful man might contribute to the folklore or cultural tradition connected with the landscape. Some of the land might be remapped in the minds of the Nunamiut in terms of some of this hunter's exploits; key points, such as the location of rocks marking points where streams can be crossed, might be renamed after him. After about the age of forty, a hunter's skill declines rapidly, because most males begin to lose their eyesight, have difficulty climbing mountains, and

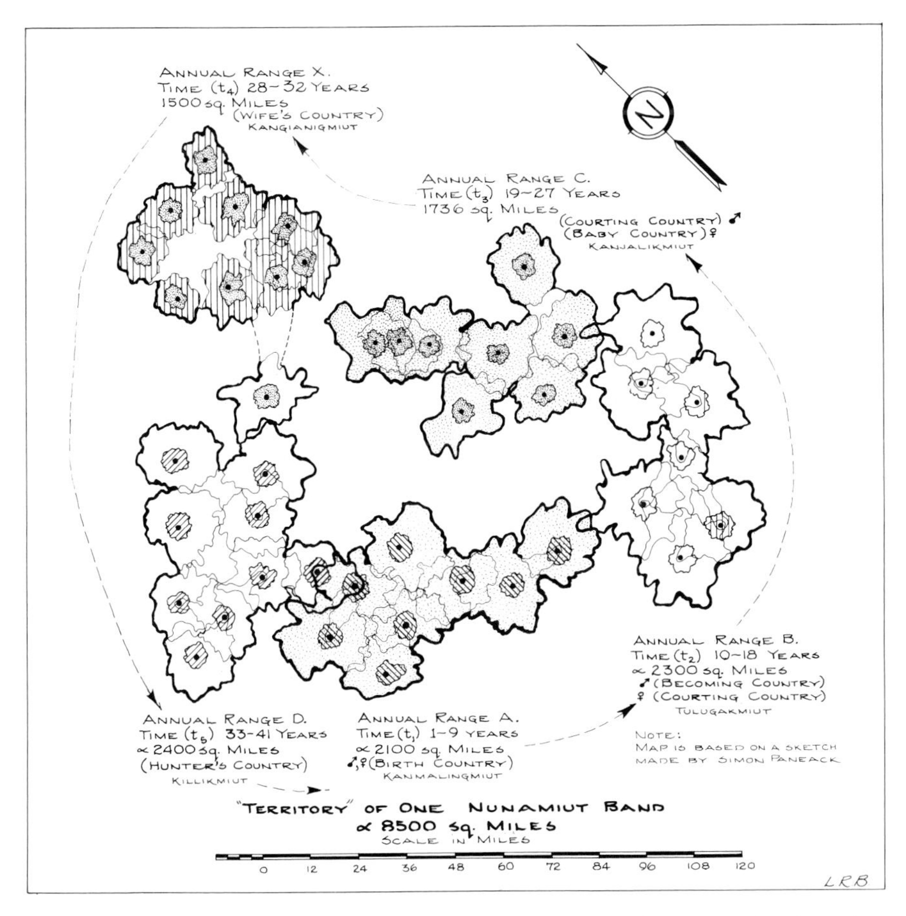

52 Idealized model of Nunamiut land use during one person's lifetime, based on interviews with Eskimo informants.

so on. At this point in his career, a hunter will probably move back into his birth territory, completing the cycle of long-term land use; and with old age setting in he will gradually become dependent on others for his basic subsistence needs.

In summary, the overall area in which a single male resides during his life consists of around five different territories and can extend to as much as 22,000 square kilometers. During his lifetime, however, a typical Nunamiut male will have travelled over more than 300,000 square kilometers in the normal course of hunting for game. As a result, at any point in time, a group of Nunamiut Eskimos has available to it approximately four times as much land as it is currently using. The same pattern of land use can also be found among the Aborigines in the Central Desert of Australia and the Naskapi in Newfoundland. Hunter-gatherer

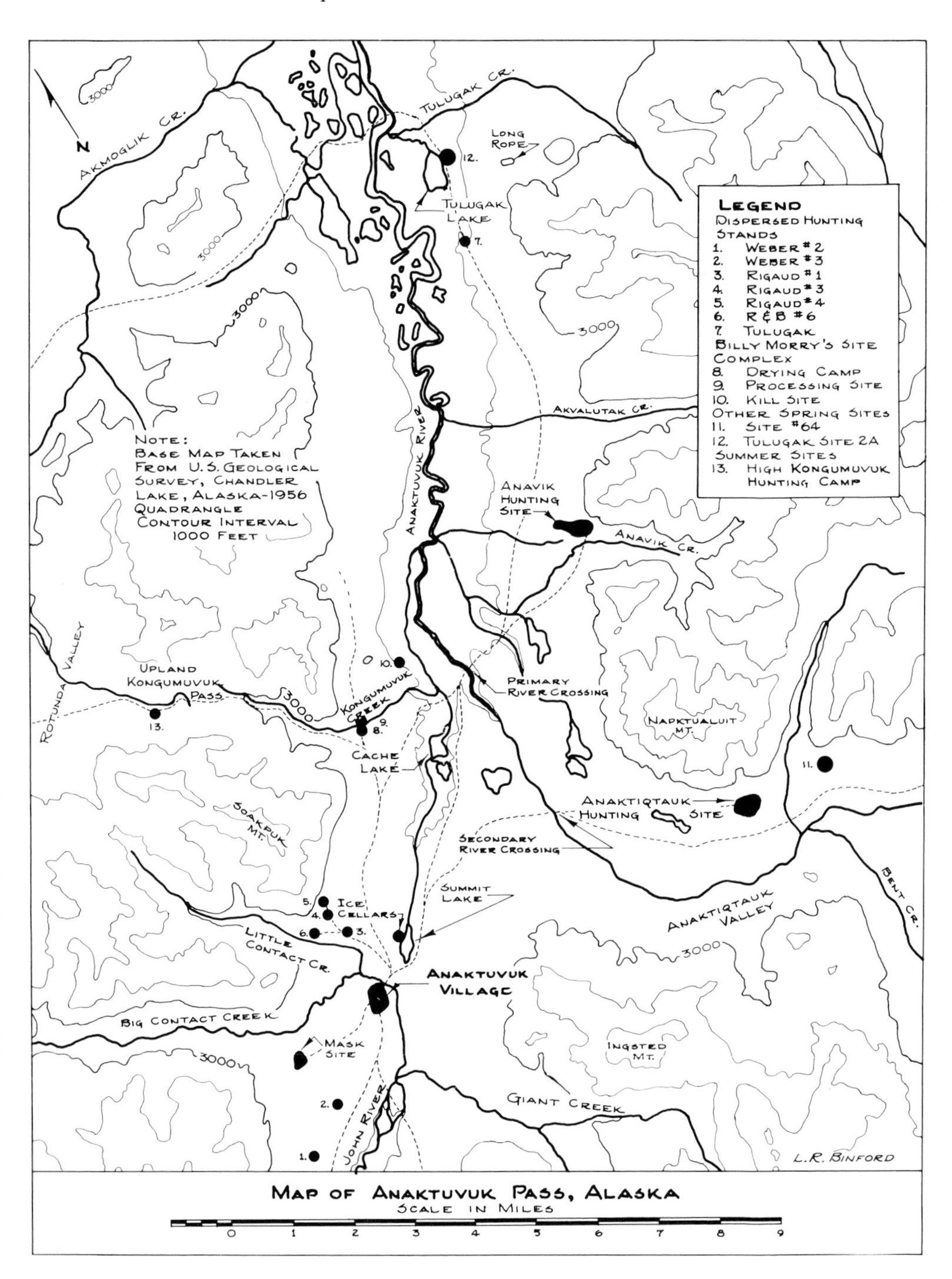

53 Map of Anaktuvuk Valley, Alaska, showing the location of sites mentioned in the text.

groups such as these utilize an enormous range of space which is occupied over a long period of time by means of a series of smaller discrete territories. Such is the vast scale we must consider, if we are to understand variability in the archaeological sites of mobile hunters and gatherers.

Anavik Springs Site Complex

Having looked at how hunting and gathering groups exploit a series of discrete territories, we can now examine the way tasks are organized within the boundaries of a single residential core area. One productive way to view the organization of activities at this level is as a cluster of localities which I call the *site complex*. When a series of events are linked together as part of an overall strategy, the separate locations where the integrated set of activities takes place together comprise a site complex. Several examples of these major 'building blocks' of territories can be provided from my ethnoarchaeological study of Nunamiut Eskimo settlements. 53

The Anavik Springs site complex is composed of three distinct sites which are utilized in conjunction with each other during the hunting of caribou on their spring migration northward through Anaktuvuk Pass along their route to the flat, open tundra. The sites belonging together in this case include (1) a hunting 54

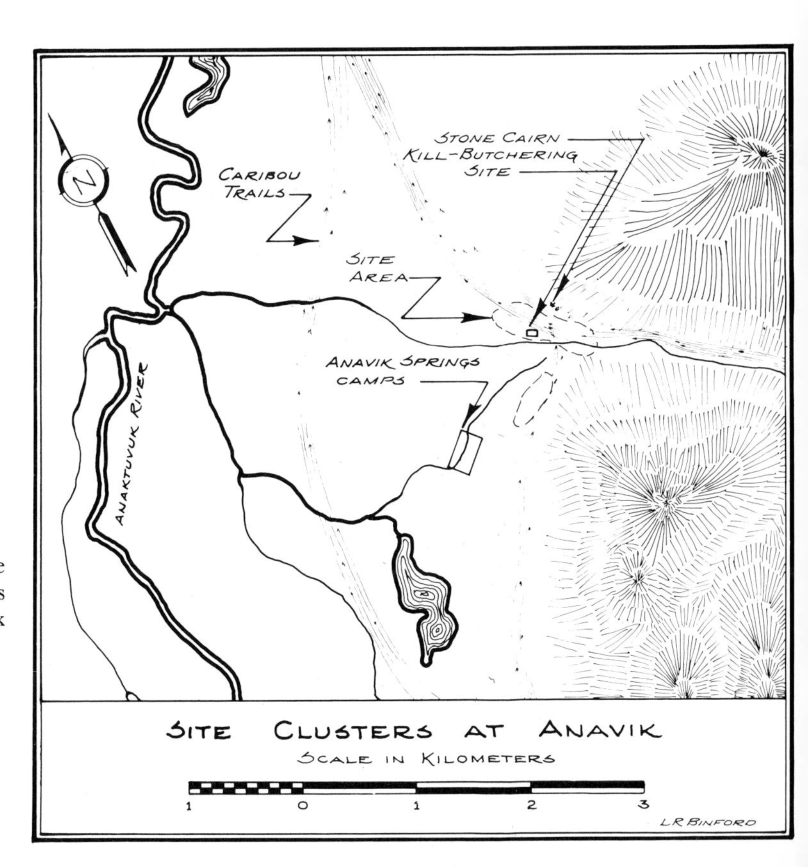

54 Location of the various components within the Anavik Springs *site complex*.

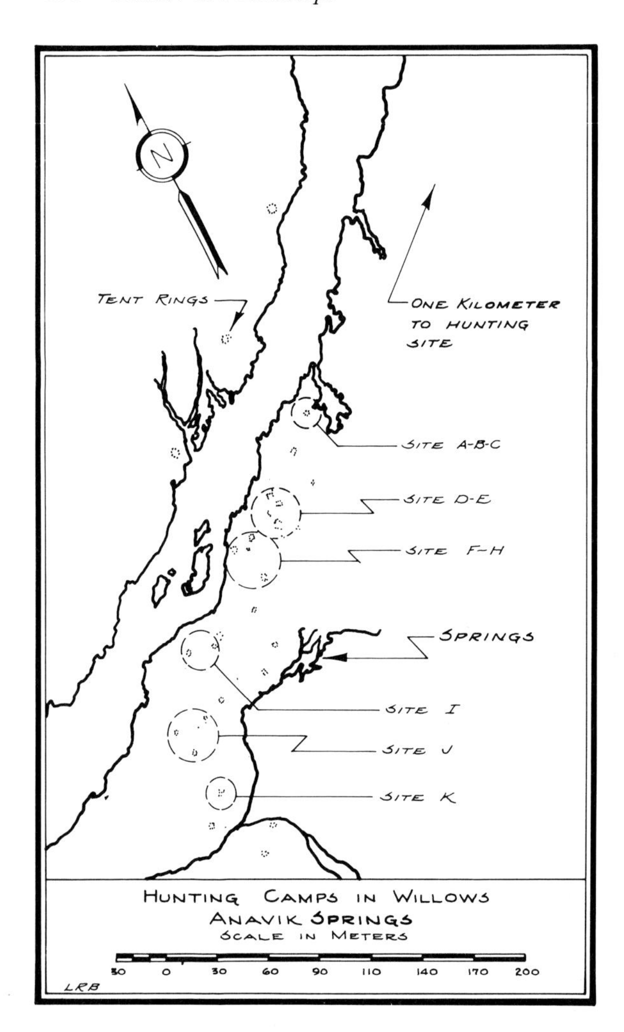

55 Hunting camps located in a stand of willow trees at Anavik Springs.

56 *(Opposite)* Lovers' Camp. Plan of the late summer hunting camp J at Anavik Springs.

camp (including a specialized 'lovers' camp'), (2) a kill site with specialized areas for butchering, and (3) a series of stone caches where meat was stored. Completely different activities took place at each of the locations, which are separated by as much as one kilometer, but all three sites are components of the same major task (the exploitation of caribou) and commonly all have been used on a single day by the same group of people.

Temporary Hunting Camp

55 The first constituent of the site complex is a temporary camp used mainly during the caribou migration. From an archaeological point of view, this location at Anavik Springs appears to consist of one single site extending for half a kilometer,

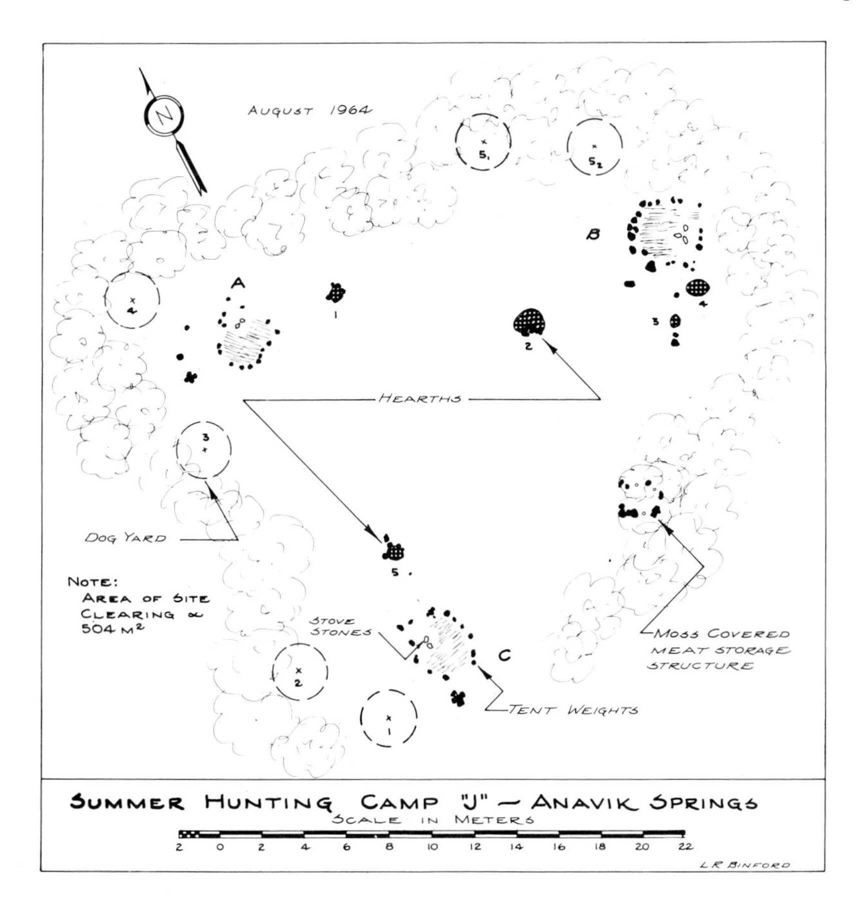

over which an uninterrupted distribution of debris can be monitored. In fact, the continuous scatter is not the remains of one occupation by one group at one time, but represents the re-use of the location over a period of at least 100 years. Since the remains of the many separate occupations over this long period of time overlap with each other, the result is an enormous palimpsest of archaeological materials.

The Lovers' Camp

56

Fortunately, with the aid of informants who had camped at Anavik Springs, I was able to separate out several discrete camps from among the continuous distribution of archaeological materials. At one of these,[5] called site J, one can observe that a pattern – a ring of stones for weighing down a tent and an outside hearth – is repeated three times. This group of tent rings represents a single period of occupation. Site J is not part of the spring caribou hunting complex; it is, nevertheless, interesting in itself, because its history illustrates a division of labor which is common among hunter-gatherer groups, although not discussed in any detail in the ethnographic literature.

By the late summer the stores of dried meat put up by the Eskimos after the caribou migration have become depleted and are unpalatable: the remaining meat is tough, the flavor has been leached out by the rain, and all the tasty fat will have been consumed. Furthermore, at this time of the year there is no game readily accessible in the local environment. The majority of the caribou, except for a few bulls which can only be found in the vicinity of glaciers located high in the mountains, are grazing far to the north, while mountain sheep are difficult to locate in this season. In order to encourage *someone* to go hunting despite the difficulty of achieving success, the Nunamiut have created a fascinating incentive. At the end of the summer young lovers are allowed to live together –not in the main residential camp, however, but only in hunting camps a long way away. The result is that in the long run everyone benefits: the old people subsist on the dwindling supplies of stored meat and the youngsters feed themselves out in the bush. If the young people are successful at hunting, they will bring fresh meat home to share with everyone; if they do not find game, they are hungry but nevertheless happy! The same type of strategy has been reported for the Washo Indians, hunters and gatherers who lived near Lake Tahoe in California.[6] During the hungry period in the early spring when food stores were low, young lovers there were also allowed to set up camps in distant areas where the chances of obtaining food were quite low. This strategy of hunters and gatherers is based on the ability of the young people with the greatest physical skills and endurance to take risks – given the right incentives.

Since camp J is one of these lovers' camps, the distribution of archaeological materials across the site does not conform to other types of hunting camps, such as the majority at Anavik Springs. Normally the choice cuts of meat would be shared at a corporate hearth. In this case, however, each group of young lovers consumed their meals separately in their own tent. The archaeological remains at site J also contain no debris from the manufacture or repair of tools. Although these differences are minor, they are exactly the type of data which archaeologists could use to identify this type of division of labor by age groups in the past.

Processing the Kill

The second component of the Anavik Springs site complex, the location where the killing and processing of caribou took place, is completely different from the small clusters of tent rings observed at the temporary hunting camp. When the caribou move through the valley, they are shot from hunting stands located on a knoll.[7] After the animals are killed, they are dragged to another location for butchering. The scatter of bones recorded at this location after the spring hunt

57, 58

57 Nunamiut Eskimo kill-site. View looking into the mouth of Anavik Valley.

58 View across the caribou butchering area at the Anavik Springs site.

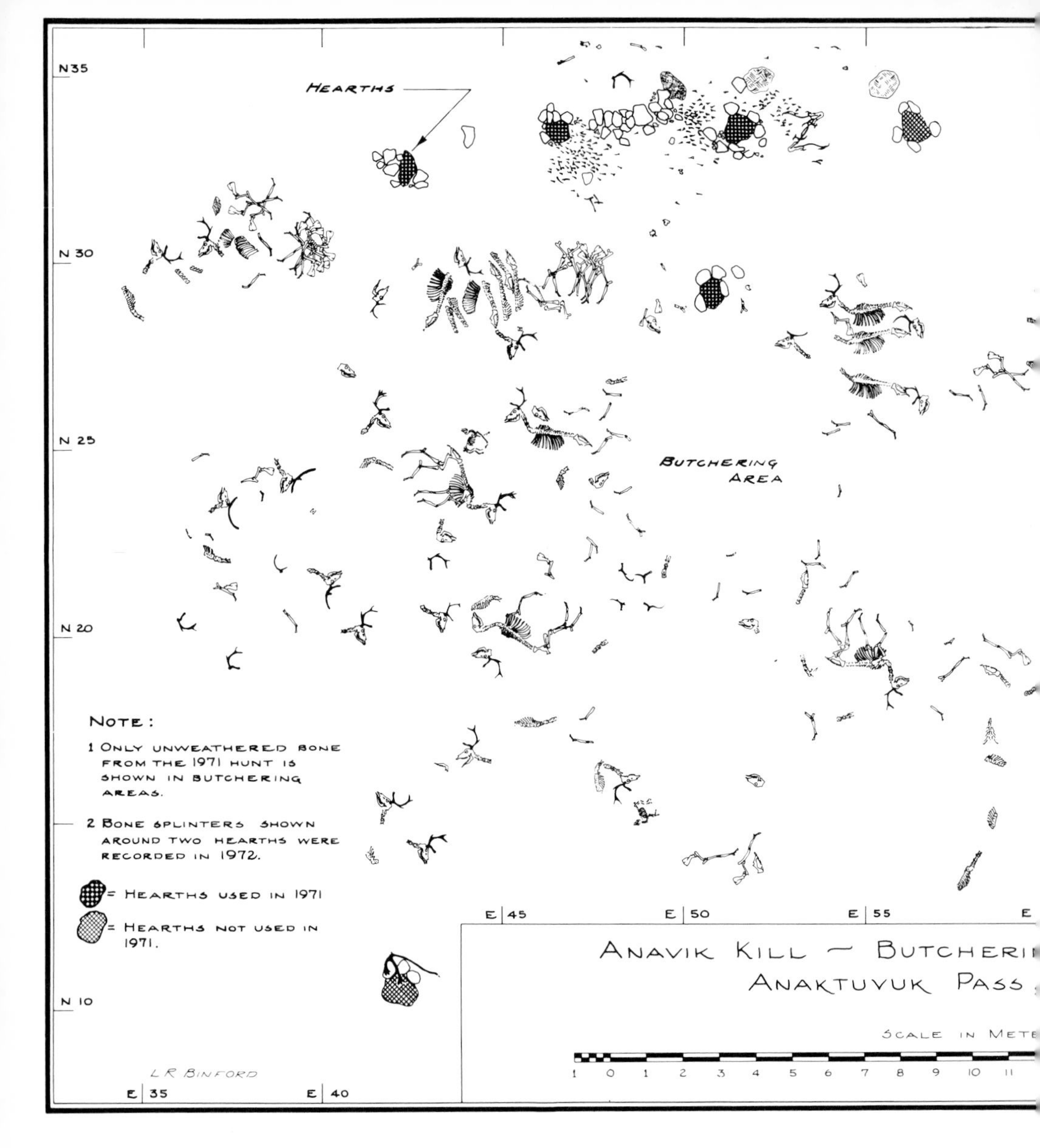

59 Plan of the Anavik Springs kill and butchering site after the spring caribou hunt, showing the distribution of hearths and faunal remains.

60 Detailed plan of the hearth and conversation area at the Anavik Springs caribou butchering site.

61 Close-up of the butchering area at the Anavik Springs site showing the circular areas in which the caribou were dismembered and the location of the waste by-products.

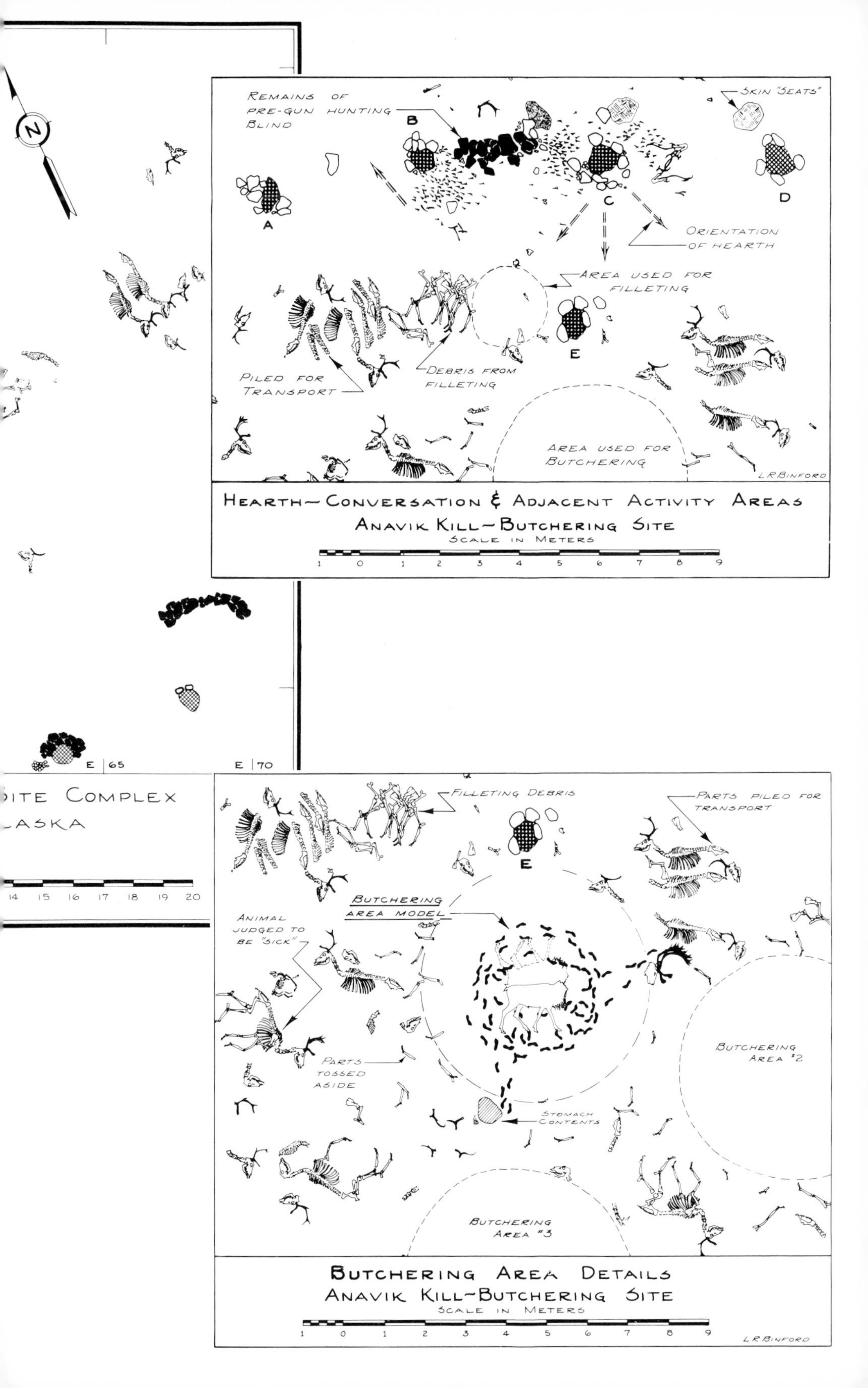
N
E 65
E 70
SITE COMPLEX
LASKA
14 15 16 17 18 19 20
REMAINS OF PRE-GUN HUNTING BLIND
SKIN "SEATS"
B
A
C
D
E
ORIENTATION OF HEARTH
AREA USED FOR FILLETING
DEBRIS FROM FILLETING
PILED FOR TRANSPORT
AREA USED FOR BUTCHERING
L.R.BINFORD
HEARTH—CONVERSATION & ADJACENT ACTIVITY AREAS
ANAVIK KILL-BUTCHERING SITE
SCALE IN METERS
1 0 1 2 3 4 5 6 7 8 9
FILLETING DEBRIS
PARTS PILED FOR TRANSPORT
BUTCHERING AREA MODEL
ANIMAL JUDGED TO BE "SICK"
PARTS TOSSED ASIDE
STOMACH CONTENTS
BUTCHERING AREA #2
BUTCHERING AREA #3
BUTCHERING AREA DETAILS
ANAVIK KILL-BUTCHERING SITE
SCALE IN METERS
1 0 1 2 3 4 5 6 7 8 9
L.R.BINFORD

represented a minimum of fifty-four caribou, although in all we know that 111 caribou had been butchered by the Nunamiut at this one site. On the plan of the site the hollow spaces within the distribution of bones represent discrete areas where one caribou was dismembered. In order to remove the skin from a caribou and prepare the joints of meat, the animal is laid down in a clear area and a man works around it. The result of this behavior is that a circle is created, with the waste products deposited on the periphery away from the area where the butchery took place. Similarly, the by-products from retouching and resharpening the stone tools used in butchering would also be deposited on the edge of the circular area used to process the animal.

At the butchery area four hearths were used by the hunters. A windbreak was placed around them using bull antlers shed in the fall (on a site utilized in the spring!). While butchering, one's hands get very cold and so occasionally the men sit out of the wind to warm their hands over a fire and perhaps eat some marrow removed from the fresh bones of the kills. Around the hearths one would find a completely different distribution of bones than in either the butchering area of this same site or at the associated hunting camp where the men would return after finishing the various tasks here.

Storing the Meat

The third member of the site complex is represented by the site where meat was stored in a large stone structure up to 4 meters in diameter. Stone meat caches[8] are permanent facilities which are usually located near kill sites. They act as central places to which individuals can return throughout the year to collect food for the group, thus avoiding the burden of carrying all the meat with them to each of the several residential sites they will occupy as part of the seasonal round of activities. Layers of meat, inter-bedded with stones or strips of wood to ensure air circulation, are placed in a radial pattern inside the cache and then are sealed off with additional stones. The reason for the high investment of labor in the construction of stone meat caches is the critical importance of stored meat in the subsistence pattern of the Nunamiut.

62 Large stone meat cache like those located in the talus along the north side of the valley above the Anavik Springs kill site. The example illustrated here is actually part of a similar site complex located at the mouth of Kongumuvuk Valley. (See ill. 53 for exact location.)

63 Alleged house-pits excavated at a Russian Palaeolithic site. (Photo courtesy of Olga Soffer.)

64 Caribou meat drying rack from a spring kill site at Kongumuvuk Creek. (For location see Site 8 on ill. 53.)

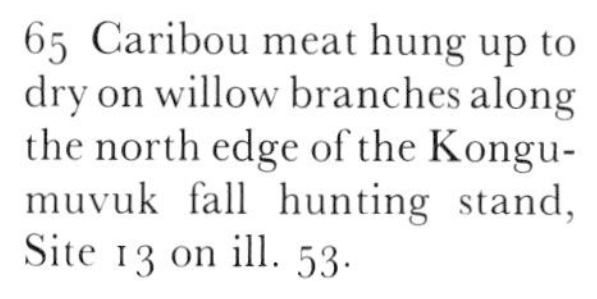

65 Caribou meat hung up to dry on willow branches along the north edge of the Kongumuvuk fall hunting stand, Site 13 on ill. 53.

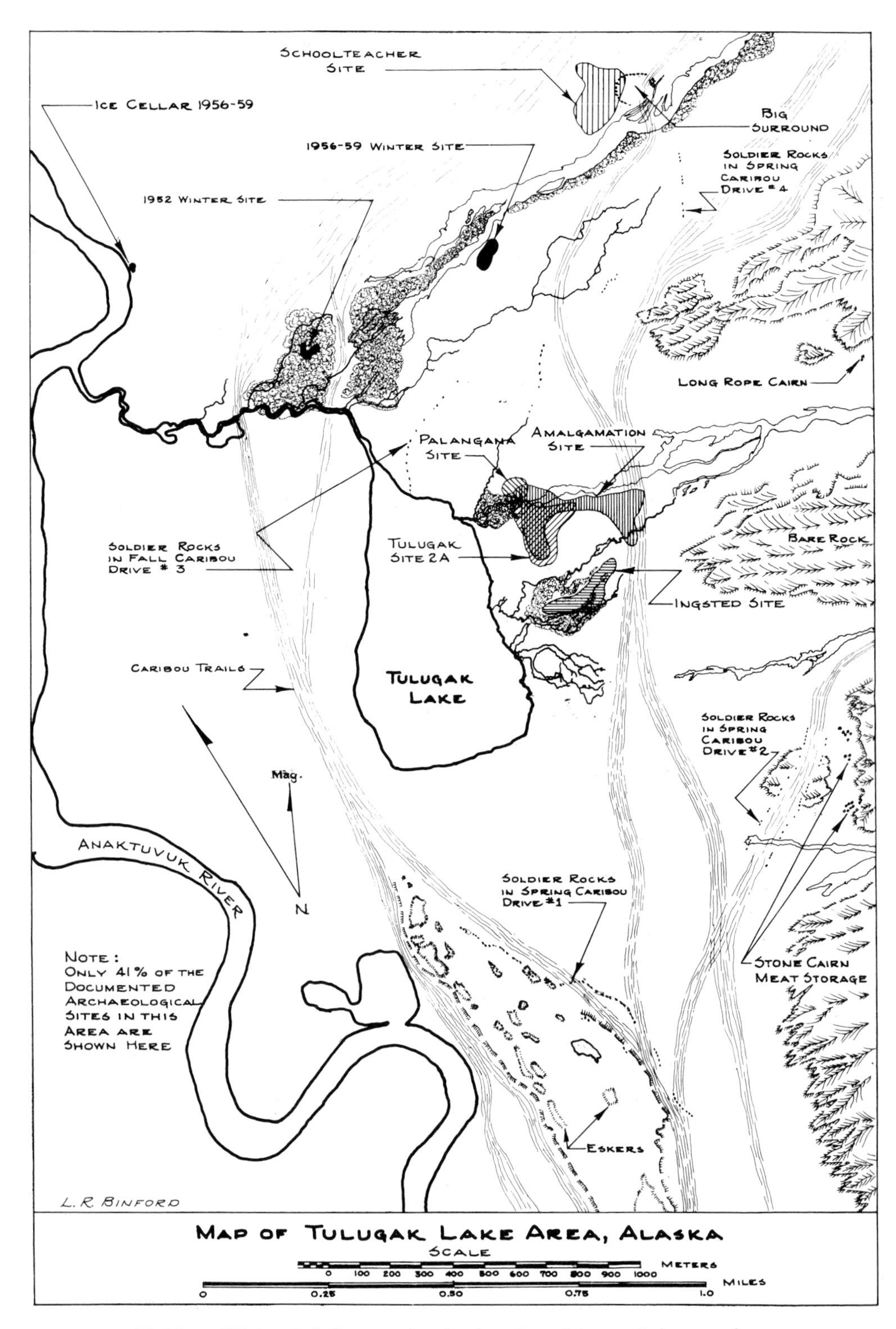

66 Map of Tulugak Lake area showing location of sites and site complexes.

To an archaeologist these impressive stone structures might resemble a house, but they were never used as such by the Nunamiut. The use of stone caches near kill sites is reminiscent of some of the 'pit-houses' described for certain Palaeolithic sites in Russia,[9] suggesting that these structures too were really not houses 63 but, as with the Eskimo stone structures, simply meat caches.

Meat can be stored at kill sites in a variety of ways besides the stone cache. When the temperature is below freezing, butchered meat or even whole animals can simply be stacked on the ground. Antlers usually serve to mark the location so that hunters can return even after it has snowed. At other times of the year meat 64 is placed on wooden racks to dry. Temporary meat caches used at hunting camps often consist merely of joints of meat strung out on a line or placed on the branches of trees along the edge of a stand of willows. Archaeologically, the remains of these 65 caches would be indicated by a linear distribution of large bones. Meat caches of all types provide important centralized, secure resources which the Nunamiut can draw on as they move around the habitat in search of additional food.

Tulugak Lake Site Complexes

My study of groups of interrelated sites has revealed that a sequence of activities in any one task did not necessarily take place all at one site. Furthermore, sites which appear to be very different may in fact belong to the same general category of behavior which was highly differentiated into various sets of activities. One of the most fascinating group of site complexes used by the Nunamiut Eskimo is located in the region around Tulugak Lake, an area very rich in resources. The 66 lake is deep enough to support a type of highly desirable, fatty fish called lake trout; spring-fed streams which flow into the lake are surrounded by large stands of willows, an important source of firewood; there are also a number of caribou migration trails which pass by the lake.

Drive Lines

The complexity of archaeological remains resulting from the exploitation of caribou in the vicinity of Tulugak Lake is tremendous. Caribou were driven between linear barriers which take advantage of natural features in the landscape, such as parallel rows of glacial hillocks (called eskers), but also incorporate man-made features which would have been very difficult to detect without ethnographic information. When not in use, the basic components of a drive line simply 67 look like piles of stones which I call *soldier rocks*. In contrast, during their use by the Eskimo to help channel caribou up a hill or into partly natural enclosures located at one end of the lake, the hunters placed moss around the rocks to form

67 'Soldier rocks' forming a caribou drive line running up the mountainside east of Tulugak Lake. (See ill. 66 for exact location.)

the shape of a man; old clothes were added on top of the moss to scare the caribou, keep them moving, and restrict their movement to the path chosen by the hunters.

Hunting Blinds

Along one caribou drive which goes up the mountain adjacent to the lake (taking advantage of a caribou's natural instincts to run uphill when threatened), we located seventy small hunting blinds from which two Nunamiut men could ambush game. Each of the blinds consists of a permanent structure made by excavating a hollow into the rock talus slope or by building a low wall. They have a dual function: not only can the hunters hide there, but the shelters also provide a measure of protection from the wind while the men wait for the game to appear – as long as eight or even twelve hours, if necessary. Obviously, they can get very cold in that time, but since lighting a fire is not conducive to attracting caribou, they have devised a different means for providing heat. Upon arrival at the blind, the men take down its walls and build a big hearth. After the fire is burning well, they pile the stones back on top of the fire and let it burn down. As the warmth of the fire heats the stones, the men can huddle up against the wall and keep warm while maintaining their vigil for the caribou. Again, the association of hearths in the walls of structures has also been noted for some Russian Palaeolithic sites.[10] One wonders why on earth anyone would build fires in the walls of houses, particularly if the proposed reconstruction with a skin tent atop the stone walls is

68

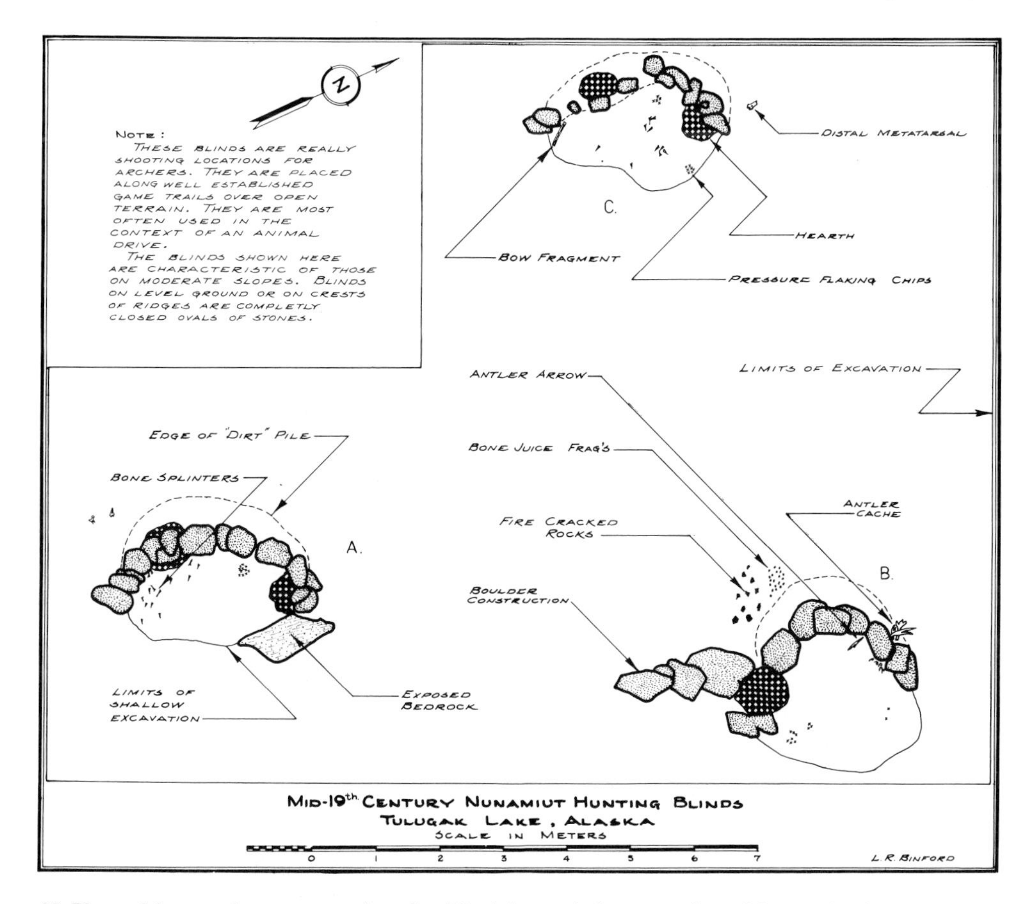

68 Plans of three 19th-century AD hunting blinds located along a caribou drive on the slope east of Tulugak Lake. (Exact position is marked on ill. 66.) Note the presence of waste by-products from snacks and tool repair, as well as a cache of antler for use in the manufacture of arrowheads. The hearths (represented by checkerboard shading) have been placed within the walls of the blinds to warm the hunters while they wait for caribou.

correct. Could these sites actually be hunting blinds similar to those used by the Nunamiut?

In plan the Eskimo hunting blinds appear as small semi-circles about 2.4 meters across.[11] The debris found in one of them, dating to an era before guns were used by the Nunamiut, demonstrates the types of activities which took place at these locations. Bone splinters from cracking bones for marrow, together with tiny bone fragments from pounding up articular ends of bones to make broth, represent the 'snacks' that were consumed. Industrial debris from tool manufacture and repair is represented here by a broken bow and some lithic flakes. The tools necessary for hunting are not made at hunting blinds, but would have been prepared before-

69 Hunting stand R & B at Anaktuvuk Pass showing a caribou skin bed where a man slept while his partner watched for game. (Exact location is noted on ill. 53.)

hand so that the hunter would be constantly ready for any animals that might appear along the migration route. This means that debris from the primary stages of production are rarely represented at hunting blinds. Instead, to while away the time the men usually brought along a broken tool needing repair or performed some other partially completed task. The activities carried out at this type of site were thus not directly related to the task at hand (hunting caribou), but were directed simply to the reduction of boredom. Another type of artifact found at the hunting blind shown in ill. 68 was an antler arrowhead which has been cached for future use, but was never needed.

Men occasionally will stay at a hunting stand overnight, rather than return to the base camp. Usually, one man stays up and watches for game, while another sleeps in his clothes on a caribou skin in a different area of the site; after a while they change places. Since they remain there over a relatively long period of time, the hunters will generally make a separate hearth away from the wall of the blind, so that they can prepare a meal of broth or roast meat. Although similar to the hunting blinds described above, the site generated in this way will be more complex in archaeological terms and one would have to be careful not to confuse the hunting blind and hearth with a base camp occupied by a family group.

69

Base Camps

Another component of the site complexes at Tulugak Lake are the residential camps situated near the lake, where firewood and fresh water are in ample supply. The Nunamiut select locations for base camps largely on the basis of the heaviest resources that they exploit, rather than merely the presence of food. Food-getting allows a flexible strategy because, as we have already seen, it can be cached and then transported; water and fuel are more difficult to move around. Residential sites, then, are positioned with respect to these basic resources and people adjust their trips out from the base camp in terms of the distributions of sources of food.

At Tulugak Lake we find a continuous distribution of archaeological remains, rather like the overlapping camp sites at Anavik Springs. There, however, the site was repeatedly used for the same basic function: the lakeside at Tulugak, in contrast, has been occupied at various times of the year for different reasons. For example, settlements in the summer were located here to take advantage of the lake trout, whereas winter villages were situated close to the abundant source of firewood. If this site were excavated, one might expect to find a summer residential camp on top of a fall hunting stand, or a winter village overlying a spring fishing camp.

As archaeologists how would we distinguish all the overlapping components of a complicated site such as Tulugak Lake? Could we recognize all the specialized types of site in the vicinity: the caribou drives, meat caches, and hunting blinds? Would we be able to reconstruct the associations between various locations and recreate site complexes? At present, archaeology lacks methods for coping with the complicated archaeological residues typically created by hunting and gathering peoples. We must begin to devise a means to untangle the palimpsests of overlapping occupations and to discover ways to recognize associated activity areas separated by as much as several kilometers.

Putting the System Together

One of the most important lessons to be learned from my ethnoarchaeological research among the Nunamiut Eskimo is that one has to conceive of all their sites as part of a larger system. Besides residential locations, an enormous variety of areas were used for special-purpose tasks which are merely parts of the overall pattern of making a living in the Arctic. We have seen how individual sites fit together to form site complexes, how site complexes can be grouped together within the territory exploited by one band of people and, finally, that several territories can be utilized sequentially during the course of a single person's lifespan. In order to reconstruct the entire pattern of land use, archaeologists have to be able first to identify the specific function of each separate site and then to fit all the individual parts together. The difficulty involved is rather like attempting to reconstruct an automobile engine on the basis of disconnected parts: one needs to know how the engine operates, in order to identify its relevant components – the carburetor, battery, cylinder, and so on – and to put them together correctly. In the same manner, archaeologists must identify each type of behavior that took place at each site they find and then begin to fit the pieces into place to make up a prehistoric system of land use. In other words, archaeology's basic unit is the individual site, but its goal is to employ these units to study past human behavior; and in order to accomplish this task, we need to develop an appropriate methodology for identifying the role of single sites within an overall system.

70 Plan of the fall hunting stand in Kongumuvuk Valley, Site 13 on ill. 53.

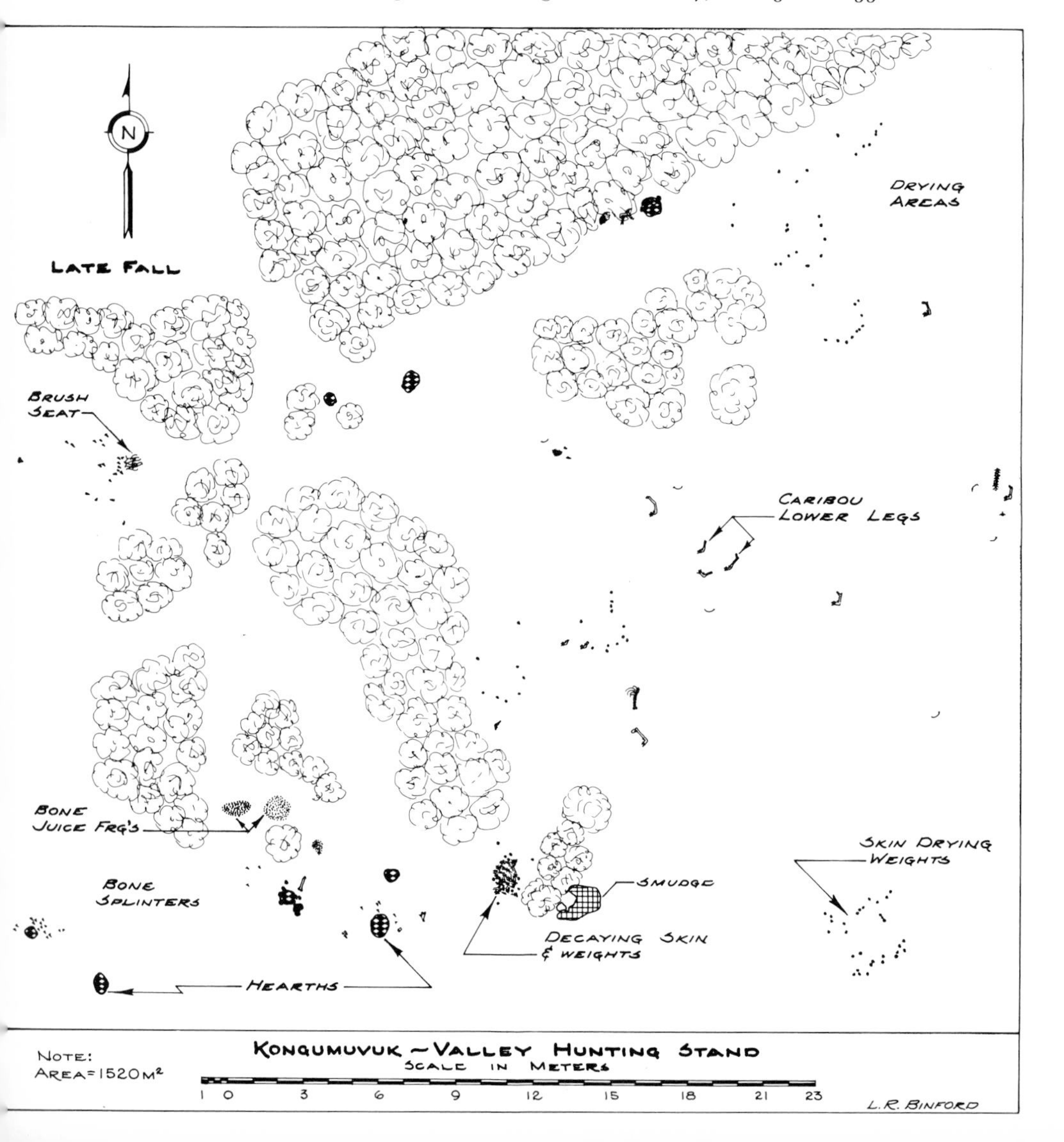

71 Circle of small stone weights used by the Nunamiut for holding down caribou skins while they are drying. (See ill. 70 for exact location of this feature at the Kongumuvuk fall hunting stand.)

Special-Purpose Sites

The value of archaeological studies of modern peoples is that, by observing the different types of sites which they occupy, we can begin to appreciate the range of variability which we are likely to encounter in the archaeological record. As a further attempt to make my point clear, it would be helpful to describe some additional special-purpose sites which I documented among the Nunamiut.

Some of these sites were surprisingly large. Typically, archaeologists expect activity areas to take up small amounts of space and to be internally homogeneous; but in the case of one non-residential site which I documented, a wide range of tasks took place over an area covering about 1500 square meters. At this site at Kongumuvuk, utilized during the fall migration of caribou, men hid in a stand of willows in order to camouflage themselves. While waiting for the game, some consumed snacks (such as marrow from fresh bone) around a small hearth and others repaired tools. The caribou were actually hunted and killed at quite some distance from the site itself. So as not to interrupt the movement of herds of caribou arriving subsequently, the Eskimo hurriedly butchered the animals in the location where they were shot and then dragged the desired portions of the animal back behind the willows to the Kongumuvuk site. Once out of the path of the migration, the men finished butchering the caribou, some of the meat being cached or placed on temporary drying racks. One major activity that took place at this site was the preparation of skins. The hides were laid out to dry and were

70

71

weighted down with stones to keep them from blowing around, with the result that there are large numbers of small circles of stones, all of about the same size, distributed over the site. As archaeologists, would we recognize that the distinctly different areas at this large site – the eating area around the hearth, the location of craft activities, the meat caches and drying racks, and the places for preparing skins – all fit together, or would we divide them into separate sites?

Tent Rings

Small rings of stones also occur on other sites occupied by Nunamiut hunting parties, but they could have been created by one of several activities besides drying fresh hides. For instance, at a site high in the mountains, normally occupied by parties of hunters seeking caribou bulls in summer, one finds small stone rings, about the same size as the circles at Kongumuvuk, associated with a small hearth. In this case, however, the size of the stones in the rings is larger than in the previous site because they were used to weight down the sides of caribou skin *tents*. The site differs from the hunting stand at Kongumuvuk in another way too. Unlike the combination of highly differentiated areas seen there, this site is composed of a series of identical units – a tent ring and a hearth – repeated over and over across space. Special-purpose sites, then, may vary in the degree to which the modules of which they are composed are homogeneous or are highly variable.

72 Hunting stand positioned in a natural swale near Little Contact Creek in Anaktuvuk Valley. (See ill. 53 for location.) This site is functionally identical to the site illustrated in ill. 69, but is located in different terrain. Note that some firewood and two old coffee cans used to boil water for tea have been cached at the site for future use. The sled was also cached here in the spring after the snow melted.

73 Deadfall trap constructed for catching a wolf. These traps are always built in the fall before the first heavy snowstorms.

Hunting Stands

Hunting stands are one of the most common types of site in the cultural landscape of the Nunamiut. They may be very complex (such as the site at Kongumuvuk, or the Mask site[12] to be discussed in the next chapter), relatively simple (as with the ambush locations at Tulugak Lake), or extremely ephemeral. As an instance of this last category, one can find locations where a hunter merely hid behind a large boulder and, perhaps, built a small fire. Natural features of the landscape, such as boulders or swales, are commonly used for hunting stands. At such sites one may find only a small hearth, some fire-cracked rock from stone boiling, and a series of tools which have been cached for later use. 72

Facilities

The soldier rocks along the caribou drives at Tulugak Lake can be classified as a particular type of tool called a facility (see further discussion in Chapter 7). Another member of the same class of artifacts are traps. The Nunamiut employ a wide range of these, of which the deadfall is one of the most common. The location of each deadfall trap should be considered as a special-purpose site. Often they are constructed in association with meat caches, in order to keep competitors 73 away from the stored food – although, in another sense, the meat cache is itself a source of bait to lure foxes and wolves into the area of the deadfall. Small walls are constructed around the deadfall to ensure that the animal enters in exactly the desired manner. The trigger for the trap is positioned far enough inside (i.e. beyond the length of the animal's neck), so that it has to place its front feet over one of the sills before the huge rock on top crashes down on top of it. Even if the stone does not kill the prey, it should land on its shoulders and prevent it from getting away.

Deadfall traps such as the ones constructed by the Nunamiut are probably very common in the archaeological record. I have observed similar constructions in sites associated with Neanderthal man and it is also clear that many sites described

74 Plan of the Tulukkana site where fifty caribou were processed for storage during a period of only twelve days. The enormous accumulation of bone is due to the preparation of the meat: it is *not* a reflection of either the number of people who occupied the site or the length of its occupation.

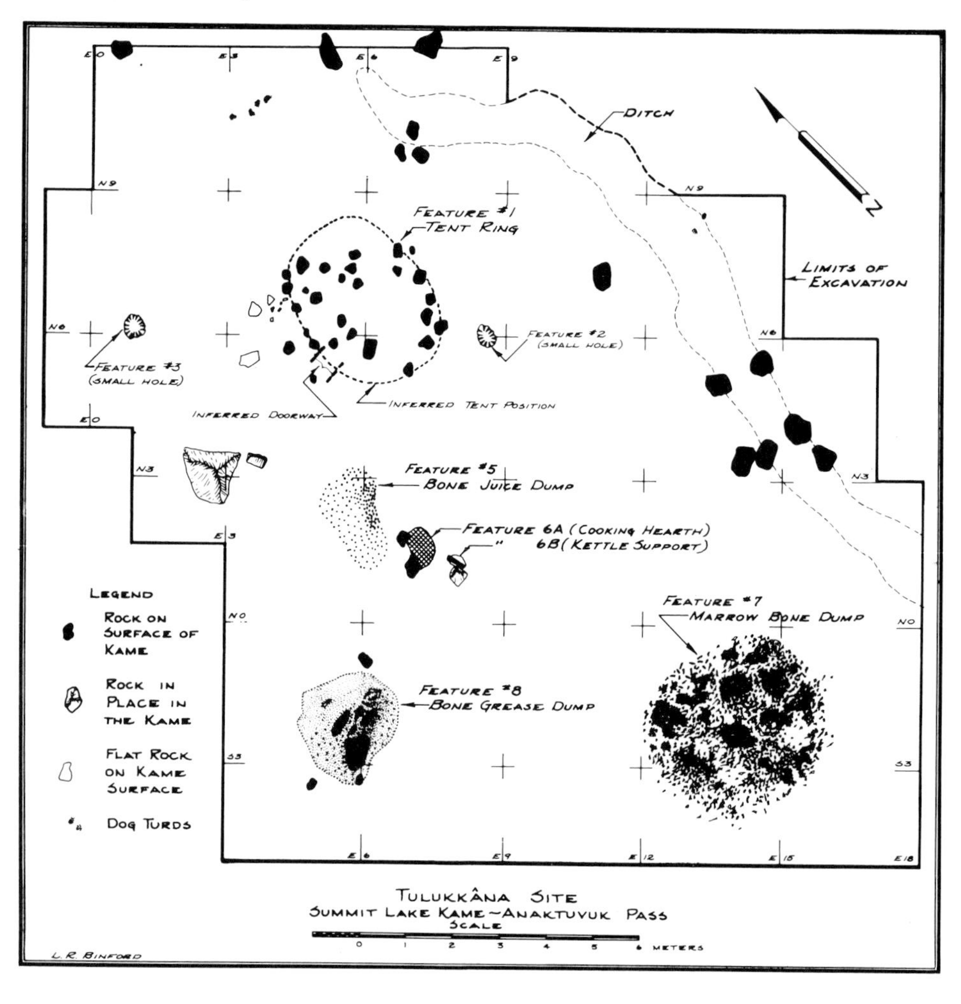

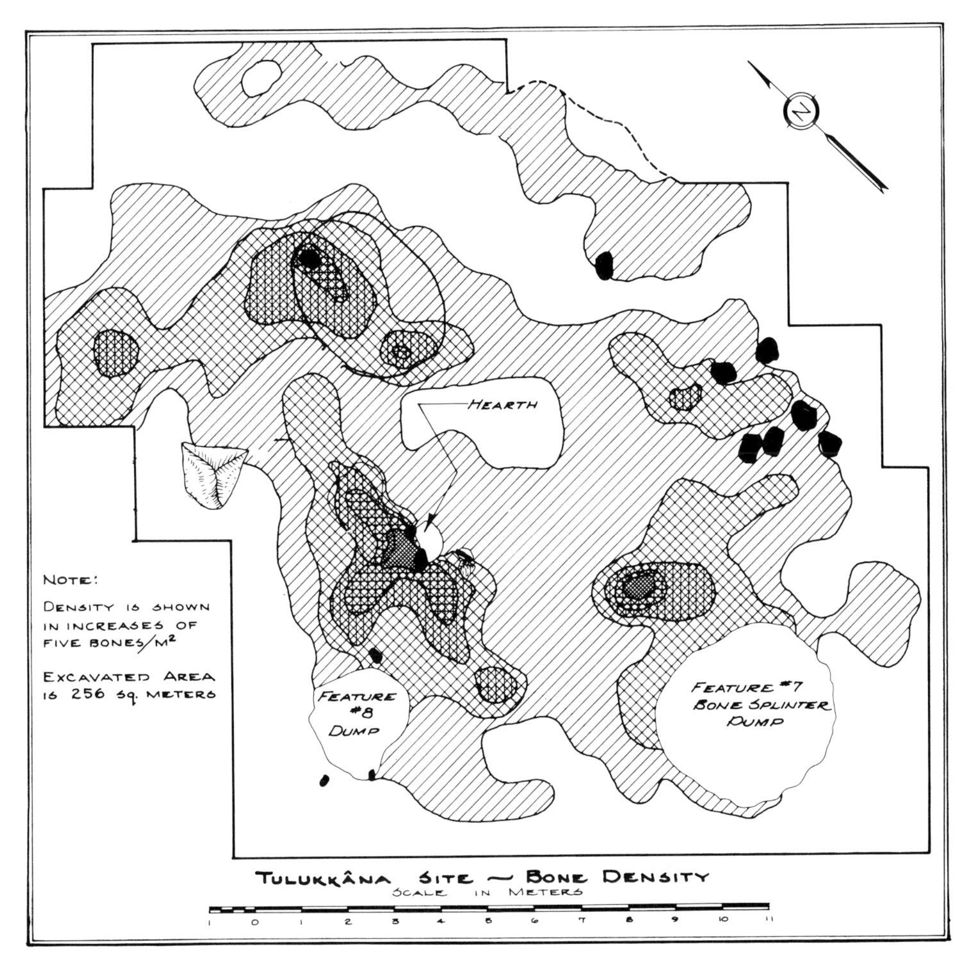

75 Contour map of the density of caribou bones found on the Tulukkana site (cf. ill. 74).

in the archaeological literature of North America as children's burials, ritual cairns, or storage pits are really deadfall traps. Archaeologists need to be able to identify accurately the very small and highly specialized sites of this kind used in the past.

Processing Sites

Although a large number of Nunamiut sites relate to the hunting of caribou, there are also many others where the processing of game took place. I have already mentioned the butchering site at Anavik Springs and the hide drying location at Kongumuvuk. Another example of this type of site documents an occasion when 74 a family had killed about fifty caribou by driving them into a nearby lake. All the processing of meat for drying took place during a period of only twelve days or so, yet the amount of debris deposited at the site was absolutely staggering. Two huge dumps of marrow cracked bone were created; the meat represented by this enormous quantity of bone, however, was not consumed there and the dumps, therefore, do not signify the remains of separate meals. For this reason, the quantity of debris provides an accurate measure neither of the number of people who occupied the site, nor of the length of time they resided there. This site, in fact, illustrates the danger of using a simple equation, such as that proposed by Yellen,[13] for relating quantity of waste to duration of occupation. Before we can interpret the nature of the data found on archaeological sites, we must determine the types of behavior which generated them in the first place – we must reconstruct the function of the site. Certainly, my research among the Nunamiut has demonstrated that archaeological sites are formed by a wide variety of different activities. It has also demonstrated, however, that because these variable types of behavior leave different traces in the archaeological record, it will be possible to develop techniques that will allow us to recognize similar special-purpose locations used in prehistoric times.

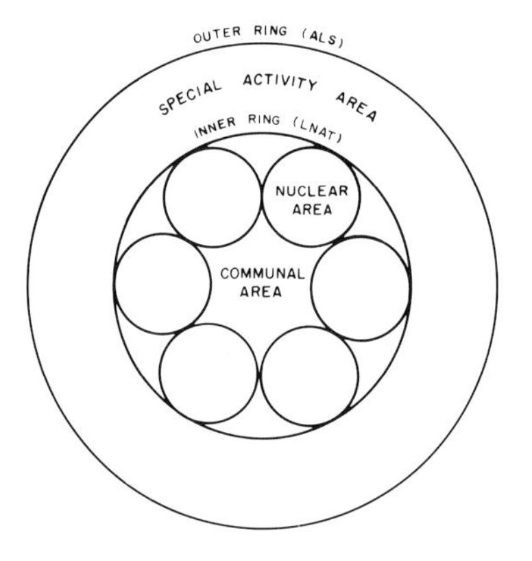

76 Model proposed by John Yellen of an idealized !Kung Bushmen camp. (Reproduced with permission from Yellen 1977, fig. 12, p. 126.)

The Layout of Residential Sites

At a still lower level of analysis, archaeologists need methods to study the patterns of use that take place *within* individual sites. Residential locations, as well as special-purpose sites, can be conceived of as being composed of small 'modules'. One of the most basic building blocks of sites are the structures in which people live. Studies of hunting and gathering groups demonstrate that, since the nature of the residential modules and the way they are distributed in space can vary

77 Residential camp occupied by Nharo Bushmen living in the central desert of Namibia *c.* 1927. The Ring Model described by Yellen (ill. 76) is clearly illustrated in this photograph. Note the meat hanging in the tree to the right (cf. ill. 65). (Photo by L. Fourie, courtesy of the Africana Museum, Johannesburg).

widely, archaeologists must be able to recognize all the possible permutations in their data.

Yellen[14] has proposed a general model for !Kung Bushmen residential camps in which the huts housing individual families are tightly grouped in a circle. In the middle of the ring of huts is an empty space used communally by all the people in the group; scattered around on the periphery of the ring of huts is an area where special-purpose tasks are carried out. The Bushmen camp pictured in ill. 77 provides a good example of the spatial structure summarized in Yellen's model. Similarly, a very tight cluster of huts with the hearths only about 3 meters apart can be observed at dry season camps of the Birhor, a group of hunters and gatherers in India.[15] 76 1

Not all Bushmen camps, however, conform to this idealized pattern.[16] And other hunter-gatherer groups exhibit forms of internal site arrangement which deviate from Yellen's model: for example Seri Indian camps in Mexico are laid 78

78 Seri Indian camp located on Tiburon island, Sonora, Mexico. The structures in the settlement are laid out in a linear fashion which contrasts strongly with Yellen's Ring Model of settlements (ill. 76). The huts currently in use have been placed in and among the remains of previously used structures, some of whose remains are visible in the far right of the photograph. For an excellent description of Seri settlements, see Ascher (1962). (Photo by E. H. Davis, 1922, courtesy of the Museum of the American Indian, Heye Foundation.)

out according to a linear pattern and considerable space is left between the shelters of different residential units. As with the Bushmen sites, the distribution of single dwellings varies among different Birhor settlements. For instance on one occasion when four bands were camped at the same location, each of the bands maintained its individual integrity by establishing a separate camp. In addition, the huts were not placed according to Yellen's ring model, as on other occasions, but in a semi-circle. Although this is clearly a single settlement despite the spatial separation of the different groups, the archaeological remains of such a site could easily be misinterpreted as a series of discrete unintegrated settlements, for there would be clear gaps in the distribution of debris between the clusters of huts represented by the different bands.

79

The use of physical space to represent social distance, as demonstrated in the Birhor case, may be a principle common to all hunter-gatherer sites. If true, this generalization could be useful for guiding the interpretation of archaeological sites. There is, however, a further complication that is well illustrated by Nun-

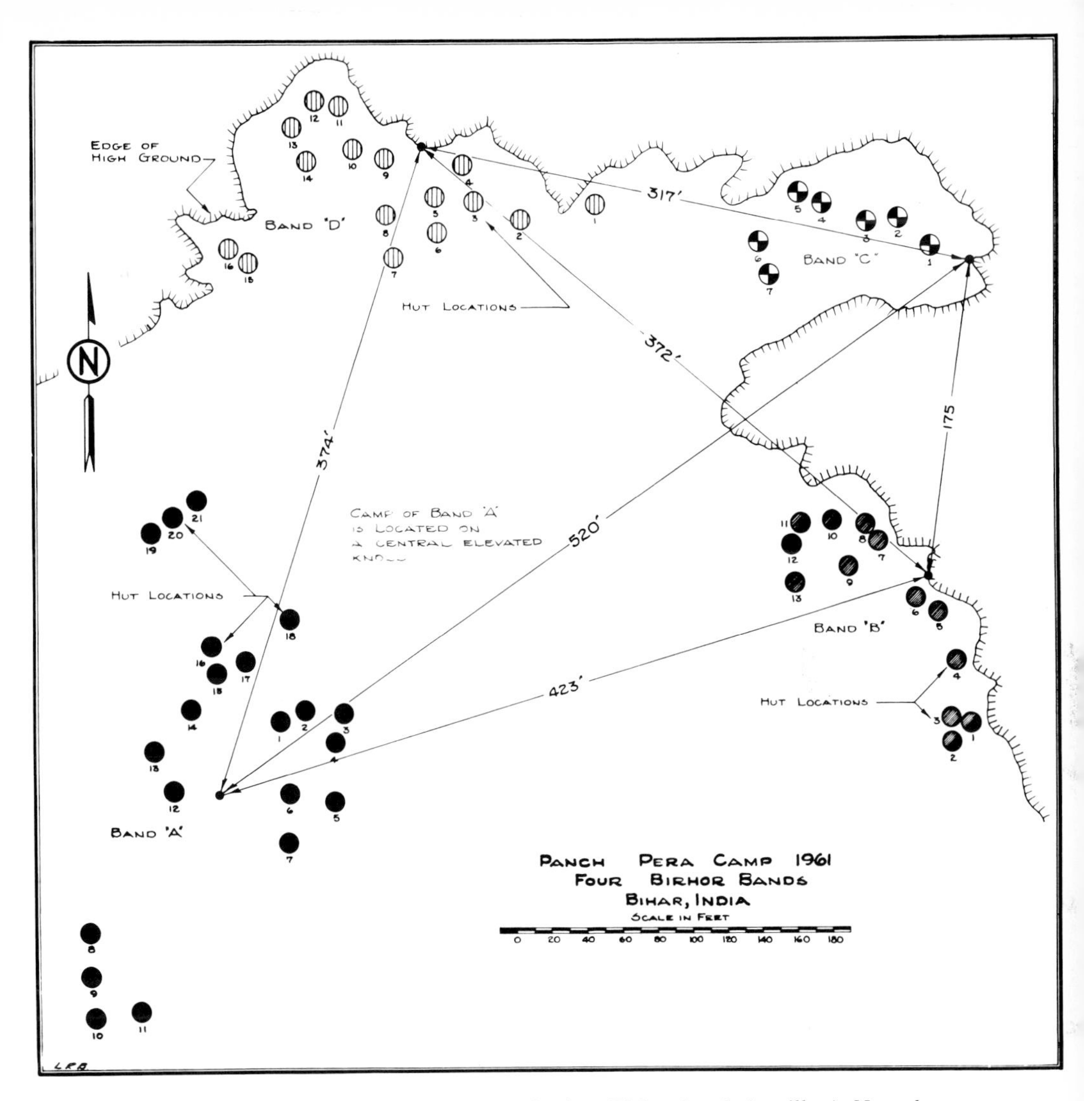

79 Map of the camp occupied simultaneously for four Birhor bands (see ill. 1). Note the large distances between each band and the non-circular grouping of the huts in relation to each other. (Cf. Williams 1968.)

amiut summer residential sites. At these locations, although the distinct social groupings or bands set up camp in different areas of the same site, the various houses within each band are often spaced out over large distances. At one site, for which the documentation is particularly good, there was an average of 90 meters between the residences of members of the same social unit. How would an archaeologist interpret this spatial distribution represented by separate scatters of debris: as different sites, as many separate social groups, or, as it actually was, two bands composed of several families?

If we were to examine a large number of additional ethnographic cases, great variability would be apparent in the way residential modules are distributed through space. Both the arrangement of the structures (clustered or dispersed, in circles or semi-circles, etc.) and the distance between each unit varies from group to group and within the seasonal cycle of any particular ethnic group or band. Archaeologists have to recognize that this type of variability exists, to understand the factors that cause it, and to create methods for monitoring it in the archaeological record.

The Challenge to our Methodology

As I have documented in this chapter, the settlement pattern of hunting and gathering groups may be seen as being organized on a series of levels ranging from the enormous area covered by a group in the lifetime of one of its members, through the residential core area and site complex, down to the distribution of houses and hearths at a single site. (The analysis of features on individual sites is considered in greater detail in the next chapter.) In order to understand the archaeological record of hunter-gatherers, therefore, we have to conduct research on all these different levels. Not only do we need to develop methods which will allow us to recognize the kinds of organized dynamics which took place at each scale of landscape use, but we must also be able to detect variations through time between different groups of hunters and gatherers in the organization of behavior at the regional level, the residential core level, the site complex level, the individual site level and the activity level.

It will be clear that in this chapter I have not attempted to develop methods for inference in relation to patterns of prehistoric land use, although hopefully some of this material will indeed eventually be used to achieve that goal.[17] For the present, I have merely tried to illustrate something of the nature of the problem which faces archaeologists. It is possible, however, on the basis of the examples presented here, to summarize several lessons to be learned by archaeologists and to suggest some ways forward.

In the light of the Nunamiut data presented here, the assumption that a single group of people generates sites which are internally homogeneous is not realistic. Similarly, the expectation that the closer sites are to one another, the more they should be alike, is also not sustained by the experiences reported above. The existence of site complexes, in which behavior related to a single activity is in fact carried out at three or more distinct places, is inconsistent with the way many archaeologists in the past have attempted to give meaning to similarities and differences in artifact assemblages. At least in some regions and with some hunter-gatherer societies, we may expect that the more intense the utilization of a particular locale, the more diverse will be the separate types of settlements and sites placed in the locale – as for example at Tulugak Lake, which merits consideration in more detail. For instance, it is generally true that within the environment exploited by many hunting and gathering peoples there are certain places like Tulugak Lake which provide both a greater nucleation of critical resources and also better chances for success in obtaining mobile resources. Archaeologically, such places will be extremely complicated.

Each site thus reflects the unique sequence of uses to which that particular place has been put in the past. Clearly, the internally differentiated nature of activities and the spatial segregation of the places where different tactics are executed is consistent with some of the problems in the Mousterian data reported by Bordes (Chapter 4). But make no mistake: these ethnoarchaeological experiences do not provide direct solutions to the 'Mousterian problem'. The conclusion we can draw from my work among the Nunamiut is not that my functional arguments about Mousterian variability were correct, but rather that archaeological methods for inference are *in general* very inadequate. Clearly, the conventions used by most Palaeolithic archaeologists have been shown to be incapable of coping with the variability and diversity of land use illustrated by the Nunamiut case. The challenge provided by ethnoarchaeology of this sort is to forge better methodologies.

How can we take the lessons derived from this research about the dynamics of land use and apply them to studies of prehistoric stone tool assemblages?[18] How should we move from the overall ethnographic picture of one complete dynamic system to the stationary, site-based perspective utilized in archaeology? What is clear is that the individual sites which belong to the same hunter-gatherer system of land use are in fact different. For this reason, a site classification scheme using similarity in structure as its criteria is not likely to group correctly sites which were produced in the context of one type of environmental exploitation or even within the life of a single individual. This brings us back again to the methodological challenge: how do we recognize that *different* things found at *different* places represent components of the *same* system?

Much of my own work along these lines has previously focused on animal bones,[19] because they are elements common to the present and the past. It has been possible to show that the skeletons of animals have been modified and distributed on sites according to particular principles which were ultimately determined by the basic activities which were also carried out at different places in the landscape, in much the same way as I have illustrated in this chapter. In the next chapter, I wish to turn to other avenues of research which might aid archaeology in diagnosing in other forms of data (such as lithic assemblages) variability caused by differences in the use of places, as illustrated in this chapter. This new research concentrates on the study of site structure.

7
People in their Lifespace

Site Structure: A Challenge to Archaeological Interpretation

As we saw in the first three chapters, one of the Big Questions archaeologists are currently seeking ways to understand is how early man organized his *life space* – the location and the spatial relationship of activities such as sleeping, eating, food-getting, tool manufacture, etc. We want to find out to what extent early man, like his modern counterpart, made consistent and specialized use of space. For instance, once they began to utilize tools regularly, did our ancestors organize their use of space so that tools were ready where needed, or did they simply produce and discard them in the places of their use? Did they share food, as modern man tends to do? In other words, the study of past use of space asks the fundamental question: how were man's activities organized at different places?

We saw in the last chapter how certain modern hunter-gatherers move among a number of localities, carrying out different types of activities at each one. As I tried to emphasize there, if the archaeologist is to understand the dynamics of similar systems in the past, he must be able to diagnose the nature and organization of the tasks conducted at each site. Likewise, if the 'Mousterian problem' is to be resolved, we must be able to reconstruct at least some of the activities that took place at Mousterian sites, and to do so in terms of data which are independent of the make-up of lithic assemblages, since we would like to find out if the composition of stone tool assemblages varies in regular ways with other facts which might be understandable in terms of the past. More specifically, archaeologists would like to be able to interpret *in terms of prehistoric living conditions* facts such as the various frequencies of tools, the differences in the distributions of tools and animal remains, or the relationship of particular types of debris from stone tool manufacture with respect to the tools themselves.

The study of *site structure* – that is, the spatial distribution of artifacts, features, and fauna on archaeological sites – was one of the challenges I took up when I began ethnoarchaeological research.[1] My ethnographic experiences impressed on me the fact that there were generally clusters of variables which, depending on the situation, to a large extent determined the way behavior at different locations was organized. For instance, in hunting camps the relative success of the hunting party affected very substantially the patterns of food consumption,[2] the activities conducted, and in many instances the duration of the camp's occupation. On the other hand, in residential camps such situation-dependent conditions were rarely apparent and, where they were, they reflected drastic, system-wide conditions of stress which triggered emergency strategies never seen in hunting camps.[3] In short, I observed that different patterns of assemblage variability were referable to functionally different types of sites. Nevertheless, despite these functional differences there also appeared to be an underlying stable set of traits characteristic of the internal spatial organization of life at a site. Consequently, while researching the problem of assemblage variability in fauna, I took every opportunity to document the spatial pattern of finds within sites whose function, duration of occupation, season of use, and so on, were known; I did so in the hope of building up, as it were, a 'library' of materials which could perhaps serve as the basis for developing criteria for recognizing factors which conditioned the spatial organization of activities on sites, regardless of function.

One of the elements common to all sites, past and present, is the physical size and structure of the humans who use them: perhaps this simple fact is the key to interpreting site structure? If one could show from ethnographic cases that certain types of spatial patterns are the result of simple body mechanics, then one would have a basis for making inferences about the past – or at least as far back as our ancestors had basically the same type of body. The relationship between the human body and the spatial patterns would act as an 'eternal object' (to use Whitehead's[4] term) for this research domain, because it could be assumed to be uniform between the past and the present.

Just as the bony skeleton provides the framework for the body around which the muscles and organs operate, so the arrangement of *facilities* on a site provides the skeleton around which activities are organized; the flow of persons and goods is accommodated to the facilities within a site. Phillip Wagner has defined facilities as follows:

> . . . containers like baskets, and pottery, vessels, boxes, buildings, . . . bases like roads and platforms . . . and barriers like fences, dams, walls . . . Facilities represent a rearrangement of features of the environment, or the addition of features to the environment . . . they control or prevent the movement of solid, liquid, or gaseous material and animate beings.[5]

The 'skeletal morphology' of a site – what I call the *site framework* – is the arrangement of such facilities. From an archaeological perspective, we see the facilities as *features* and the use areas and circulation pathways as *item patterning* and/or the *spatial clustering of artifacts*. I am convinced that fundamental clues to the character of activities, the labor organization employed in their execution, and the anticipated use of a location in terms of the overall subsistence-settlement system, are

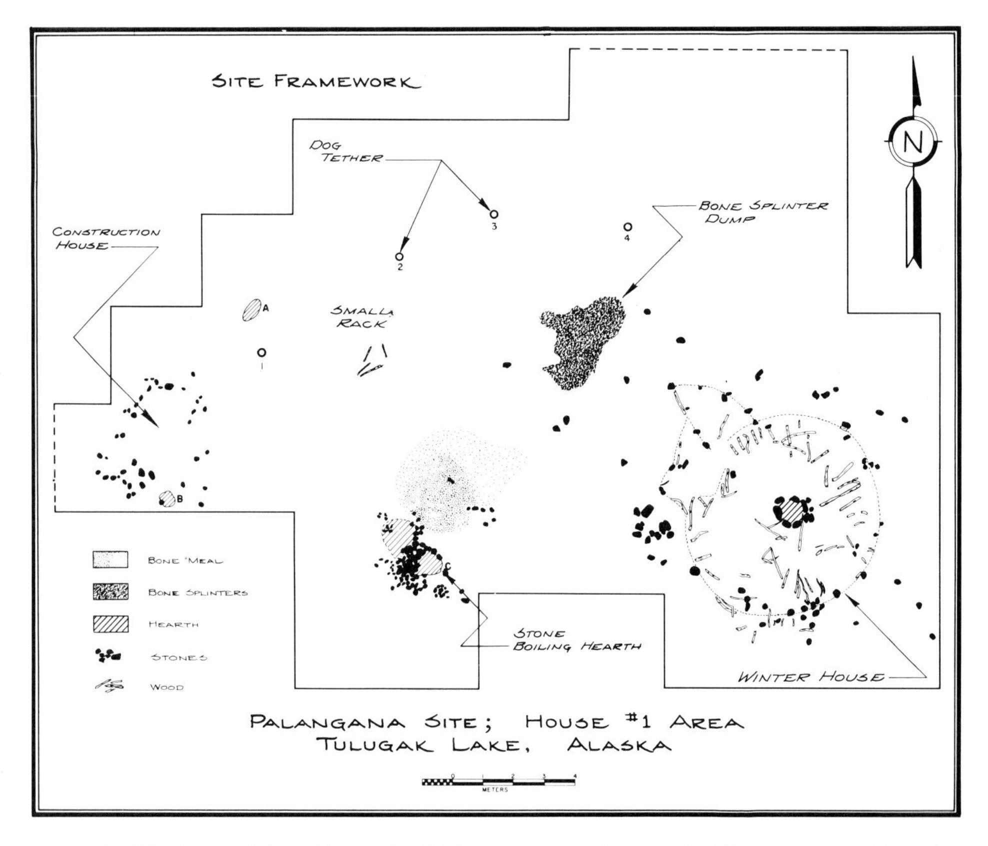

80 *Site framework* for a Nunamiut Eskimo winter settlement, the Palangana site. (Location of site is marked on ills. 53 and 66.) There was almost certainly also a meat rack here, but it was not discovered. The small structure noted as a 'construction house' was erected for the men to stay in while they built the winter house and was not in use during the occupation of the house. For a description of this site, see Binford (1978a, pp. 431–49).

coded into the organization of the site structure. We need to learn about the factors which affect how people establish, lay out and use a location; equally important is the way a group maintains a site.

80 The best way to illustrate these general points is by example. At a typical Eskimo winter house site, there is a characteristic site framework composed of several basic facilities, including a house, a meat rack, dog tethers, and outside hearths. Distributed around and among these features are a variety of specialized activity areas. These might include a household midden, a dump of bone splinters, a dog yard, work space, a wood pile and associated chopping area, a children's play area and, finally, areas for human waste disposal. Such areas are not facilities *per se*, but are places where particular functions relevant to the life of

the social unit present are carried out. The land surfaces upon which certain activities are regularly conducted may not involve their actual modification in any intentional manner, although they may be cleaned or maintained. Archaeologically, they would not appear as soil disturbances or an arrangement of natural or manufactured materials (as in the case of a house or hearth), but we would see the archaeological clues to their functions in the form of the spatial arrangements of items, both tools and debris, which had been incidentally produced at the area or placed there intentionally. Woven into the structure of facilities and use areas are paths and avenues of access for both people and materials.

From an archaeological perspective, given the outline above, what seems most appropriate is a descriptive and analytical procedure which attempts to define the site framework in terms of features and which is followed by a study of the relationships between this skeletal framework and the dispersion of items. Unfortunately, the real world of archaeological remains rarely provides such an ideal situation. It is a simple fact that in many, if not most, archaeological sites facilities are not equally preserved and identifiable, thus complicating the proposed procedure. For instance, a hearth may be recognizable, but the former presence of a house around the hearth may not be indicated by post molds or other such structural clues.

Our methods at present are inadequate for this task. For example, Leroi-Gourhan[6] has advanced a model of site structure which attempts to infer the presence of a house from patterning in the dispersion of items. Not only is his inference suspect because he chooses the cluster of items *after* assuming the existence of a house in the first place,[7] but I also find his suggestions less than convincing given my own ethnographic experiences. Archaeologists need criteria for distinguishing patterns that may appear in the absence of a house, or on sites where residential types of facilities were not present.

81

Adopting the viewpoint of formation processes, we see that sites are organized by components or modules of the kind already described in Chapter 6. In the example of the Eskimo site, I could speak quite meaningfully of the outside cooking hearths, the dumps, the dog yard, the play area, etc. Long ago I referred to such modules as *activity areas*. There has been considerable confusion in the literature about this and related concepts, due at least in part to a failure to distinguish between the properties of a living cultural system and patterning in the archaeological remains (a confusion rightly anticipated by Schiffer and Rathje[8] a number of years ago). Before continuing further, I must clarify exactly what I mean by such concepts as 'activity', 'toolkit' and 'activity area'. A *toolkit* is a set of tools used in the execution of a task. An *activity* is an integrated set of tasks, generally performed in a temporal sequence and in an uninterrupted fashion. It is recognized that identical tasks may be integrated into different activities: for example, the task of cutting meat may be integrated in the activity

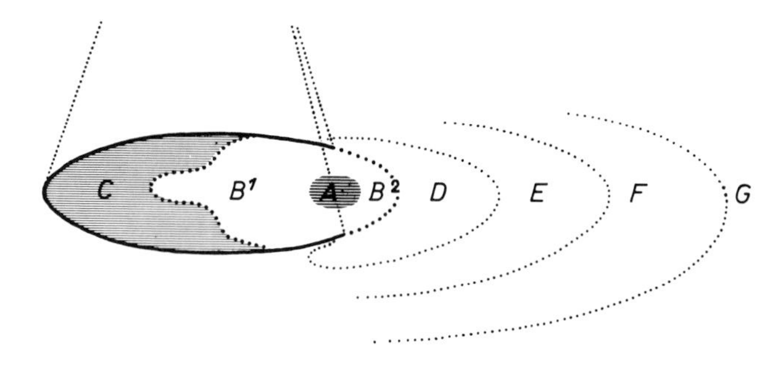

81 *Leroi-Gourhan's model for a residential site.* The hearth (Zone A), located in the doorway of the house or structure, is conceived as the focus of organized activities on the site; it marks the transition between space inside and outside a structure. The inside is conceived as the area of domestic usage and can be internally differentiated into two zones. In Zone B^1 persons sit around the fire and conduct various activities and social acts; it is likely to have been kept fairly clean as a place where the more delicate activities are conducted. Leroi-Gourhan describes Zone B^1 as the area where archaeologists will find small tools and ochre. The second area within the structure is Zone C, the sleeping area, where little in the way of artifacts or debris is to be expected. Around the hearth outside the structure is a further domestic space, Zone B^2, which is considered to be the place where more crude activities, producing larger quantities of debris, are thought to have been localized. Such things as the waste from primary flint work, antler and bone processing, and stones used in cooking could be expected outside in Zone B^2. Beyond are a series of concentric circles, Zones D, E, F, and G, which are conceived as follows: (D) zone of concentrated dumping and repeated disposal; (E) zone of dispersed dumping; (F) space of rare dumping, and (G) space of isolated finds. Given this model one can expect high and low density sides of a hearth with the high density side consisting of the area outside a house and the low density side on the inside. This is a good example of how a formation model can be used to justify a series of conventions for interpreting archaeological remains. (Reproduced with permission from Leroi-Gourhan and Brézillon 1972, fig. 174, p. 254.)

of butchering, preparation of meat for cooking or eating, etc. *Activity areas* are places, facilities, or surfaces where technological, social, or ritual activities occur. We can readily imagine individual activities which made use of a number of toolkits and, conversely, different activities which integrated one or more identical toolkits. It was because I expected this kind of mixing of components to be present in the archaeological record that a number of years ago I advocated the use of multivariate statistical techniques for the analysis of interassemblage variability.[9]

Returning to a spatial viewpoint, it is consistent to anticipate that areas within sites could be equally complex: some might be multi-purpose locations, others places where individual activities or individual tasks were conducted. This line of thought leads to the conclusion that there is not necessarily an exact correspondence between a location and a toolkit, or even a single activity. It does not follow, however, that the location of artifacts has no structure and therefore carries no information about the character of the past cultural system. Quite the reverse: the challenge of interpreting site structure is no different from the challenge of archaeology in general. How do we give accurate meaning to the patterns we observe?[10]

We can begin the search for appropriate methods by studying how patterns in site structure are formed in the present. In the remainder of the chapter, therefore, I will illustrate some of the thought-provoking observations that I have made among living peoples. I will focus on the spatial modules which underlie the structure of the position and layout of activities (*activity areas*) and the associations of items (*toolkits*), both of which archaeologists could detect through pattern-recognition studies of site structure.

Working Around a Hearth

When people are working at a job which requires the use of a hearth, they tend to carry out the task according to a spatial pattern which appears to be universal. For example, a !Kung Bushman woman living in Botswana cracks mongongo nuts on an anvil located within an arm's distance of the fire where the nuts are roasted. For this chore she does not face the fire directly, but sits obliquely to it. If she were actually facing the fire, there would not be adequate workspace in front of her and she could not, of course, work in the embers of the fire. This same

82

82 Young Bushman male using a bowdrill in a camp located at Gautsha Pan. Note that he does not face the fire directly but sits sideways to it. The hearth is located only a short distance from a shelter within which bedding is visible. A second anvil is located close to the hearth on the opposite side from the seated worker. (Photo taken in 1975 by J. Kramer, courtesy of the South African Museum, Cape Town.)

pattern is typical of work carried out by one person at or around a hearth: the worker sits with his or her body at right-angles to the hearth and within arm's 83 length of it. Similarly, an Aborigine from the Central Desert of Australia will sit with his side to the fire when he is warming resin in the embers for hafting a stone tool to its wooden handle. The same positioning can be observed when a Navajo 84 woman prepares bread at an outside hearth. The pattern has been recorded by anthropologists for a wide variety of ethnographic settings; I have also observed it frequently in the course of analyzing a substantial number of old ethnographic photographs.

Having noted a basic pattern of activity around a hearth, additional features associated with it or important differences from it become significant. Inside 85 substantially built houses, stones are typically placed next to the hearth to be used as small tables for cutting meat, laying out food, or placing containers. When a whole group of people are working around a hearth, the pattern differs from the solitary seated worker model. In order for all the people to have adequate workspace, everyone moves out away from the fire; consequently, one observes a 86 circular arrangement of debris around the hearth rather than the perpendicular distribution associated with one worker.

83 Alyawara Aborigine man from central Australia at a small processing site preparing spinifex resin for hafting stone tools. While working he sits with his side to the hearth.

84 Navajo woman from the southwestern United States preparing bread at an outside hearth. Note the position of the hearth in relation to the woman and her artifacts. (Photo courtesy of Susan Kent.)

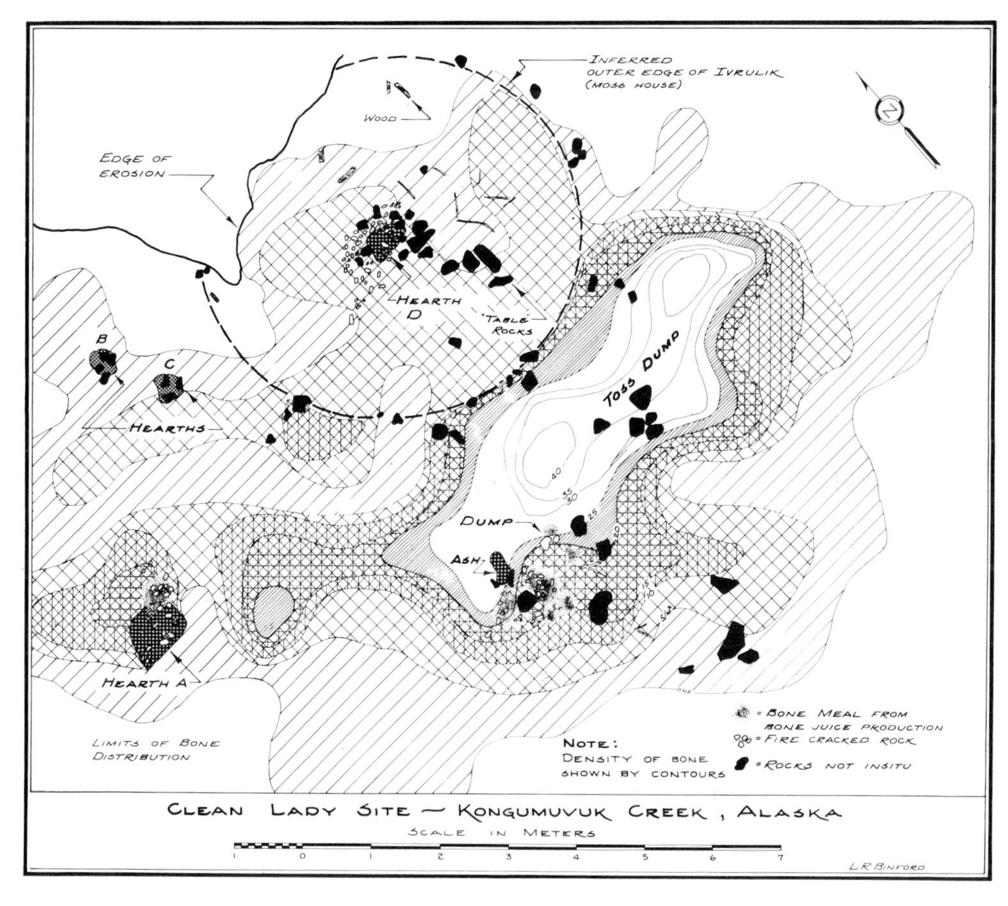

85 Map of the Clean Lady site at Kongumuvuk Creek, Anaktuvuk Pass, Alaska showing the arc-shaped arrangement of rocks forming a table adjacent to the hearth (D) inside the moss house. This pattern is typical when a single cook habitually uses a particular place around a hearth. Note how clean the area inside the rock table is. An outside hearth (A) is present on this site as are a small *door dump* to the right of the house entrance and a very large bone midden to the left of the door.

86 Family group of !Kung Bushmen processing mongongo nuts. Note the circular arrangement of the group seated some distance back from the hearth located in the foreground. (Photo courtesy of Patricia Draper.)

87 Debris from stone tool production as it lay just after a worker had finished removing flakes from a core. The activity took place in the men's camp at the Bendaijerum site occupied by Alyawara in central Australia.

Another important observation about site structure can be illustrated by stone tool manufacture among the Alyawara Aborigines in Australia.[11] In one case I watched a seated worker knocking flakes off a core. The tiny impact chips created as a result of this flaking would later provide a clue to where the man had been seated, because they fell between his legs and were left in place. The flakes, however, were arranged carefully in an arc in front of him. The shape and size of this arc were determined by the length of the man's arm. A similar pattern was also created in a very different part of the world (northern Alaska), where I have observed some very old Eskimo men working stone.

87

Spatial models of seated workers are often complicated by the presence of more than one individual. Similar but parallel actions by different individuals, as well as their different actions, generate overlapping distributions. Ill. 88 illustrates nicely a classic hearth-centered seating arrangement involving a number of individuals. I think the reader can appreciate the complex nature of the spatial patterns generated by the items dropped by such a group of seated persons. This type of distribution has been converted into an idealized model (ill. 89) based on actual observations made at an Eskimo site where a group was frequently observed

88 Classic circular arrangement around a hearth as demonstrated by Nharo Bushmen at Ganzi, Botswana, *c.* 1969. (Photo by H. Steyn, courtesy of the South African Museum, Cape Town.)

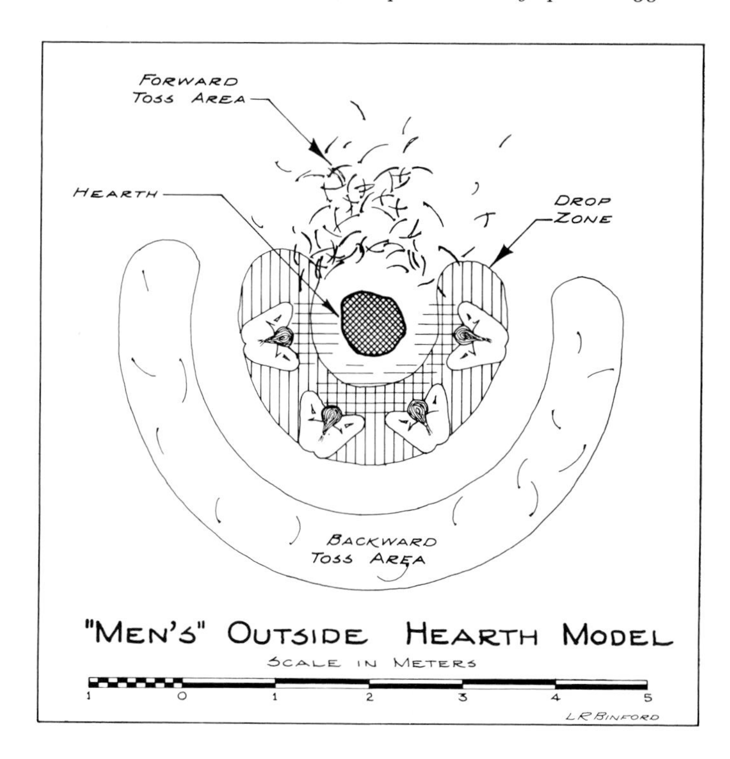

89 Model of *drop* and *toss zones* as developed from observations at the Mask site in Anaktuvuk Pass, Alaska. (Cf. Binford 1978b.)

sitting in a circle around a fire. The debris which was dropped produced a ring of small items centered around the hearth; the disposal of large items, however, was different, these objects being tossed behind the people away from the sitting area.

Let me illustrate this general seating model by reference to a specific case recorded among the Nunamiut, in which men in a hunting camp were processing caribou bone for marrow. If we look at the spatial distribution of the tiny bone chips created by breaking open the bone to get the marrow, we see that there is a concentration around the hearth – the *drop zone*. These small fragments of bone are analogous to the small impact chips formed during the reduction of stone cores (ill. 87). As in the case of the lithic waste, the tiny pieces of bone were left *in situ* by the Eskimo at the location where the marrow cracking actually took place. On the other hand, the spatial distribution of the large pieces of bone – the *toss zone* – is different, because the ends of the bones were tossed or placed behind the men in an open area after the marrow had been removed. This tossing aside of larger items is described by the Eskimo as a kind of 'preventive maintenance' of the seating area. When I asked the men about these different modes of disposal, they would say 'Who wants to sit down on a large bone?'

The presence of several individuals engaged in different actions around a hearth can contribute to variability in both content and form of the debris distributions.

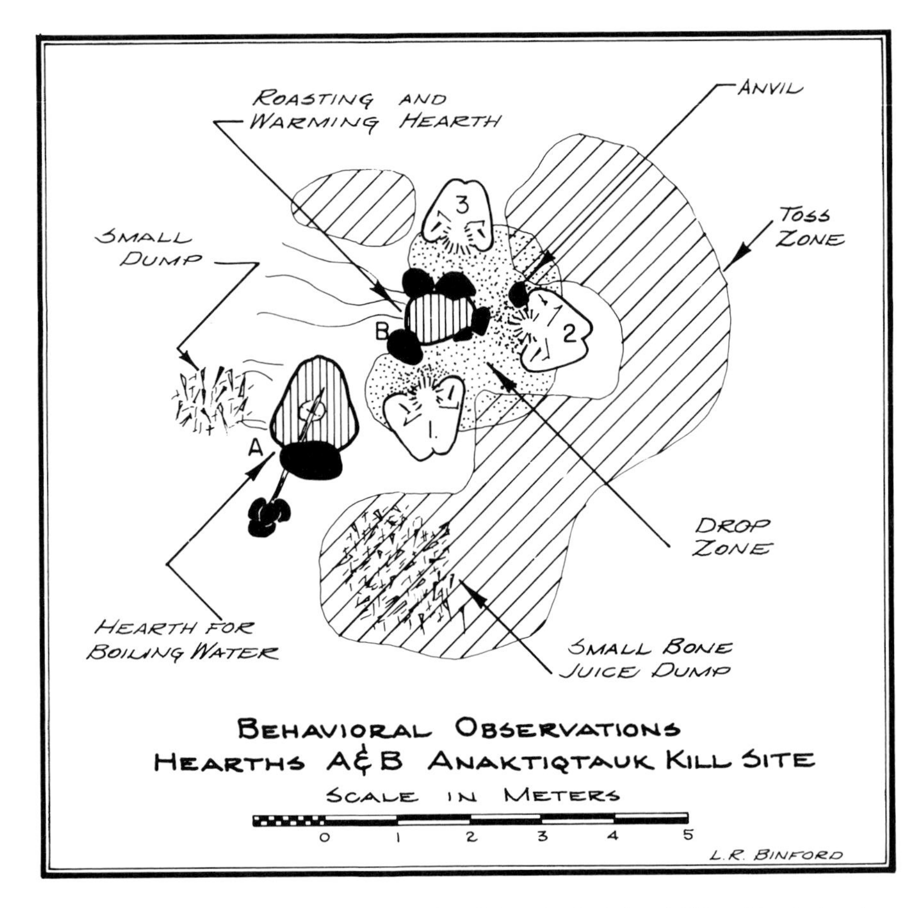

90 *Behavioral observations made at Hearths A and B on the Anaktiqtauk kill and butchering site at Anaktuvuk Pass, Alaska.* (Location given in ill. 53.) Two men (nos. 2 and 3) were seated at Hearth B cracking caribou bones and eating the marrow. Bone splinters discarded around them as the bones were broken entered the *drop zone*. Larger articular ends of the bones were placed to one side or thrown slightly behind them in the *toss zone*. Person no. 1 arrived and suggested that they prepare some warm broth from the boiled fragments of caribou ribs which he had with him, as well as from some of the broken articular ends of the long bones left over after marrow eating. For this purpose a quick flaming fire was kindled at a second hearth (A) and a coffee can was suspended over the fire for boiling the broth (cf. ill. 72). Individual no. 1 attended the fire and kept the pot boiling until the broth was considered ready. It was then poured into cups and the bone fragments remaining in the can were dumped across to the other side of Hearth A. Preparation of the broth was carried out by no. 1 in a standing position. After the broth was consumed, no. 1 collected many of the fragments from the extraction of marrow and prepared a second pot. After it was served, the scraps of bone were dumped behind the sitting position of no. 1.

In the situation illustrated in ill. 90, individual no. 1 is engaged in boiling up bone fragments to produce a kind of broth, an activity for which a separate hearth is being used (although this is not always felt to be necessary). The important point here is that, after pouring off the broth into cups for himself and the others to drink, he dumped the contents of the boiling can across the fire or threw them directly to his left as he stood and faced the hearth: these areas are labeled 'small dumps' in ill. 90. This action – the disposal of an aggregated mass of refuse, as opposed to the discrete items we have been discussing so far – obviously produces homogeneous concentrations of items. Such localized distributions break up and punctuate the pattern of dropped and tossed items accumulating simultaneously. On subsequent days at the site, when more men were present, a third hearth was built in a position towards the bottom of ill. 90. The prior existence of the small bone juice dump located behind individual no. 1 acted as a sort of 'magnet' attracting further disposal, so that most of the items tossed away by men seated at the later hearth were added to the earlier dump, still visible from the previous day.

91 Activities observed at the Mask site, Anaktuvuk Pass, Alaska, on a spring afternoon.

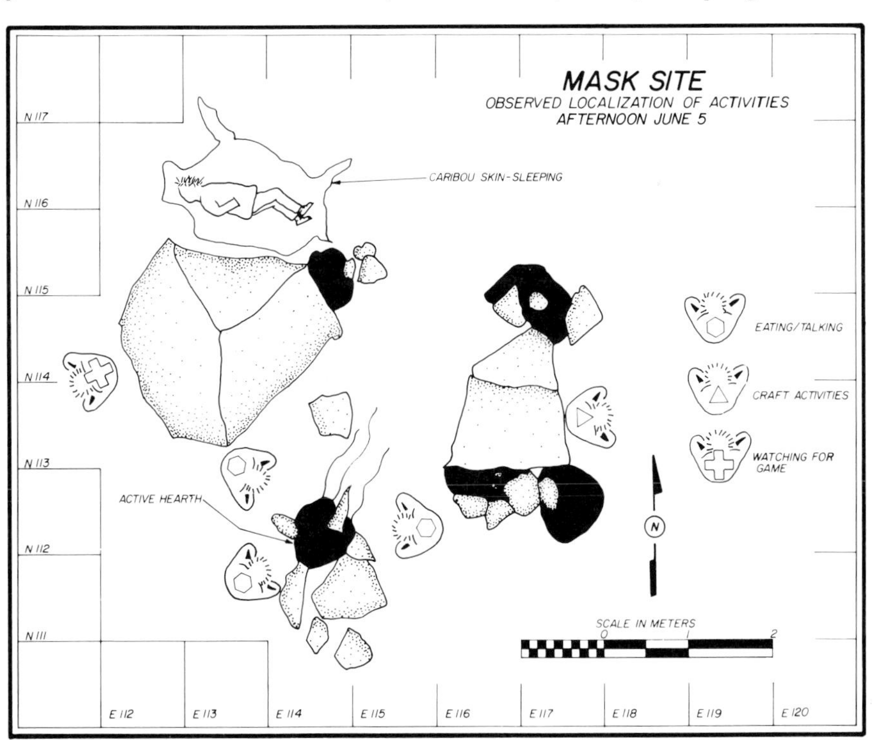

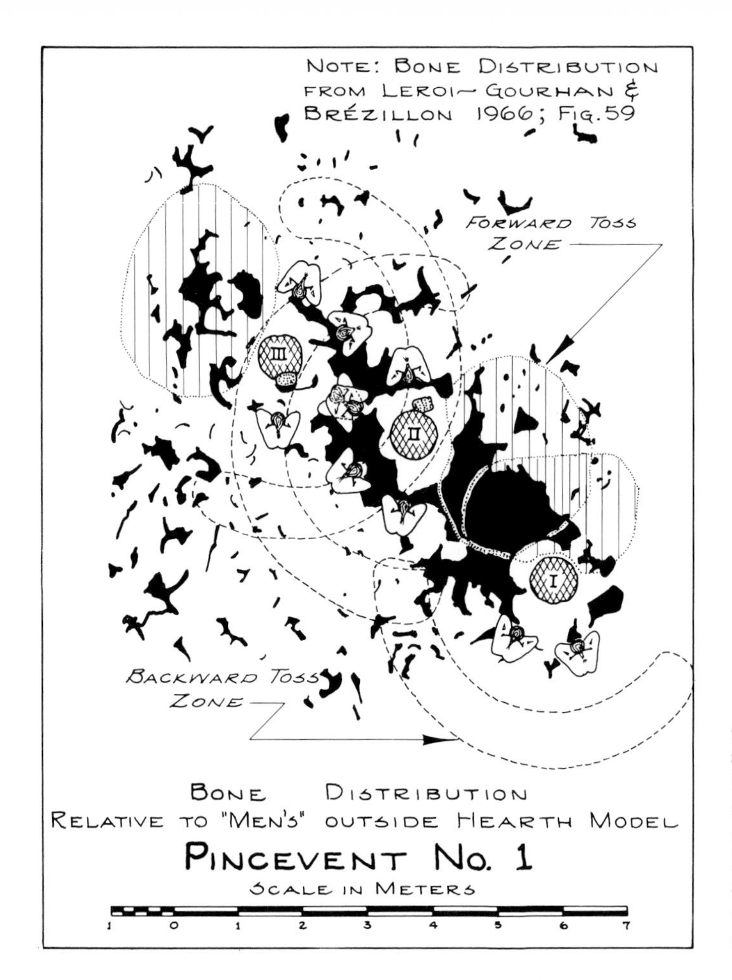

92 Toss zone model for men seated around an outside hearth superimposed on the actual distribution of bone artifacts on the site of Pincevent One. (Archaeological data based on Leroi-Gourhan and Brézillon 1966, fig. 59, p. 335.)

So far, these examples have illustrated three different modes of disposal: (1) dropping discrete items *in situ*, (2) tossing away discrete items, and (3) tossing away aggregated items *en masse*. In the case of dropping, the items tend to come to rest in the immediate area where they were processed or worked; larger items or aggregates of smaller items, in contrast, are tossed to the periphery of the work areas where they were used.

Hearths, Inside and Outside

The distribution of debris around a hearth gives us clues as to whether the activity in question took place inside or outside a house. For instance, I was able to document the way the Nunamiut Eskimo used space in a hunting camp (the Mask site) over a long period of time. On my plan of the site (ill. 91), one can see the patterns of activity which were taking place at one moment in time: one man

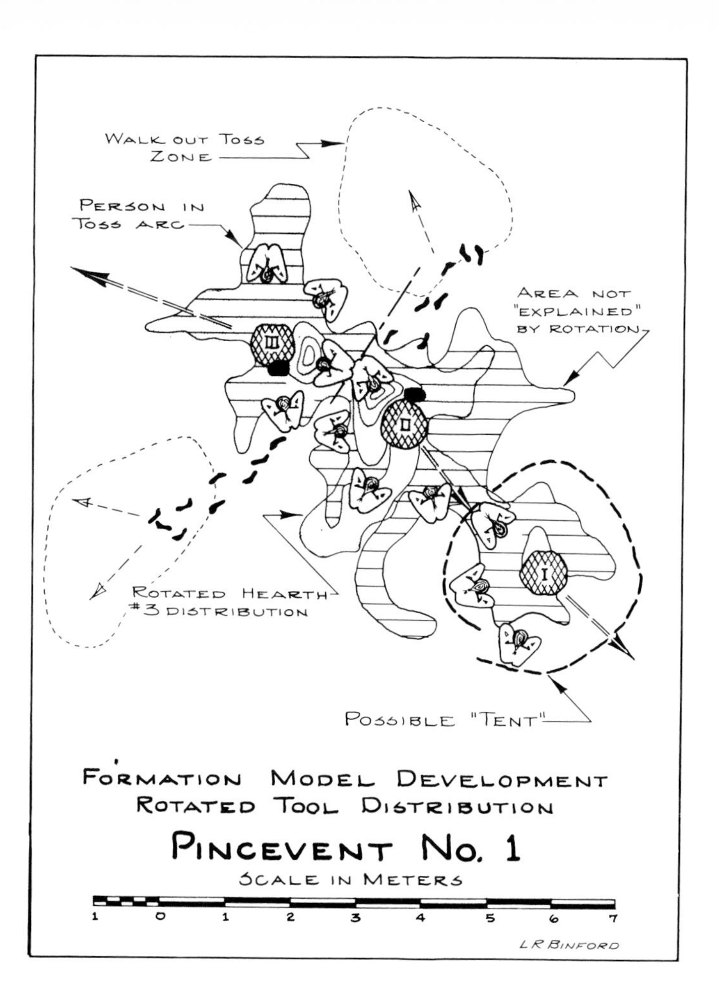

93 Formation model for the hearths at Pincevent One. In response to a change in wind direction (symbolized by the broken arrows), the occupants rotated their position from one hearth to another adjacent hearth. Such an extensive use of space would not be characteristic within the limited shelter of a house. (Archaeological data based on Leroi-Gourhan and Brézillon 1966, fig. 56, p. 331.)

was sleeping on a caribou skin; another was seated to one side, making tools; a third was watching for caribou; as in the previous example, most of them were arranged around the fire chatting. Predictably, the men seated in a semi-circle around the fire had tossed their unwanted food debris either into that area around the hearth where the smoke was most dense due to the wind direction, or else over their shoulder, thus creating a distinctive 'toss-zone' spatial pattern.

These distinctive dumps and toss zones would not occur *inside* a house, because people rarely throw waste materials against the walls of their home. Put another way, maintenance tactics in intensively used spaces inside a house tend to be quite different from those in extensively used contexts outside. As a further consequence of such behavior, outside and inside hearths vary in the degree to which the distribution of ash and other debris spreads away from the hearth. In my experience, hearths used for cooking inside houses are usually lined with substantial stones to prevent the flooring of the house (vegetation, skins or mats) from catching fire. The stones containing the hearth also prevent the ash from being dragged out into the seating and work areas which are concentrated about a hearth in the confined space of a house. On the other hand, outside hearths are generally not so contained. When plants or animals are being cooked, the constant searching in the ashes for the roasted foods causes ash and fire-cracked rock to be dragged away from the center of the hearth; over time this results in considerable smearing of ash, charcoal and other hearth debris all around the seat of the fire. Ill. 94, for instance, shows a Masarwa Bushman woman scraping ash out of a hearth in order to recover roasted nuts. As fires are kindled over and over again in the same general area and this smearing increases, the center of the fire tends to drift. Large distinctive hearth features occur solely in areas outside houses, where space is less constrained and activities may be more extensive in character.

Our knowledge about the meaning of the distribution of waste can be used to interpret the behavior that took place at the French Palaeolithic site of Pincevent, dated to the Magdalenian period about 15,000 years ago.[12] If one takes the seating model of men around a hearth from the modern Eskimo hunting stand at the Mask site, readjusts the scale, and applies it directly to the distribution of debris from stone tool manufacture at this archaeological site, it fits exactly. The excavator of Pincevent, Leroi-Gourhan, interpreted the pattern of archaeological remains at this site as evidence for a house, but I doubt that he is correct: as we have seen in the ethnographic record at least, the doughnut-shaped distribution of waste material is typical of activities which take place out-of-doors.

92, 93

Ethnoarchaeological research provides additional evidence to support my interpretation of Pincevent. When people are sitting outside with no shelter, they alter their position frequently in accordance with the wind direction. For instance,

94 Masarwa Bushman woman dragging ash out of a fire while recovering nuts which had been roasted. Note the arrangement of the hammer, anvil and nuts where a seated worker had been working earlier (cf. ill. 82). (Photo courtesy of the National Cultural History Museum, Pretoria.)

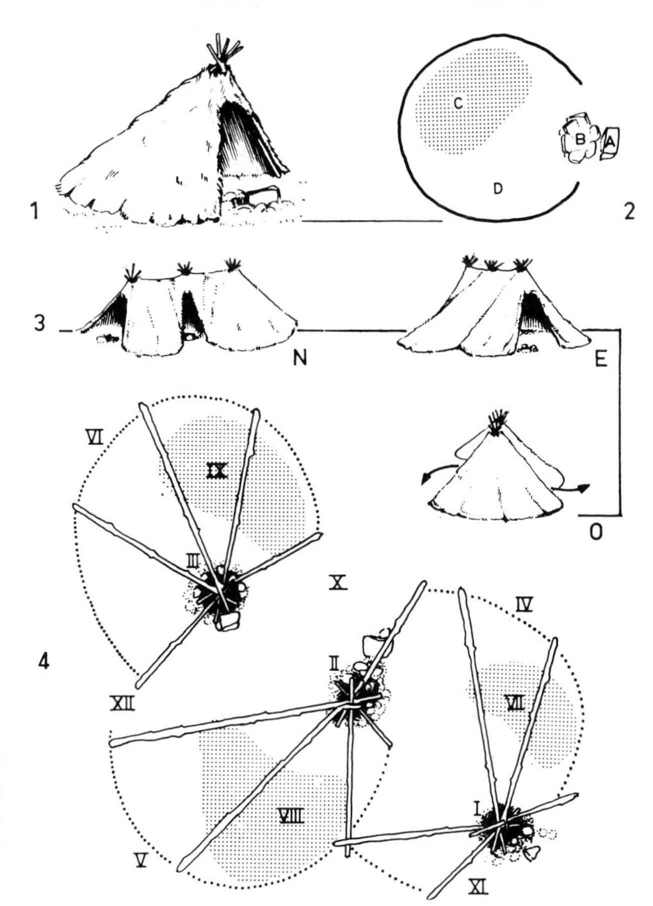

95 Leroi-Gourhan's reconstruction of the three hearths at Pincevent One. (Reproduced with permission from Leroi-Gourhan and Brézillon 1966, fig. 78, p. 363.)

if there is a flat area where people prefer to sit, they will locate their hearth accordingly; if, however, the wind direction changes so that the smoke begins to disturb them, they do not abandon their preferred position, but simply turn around on the spot and build a new fire. In this way, they do not have to move all their gear to another side of the original fire and sit where they had previously been tossing their garbage. When one is not constrained by a house or a temporary shelter, then building another hearth is easier than relocating oneself relative to existing facilities. Since wind direction has no effect on the orientation of debris with respect to a hearth within a house, the rotation of hearths would only be expected for fires used outside.

The distribution of the debris in relation to the three hearths at Pincevent suggests that only one person dominated the use of two hearths. What appears to have happened is that the wind changed direction and the seated worker simply rotated 180 degrees and built another hearth to avoid the smoke. Since wind only affects hearths outside, Leroi-Gourhan's reconstruction of a complex skin tent over all three hearths[13] cannot be sustained, at least in terms of our new understanding of site structure derived from ethnoarchaeological research.

92, 93

95

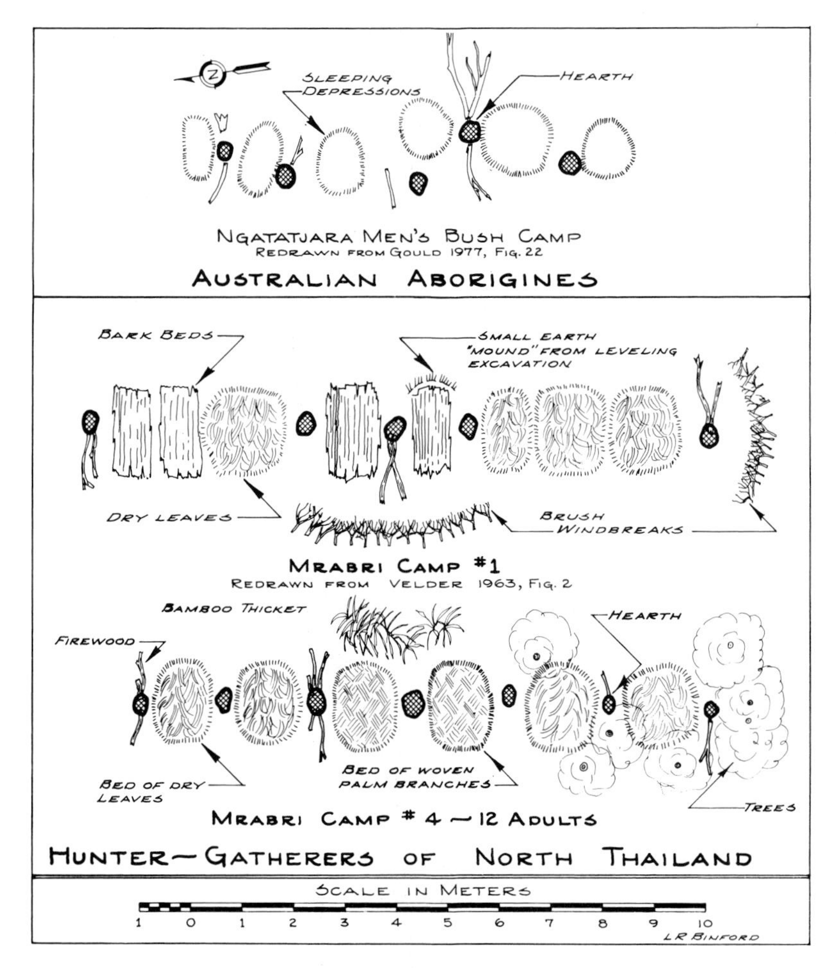

96 Comparative sleeping arrangements documented among the Australian Aborigines and Mrabri of North Thailand (see ill. 1). Note the recurrent patterns of alternating beds and hearths. (Based on Gould 1977, fig. 22; Velder 1963, fig. 2.)

Sleeping Areas

Another way in which the size and basic mechanics of the human body affect patterning in the archaeological record may be seen in terms of the space required for sleeping. Although many different arrangements for sleeping have been observed in the ethnographic record, they all depend on a limited series of known factors. For instance, in a Ngatatjara Australian Aborigine camp occupied by an all-male hunting party,[14] an alterating pattern of beds and hearths occurred. In contrast, when married couples are present at the camps, as has been recorded

96

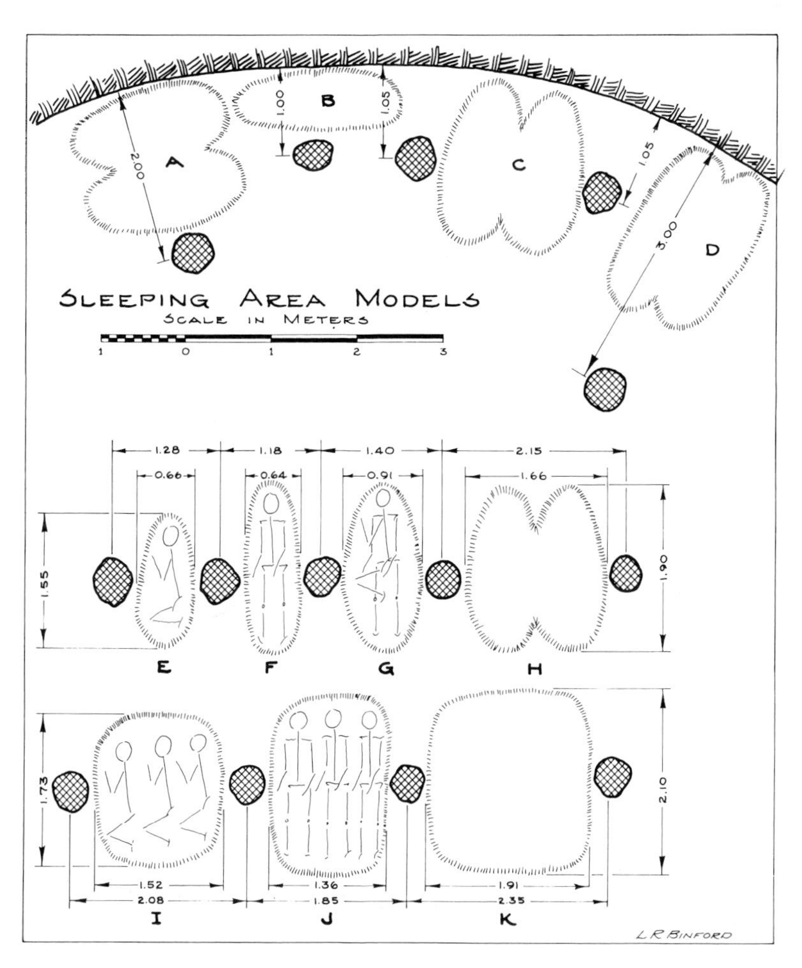

97 Sleeping area models: a generalized diagram of the arrangement and size of sleeping areas based on observations among a large number of hunter-gatherer societies.

for the Mrabri (a hunting and gathering group in the tropical rainforest in Thailand),[15] the hearths were interspersed with double rather than single beds; both single and double beds separated by hearths were laid out when the social composition of the group was mixed. Regardless of slight variations in the number of single and double beds, the basic arrangement, including the alternation of beds and hearths, appears to be found all over the world.

The size of the beds is not determined solely by the number of people sleeping on them: more space is required, for example, if people sleep in clothes, rather than under a cover. Given the relevant factors seen in contemporary situations 97

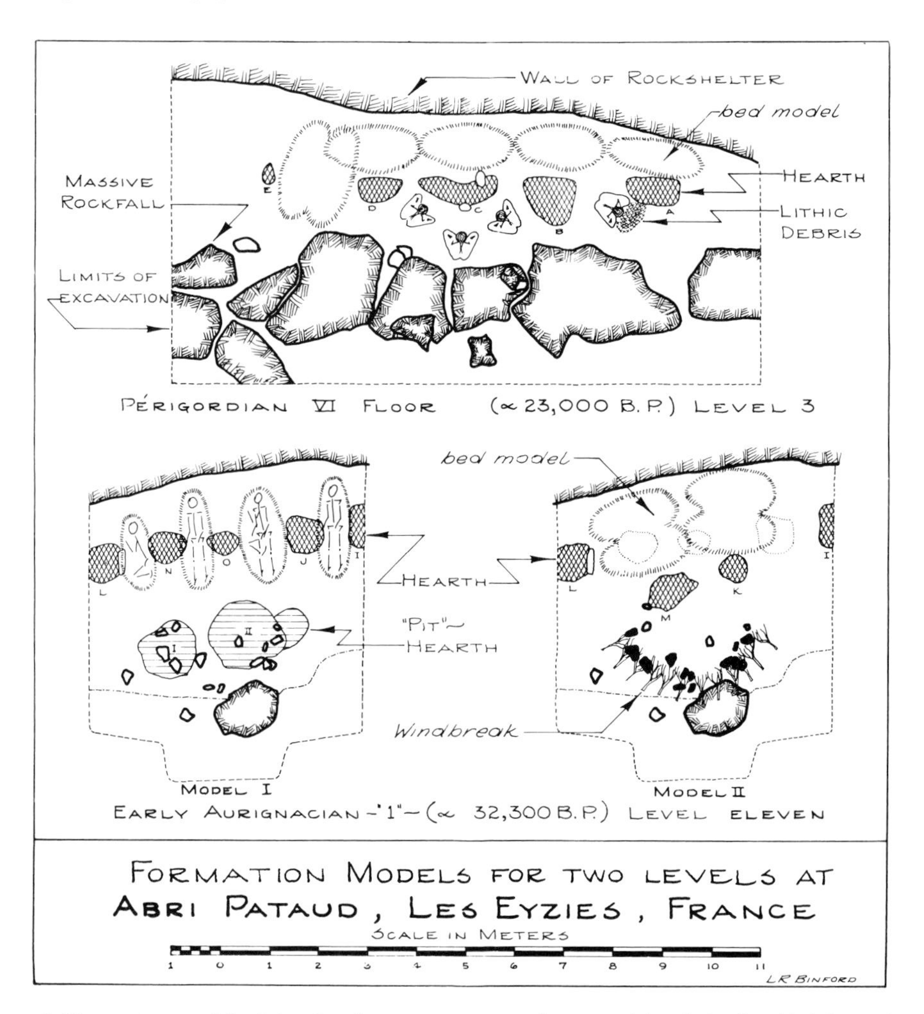

98 Formation model of the sleeping arrangements for several levels in the Abri Pataud rock shelter. (Archaeological information from Movius 1975.)

analogous to those of prehistoric times, one could hope to calculate how much space would be required for a bed, in just the same way that an architect today determines how much space to allot for particular areas within a modern house.

The sleeping arrangements typical of rock shelters are especially interesting, because variations in the positions of the beds are determined by the season of the year. In winter, beds are usually located *parallel* to the back of the shelter; for a single bed a hearth is placed about 1.20 meters from the rock, or about 2.00 meters in the case of a double bed. In summer, when ideally one would like to reduce exposure to the heat from the sun which has been absorbed by the rock, the beds are placed *perpendicular* to the back wall and people sleep with their heads away from the source of the heat; in this arrangement hearths are located between the beds.

Just as with the models of seated workers around a hearth (discussed above), these general patterns of sleeping arrangements derived from the ethnographic record can also be applied to the interpretations of archaeological sites: the basic structure of the human body, after all, has remained the same for a very long period. The value of this approach can be demonstrated by an analysis of the distribution of hearths at the Upper Palaeolithic site of Abri Pataud in France, excavated by H. I. Movius.[16] By superimposing standard bed sizes, for which I have extensive ethnographic documentation, on the plan of a level belonging to the early Aurignacian I phase at Abri Pataud, I found that an arrangement of single beds in between the hearths fits the archaeological spatial patterns extremely well. Among modern groups, as I have already mentioned, the alternation of hearths and single beds typifies the sleeping patterns of all-male hunting camps. The combination of this form of bed distribution with the presence of roasting pits located in front of the sleeping area suggests to me that, at this date, the site was not used for residential purposes (as Movius originally proposed), but was a temporary camp.

98

Another level at Abri Pataud, belonging to the Perigordian VI phase, should also be regarded as representing a temporary hunting camp, because of the spacing of the hearths. An interesting feature of the hearths in this level, however, is that the side which faces the sleeping area at the back of the rock shelter is flat; from ethnographic data, we know that hearths are often built this way to prevent bedding from catching fire. On the other hand, in a slightly different lens of the same level, there are some hearths located about 2.00 meters from the rear wall of the shelter, suggesting that double beds were positioned there. In front of the sleeping area is a group of stones which I would interpret as a windbreak. The archaeological remains of this portion of the rock shelter suggest that we are dealing with a small family camp, something quite different from the hunting camp previously described and probably representative of a different part of the overall settlement pattern of the Upper Palaeolithic people who lived in this area (cf. Chapter 6 for a description of variations in hunter-gatherer settlement patterns).

Breakfast in Bed

One further interesting fact has emerged from these ethnographic studies: the bedding area of a site is often not necessarily used exclusively for sleeping. Commonly, people conceive of a bed as a private, personal area. If, for example, a man goes and sits on his bed, it is a signal that he does not want to be bothered. He may do a variety of tasks while there – think quietly, make tools, comb his hair – but the rest of the community knows that he does not want to talk. I have found this same relationship between personal space and sleeping area among all the hunting and gathering groups with whom I have worked. I have even observed men in hunting camps make beds which are in a sense symbolic, since they are not used at all for sleeping, but simply as a place where one can repair tools in peace and quiet or just be by oneself.

99

Such use of beds as personal spaces at a camp creates some interesting distributions of material which we can also hope to monitor in the archaeological record. Hunter-gatherers usually consume a prepared meal as a group in the evening, but often everyone takes some of the left-overs from the meal, such as cold meat or a rabbit bone, and puts them by their bed so that they can have a snack for breakfast. Understandably, in the morning when it may be cold and people are likely to be sleepy and slightly grumpy, they are content to sit on their bed and eat in silence. As a result, a small midden or deposit of waste is created around each bed. In addition to left-overs from the previous day, the middens around the beds may contain the bones of small mammals which have not been shared among the group but cooked in the hearths by the beds and consumed there. The waste

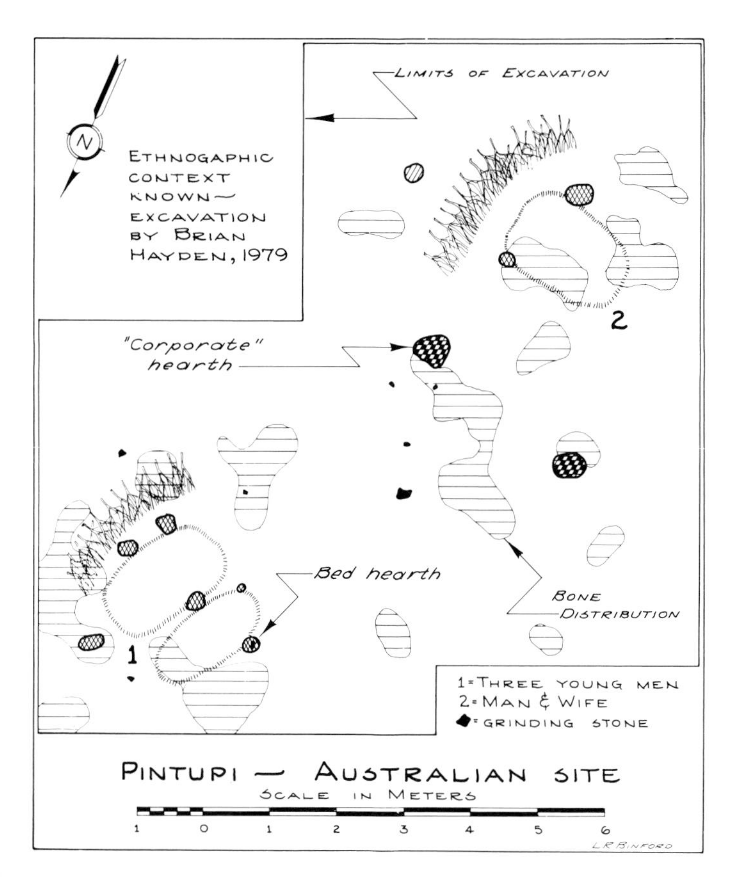

99 Pintupi Aborigine camp showing small hearths and waste fragments from breakfast snacks around the sleeping areas. (Based on Hayden 1979, fig. 125B, p. 152.)

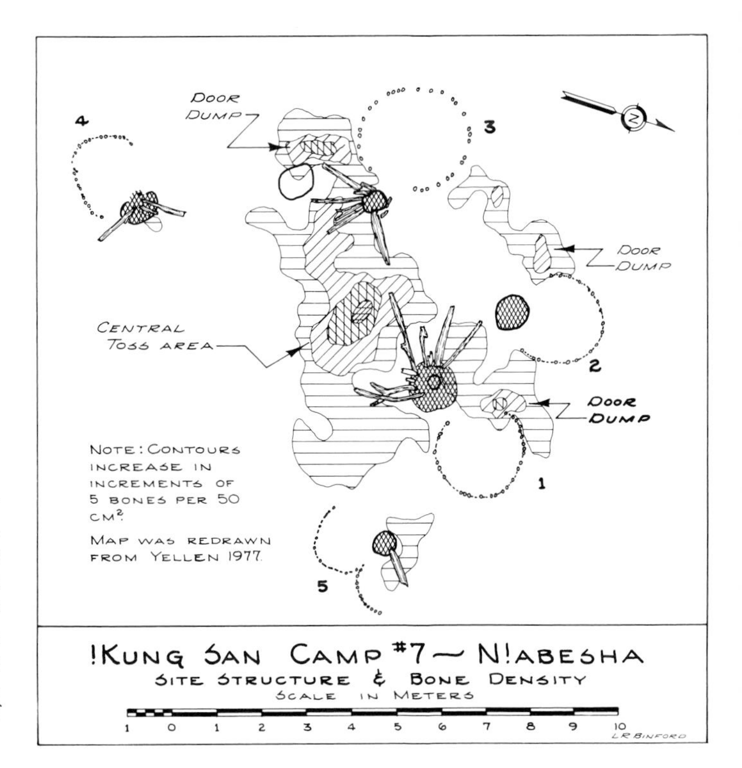

100 !Kung San camp no. 7 as recorded by John Yellen. Note the *door dumps* to the right of the entrance to the huts. These contain the waste from breakfast which was consumed on beds inside the huts. (Based on Yellen 1977, unnumbered end-plan of camp 7.)

from individual snacks and from communal meals, therefore, can be expected to be differentially distributed on archaeological sites.

The debris from 'breakfast in bed' is not always deposited around the area where the meal was consumed. At a Bushmen camp after everyone has woken up and eaten their individual snacks in bed, the debris from the meal is collected in the skins or blankets which make up the bedding, carried to the door of the hut and discarded there.[17] This behavior creates a *breakfast dump* just to the side of the sleeping area or immediately next to the door. I have also observed *door dumps* at Eskimo and Australian Aborigine camps and have additional data of the same sort from settlements occupied by horticulturalists. 100

Extensive Activity Areas

Some tasks, since they are performed from a standing position rather than when seated, create large and extensive scatters of debris. One good example of an activity which takes up large amounts of space in this way is the preparation and use of roasting pits out-of-doors. The Alyawara Aborigines with whom I have 101–6

101 *Alyawara Aborigine butchering a female red kangaroo.* A small hole is cut in the abdomen and the viscera are removed exclusively through this small opening. The hole is later closed by using a small twig as a pin; this prevents ash, soil and charcoal in the roasting pit from entering the abdominal cavity as the animal is cooked.

102 *Digging the roasting pit.* The pit is dug in a relatively clear area, the loose soil being tossed on one side of the hole with the explanation that 'it's better to heat up dry soil' (which refers to the fact that the fire is kindled alongside of the pit as well as inside it). The soil heated up on the platform next to the pit is later shovelled into the pit to seal the earth oven for cooking (cf. ill. 105). In this picture firewood is being placed on the platform next to the pit.

103 *Singeing the kangaroo.* After the firewood is arranged inside the pit and on the platform, it is ignited. Once the fire is burning well, the kangaroo is tossed on to singe the hair and then flipped out again, so the scorched hair can be scraped off. This procedure takes place because the hair is excellent insulation and, if left on the skin, tends to retard or even prevent cooking. Since the hair does not burn off all at once, the animal must be flipped in and out of the fire several times.

106 *(Opposite) Map of the Alyawara roasting pit area.* Note the location where the Aborigines consumed a snack while waiting for the meat to cook; 'LRB' and 'JO'C' indicates the area where the archaeologists consumed their own snack of canned beans! The map illustrates nicely the extensive area occupied by an activity such as cooking food in a roasting pit.

104 *Preparing the charcoal.* The burning wood is flamed up to a fast burn. Singeing the game as well as occasionally beating the burning wood results in the accumulation of a substantial bed of charcoal. Once it is judged that enough charcoal has been scaled off the burning wood, the remaining burning sticks are pulled out and tossed to the side, leaving only the charcoal in the pit and on the platform as shown here. The circular walk area around the pit can be clearly seen, as can other food to be cooked (laid on a small table of leaves to keep it clean).

105 *Placing the food in the oven.* The kangaroo is nested in the charcoal within the pit, followed by the birds wrapped in leaves to hold in the juices formed during cooking. Once the hot sand and charcoal from the platform are shovelled into the pit to cover the meat, the cooking begins.

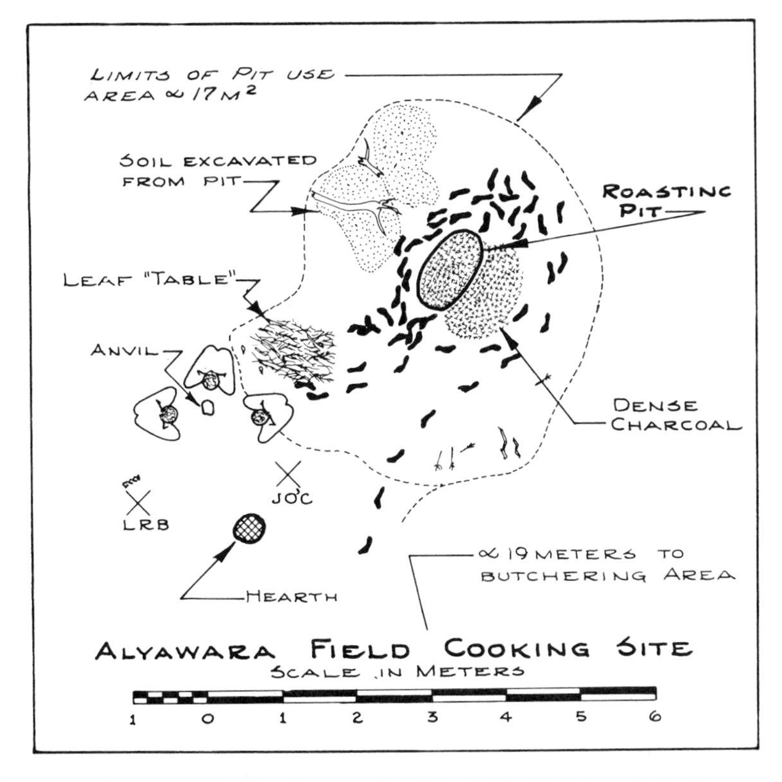

worked use roasting pits for a wide range of functions, but one occasion in particular which James O'Connell and I had the opportunity to observe illustrates nicely how the construction and utilization of a roasting pit itself contributes to the scale of the resulting activity area. At the time we were deep in the bush with a group of Alyawara males on their way to a stone quarry, but en route the men killed a female red kangaroo with a baby 'joey' in its pouch and three Australian bustards. On warm days such as the one in question, field parties which kill game some distance from the residential camp normally cook the meat in the field to prevent it spoiling before they return with it to the camp.

The men began their work by butchering the kangaroo with a stone knife and a metal ax which we had with us. Large animals of this sort are generally cooked within their own skins, so after the viscera had been removed through a very small hole in the abdomen of the kangaroo, the opening was plugged and laced up with a small acacia twig. Next, a roasting pit about $1\frac{1}{2}$ meters long and a little over $\frac{1}{2}$ meter wide was excavated to a depth of around $\frac{1}{2}$ meter. Firewood was gathered, placed on the platform next to the pit and the fire was kindled. As the firewood was burning down, the kangaroo was tossed in to singe the hair so that it could be scraped off more easily. In the meantime, leaves were laid out nearby (to prevent the cooked meat from getting covered with sand) and the birds were partially plucked and wrapped with leaves which would absorb the grease as they were roasted. When the fire had died down, the Alyawara took a stick and beat the firewood so that the scale of charcoal fell off into the bottom of the pit. Finally, having determined that the fire was ready, the men placed in the pit the kangaroo, with its legs sticking up, and the birds in their leaf packets and then added the remaining charcoal. The meat was left to roast for about an hour.

While this activity was going on, we noted the spatial patterns generated by all these tasks and we also made a map of the area, recording the location of all the features that would be potentially observable at an archaeological site. The roasting pit, the area where the fire burned, the dirt from the pit, the place where the extra firewood was tossed aside, the boughs of trees for laying out the meat

107

107 A roasting pit repeatedly used at an Alyawara Australian residential site. The substantial scatter of charcoal which accumulates around such a feature is very obvious. Such 'dirty' and spatially extensive features are almost always located away from the core activity of a living site.

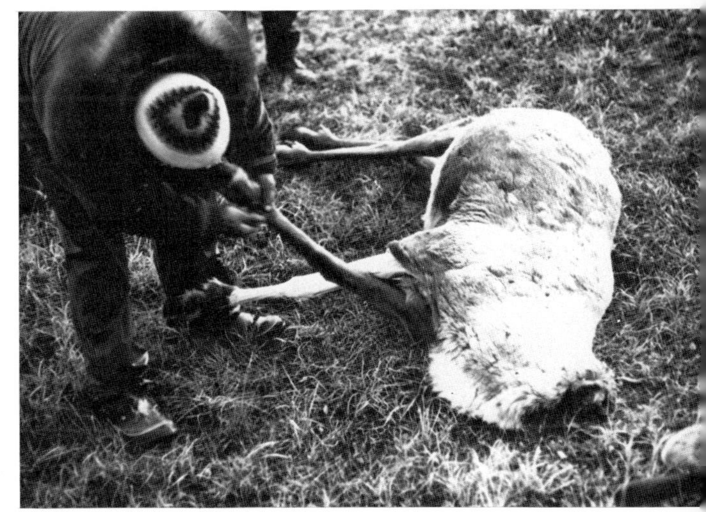

108 Nunamiut Eskimo butchering a caribou killed during the spring migration. The circular work space being used by Johnny Rulland around the animal is similar to the one around the Alyawara roasting pit shown in ills. 106 and 107.

before cooking, the place where the tail of the kangaroo was processed while the meat was cooking, even the area where Jim O'Connell and I had our own hearth to cook our beans – all these were carefully plotted on the plan.

One interesting fact that emerged from our study of this kangaroo roast is that there is some regularity in the amount of space occupied by people performing activities when standing (about 17–24 square meters of space). Furthermore, the activity sequence I have described results in a classic feature-centered pattern with the roasting pit in the middle, a work space around this feature and a ring around the periphery, where any discarded items can be expected to accumulate. The debris from the immediate use of the pit is concentrated around the pit, whereas the other waste comprises a toss zone located around the feature, but at some distance back from it.

Another standing-up activity which produces a very similar debris pattern is the butchering of animals. The principal difference between roasting and butchery is that in the latter case no central feature remains for the archaeologist to see. Typically the person cutting up the animal works in a circular area around it; he may flip over the carcass from one side to the other, using the skin as a protected work surface. The result is (1) an empty walk/work space focused around the animal and (2) debris which has been tossed away from this work zone and has accumulated on the periphery of the work area. According to my observations among the Nunamiut Eskimo, caribou butchery demands about 30 square meters of space. In ill. 59 this model of butchering behavior can be seen superimposed on the actual archaeological distribution resulting from the cutting up of caribou at the Anavik site. Butchering areas on Eskimo and Aboriginal sites are interesting for another reason as well. Meat distributions among these groups[18]

108

109

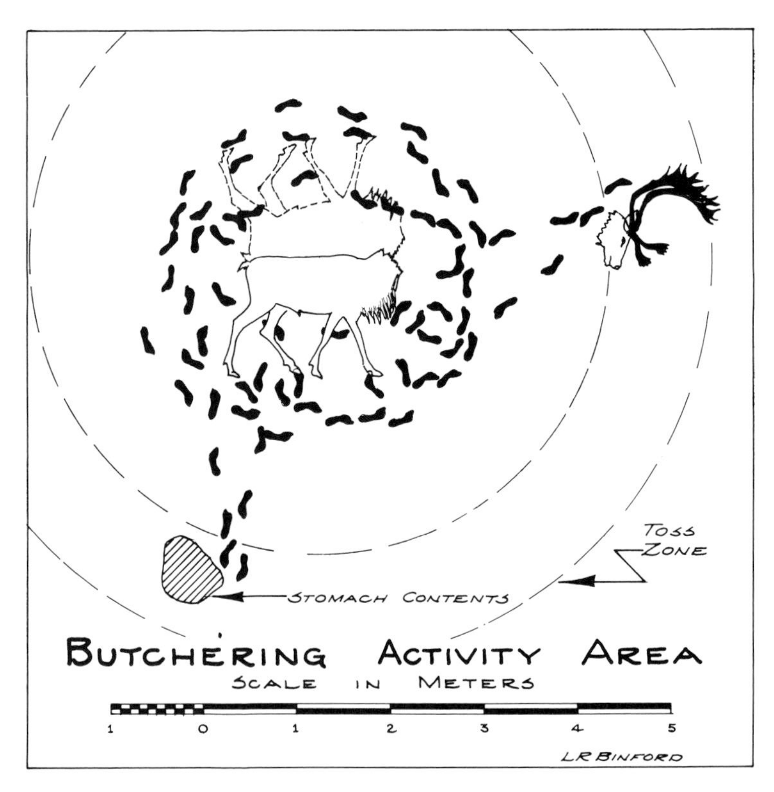

109 Activity area used by the Nunamiut to butcher one caribou. The structure of the work space is nearly identical to the Alyawara roasting pit pictured in ills. 106 and 107. The total area used is slightly greater in this case because unwanted parts have been disposed of on the periphery of the walk/work area.

generally take place at the butchering areas themselves rather than in the residential area, because (as informants noted) sharing meat was the occasion for a different kind of visit than when kinsmen come to 'talk', implying that the etiquette of hospitality applied only within the confines of the 'home'.

110

Analogous distributions of debris at spatial scales similar to the butchering areas have been observed by Robert Hard among the Tarahumara of Mexico. These people cook desert plants in large roasting pits, which are usually positioned behind the house and away from the doorside activity areas. It is generally true, in fact, that activities like roasting and butchery, which monopolize considerable amounts of space, are located away from areas used intensively on a day-to-day basis. For instance, even on sites where only a minimal stay is anticipated, Australian Aborigines nevertheless construct their roasting pits in positions peripheral to the focus of camp life – areas used for sleeping, conversation, and small-scale food preparation and craft activities. I have observed a similar

112

110 Alyawara Australian distributing meat from a kangaroo which was roasted at a pit located on the periphery of a residential camp. Children are frequently used as runners for carrying meat to persons not present to receive their share.

111 Bushman scraping an animal hide at the Mokudi camp in the *Nyae Nyae* area of Namibia, 1976. (Photo courtesy of the South African Museum, Cape Town.)

112 Large roasting pit located behind a Tarahumara house in northern Mexico. The walk/work area around the pit is clearly visible. Here we have a spatial analogy to the butchering area seen among the Eskimo (ill. 109) and the roasting pit used by the Australian Aborigines (ills. 106, 107). (Photo courtesy of Robert Hard.)

strategy of placement among the Eskimo and the Navajo: commonly their roasting pits are located adjacent to places used as minor dumps or for wood chopping, so as not to interfere with the normal activities of camp life. Along these same lines I have found that at Australian and Eskimo sites, spatially extensive, stand-up work areas are often next to each other. For example, in Eskimo sites butchering areas are frequently located adjacent to sled loading and storage areas, all of which will be found on the edge of the residential core area, because they all require a large amount of space.

71

Hide working is yet another activity repeatedly seen to occur in areas peripheral to the central parts of residential camps. When only one or two hides are being worked, they may be staked out just to the side of or slightly behind shelters, but if larger quantities are involved, they will be carried a greater distance from the center of residential activities. It is not uncommon for rather flat ground to be selected for hide working and for stones to be cleaned back from the chosen area if it is rocky; the 'ring' of stones produced in this way may subsequently be used as weights to secure the hide. In most cases, an archaeologist would interpret such a pattern as a tent ring or would infer the existence of some kind of structure from piles of stone which in reality had simply been removed to clear a surface for hide working.

111

Site Structure: Combining the Models

As described previously, sites are composed of different arrangements of facilities, surfaces and items. So far we have seen how these basic elements can be combined into general spatial models relating to particular activities (e.g. seated worker arrangements, group seating arrangements, sleeping areas, extensive standing-up work places, etc.). At this point we can now turn to the analysis of archaeological sites as wholes and begin to investigate how the models identified previously fit together to comprise a complete site. This is what I call the *analysis of site structure*: how spatial models mesh within the structure of a site as an entity in its own right. While there is no room here to consider the entire range of variability in site structure observed ethnographically, we can begin to use some of the knowledge gained so far in order to give meaning to some of the spatial patterns observed in the archaeological record.

As a first example, let us consider how activity models can be used to analyze the site structure of a typical Bushman camp. In the Kalahari Desert, people construct small huts more for protection from the sun than for warmth. The temperature can rise quite high at midday and at this hottest part of the day the Bushmen generally sit inside on their beds. Since they may use the time to make tools or carry out other tasks, debris from the activities which take place in the

113

113 Bushman camp in Angola, *c.* 1930. These are the so-called 'Yellow Bushmen', also known as Sekele. (See Almeida 1965 for further details.) Note the position of the hearth in front of the shelter erected to provide shade during the hottest part of the day. (Photo by J. Drury, courtesy of the South African Museum, Cape Town).

shade is distributed in the sleeping area. In contrast, the cooking hearth used for corporate meals is located just outside the hut near the door; when food is eaten at this hearth a doughnut-shaped ring of food remains is formed around it. 114

This same pattern is found at many other sites. Examining data from three different hunter-gatherer groups, !Kung Bushmen, Nunamiut Eskimo and Ngatatjara Aborigines, one can see that the spacing of the house, sleeping areas and external hearth is very similar. The reason for the considerable consistency in the measurements is simply that the factor which conditions them is the same in all cases – the human body. In this instance, it is simply a function of the amount of room required to seat a group of people around a hearth and still allow reasonable space for access to the hut. The sizes of the huts at the Bushmen camp are also nearly identical; variation is due simply to the number of people occupying them. The simple mechanics of the body contribute to both these basic repeated situations and, since these properties are the same for all humans, it is no wonder that there is a tremendous degree of repetitiveness in the spatial measurements of camps used by hunters and gatherers. 115

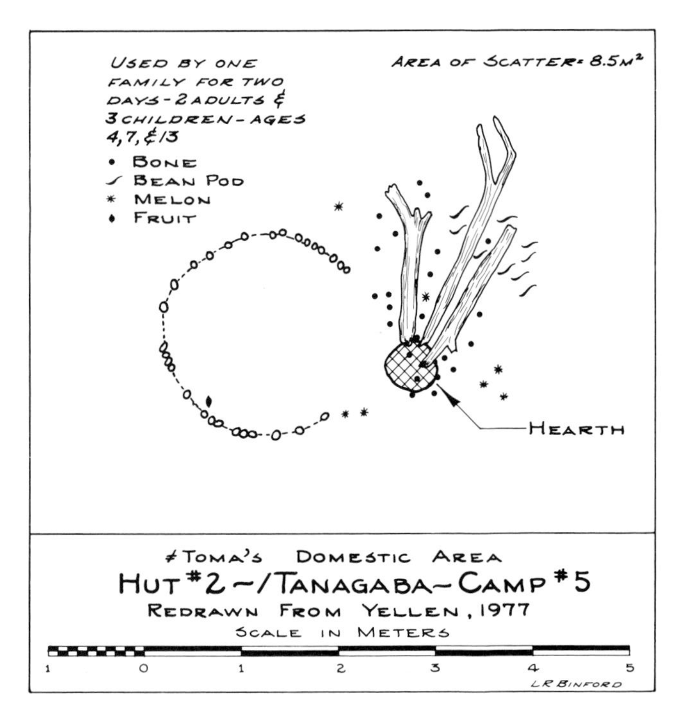

114 Map of a typical !Kung Bushman hut with associated hearth. (Based on Yellen 1977, unnumbered end-plan of camp 5.)

Now, although the actual form of the various models is highly repetitive from site to site and from one group of people to another, differences among them can also be extremely informative. For instance, at the corporate Nunamiut hearths (ill. 115) the most common seating pattern is a circle, with the attendant drop and toss zones as discussed previously. There are, of course, other ways of organizing food preparation and consumption, for instance, when there is a strong division of labor in terms of who cooks the meals. In many types of Nunamiut camps, females cook food at an outside 'kitchen' hearth, but serve the meal in a different area. Where this arrangement exists, a small brush windbreak is often placed around the hearth or, if it is very hot, a kind of ramada or sunshade may be erected over the kitchen to protect the cook. For example, ill. 75 depicts the distribution of items with respect to an outside kitchen hearth among the Nunamiut. Access to the hearth is almost exclusively reserved for the cook and this area is generally kept quite clean. Debris from food preparation may be dumped across the hearth, resulting in what I call a 'butterfly distribution' of waste. Once prepared, the food is then served to the men in a separate area which is outside

88, 89

116

115

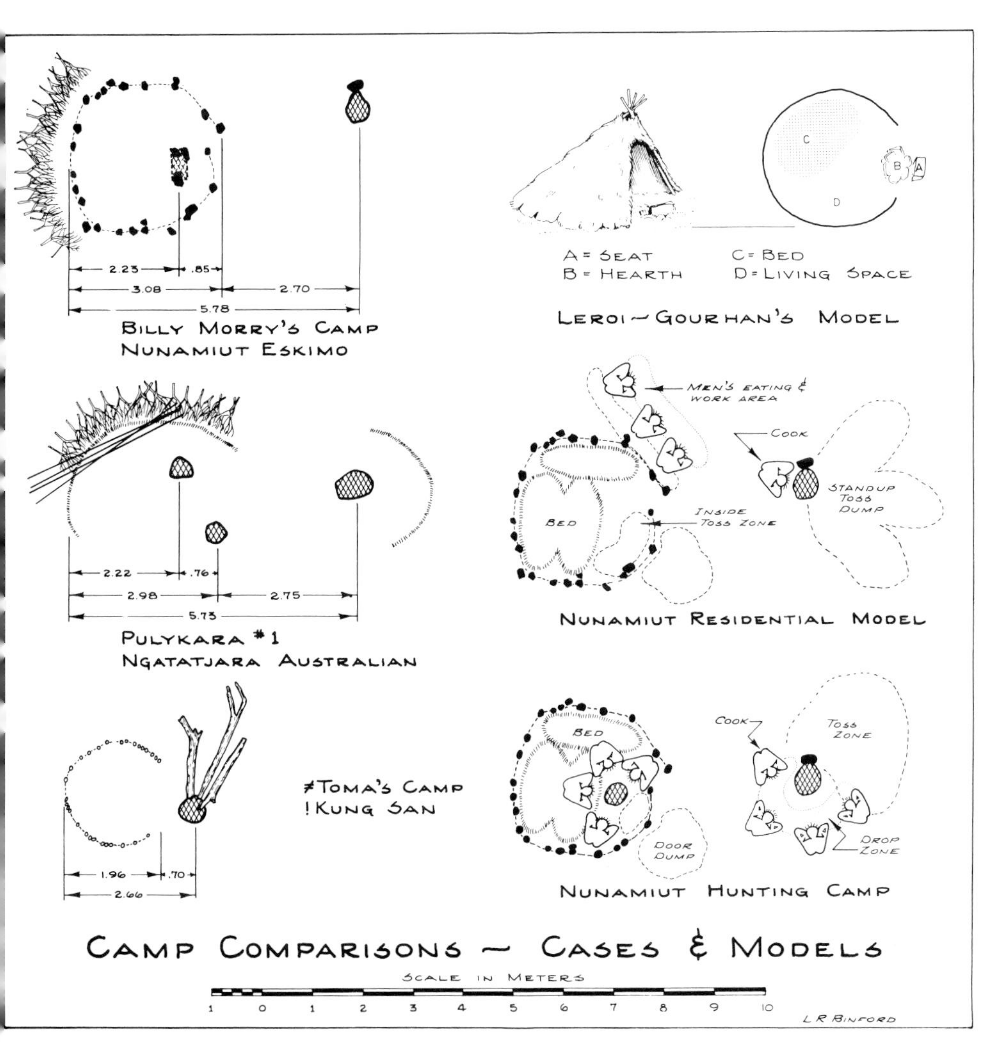

115 On the left, comparative sizes and layout of houses and hearths for three different hunter-gatherer groups, the !Kung Bushmen, Nunamiut Eskimo, and Ngatatjara Aborigines. Depicted on the right are three hypothetical models for site structure, the lower two of which are based on ethnographically documented sites.

116 Blackfoot American Indian camp *c.* 1920 showing the outside kitchen hearth on the left, with a tripod supporting a sun shade. The house itself is located to the right. (Photo by H. F. Robinson, author's print.)

if the weather is fair, but is near their beds within a shelter if the weather is inclement. As a result of this behavior, in which meals can be eaten either inside or out-of-doors, a disposal zone of debris is formed on both sides of the wall of the tent.

Inside Palangana's House

One of my most detailed studies of space use has focused on an ethnohistorically 80, 117 well-documented Eskimo winter dwelling, Palangana's house.[19] The distribution of small splinters, produced as a result of cracking marrow bones, forms a well-defined semi-circular pattern around the north side of the hearth; the position of these bits, which fell in the drop zone between the knees and alongside the legs of the seated men, betray the seating arrangement of those consuming meals. In contrast, the southeast side of the hearth contains far fewer chips and parts of its rim lack them more or less completely. This paucity of bone splinters identifies the place where the cook had access to the fire for preparing and serving meals. Although the larger bones are not shown in ill. 109, there is no toss zone associated with this bone splinter drop zone, for the Eskimo never toss the larger bones back on to their beds and into the recesses along the house walls where their belongings are normally stored. Two facts, both related to maintenance of this living space,

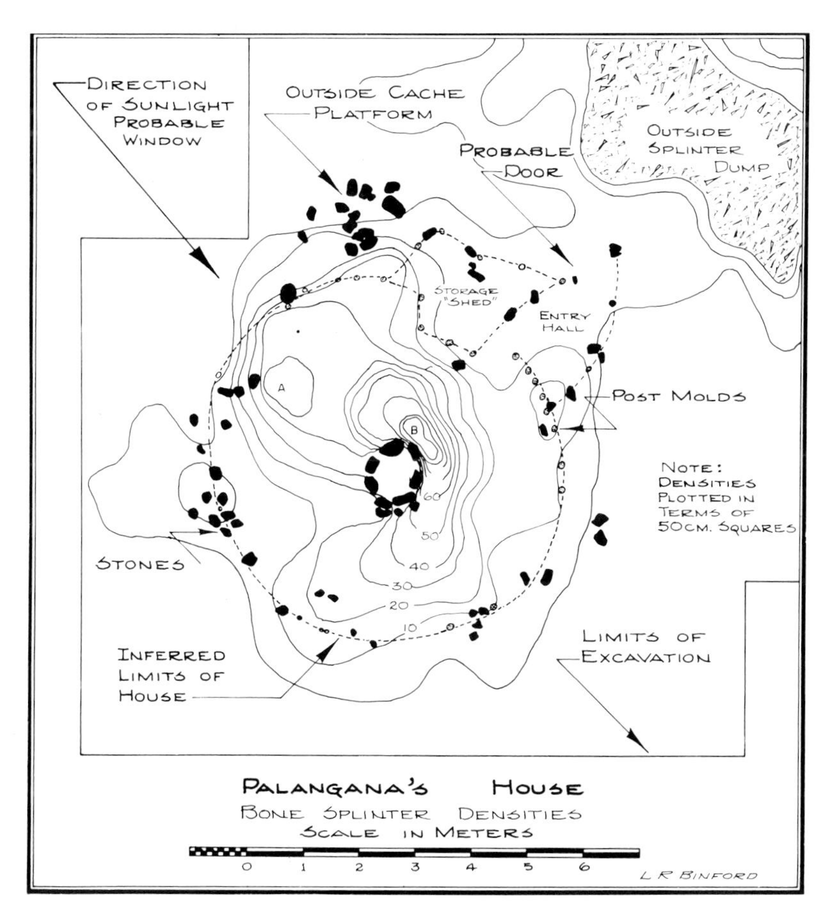

117 *Contour map showing the density of small splinters of bone in and around an Eskimo winter house (Palangana's House) at Tulugak Lake, Alaska.* (See ills. 53 and 66 for exact location of the site.) The highest densities identify the general seating locations of male consumers during meals and when eating snacks during the day. The distribution of splinters is mainly centered around the hearth, although it is concentrated on the left-hand side, leaving free an area of domestic work space largely used by the women during the preparation of meals. The positions marked 'A' and 'B' almost certainly represent the habitual seating spots of the man (B) and the woman (A) of the house.

reveal the distribution of bones and splinters as one produced inside a structure. (1) The presence of a drop zone composed of debris biased toward the smallest bone splinters indicates that regular cleaning of the area took place; this size bias, coupled with the existence of a large outside door dump, further demonstrates the tidying up of the intensively used space around the hearth. (2) The tell-tale absence of the toss zone is also associated with 'preventive maintenance' following consumption.

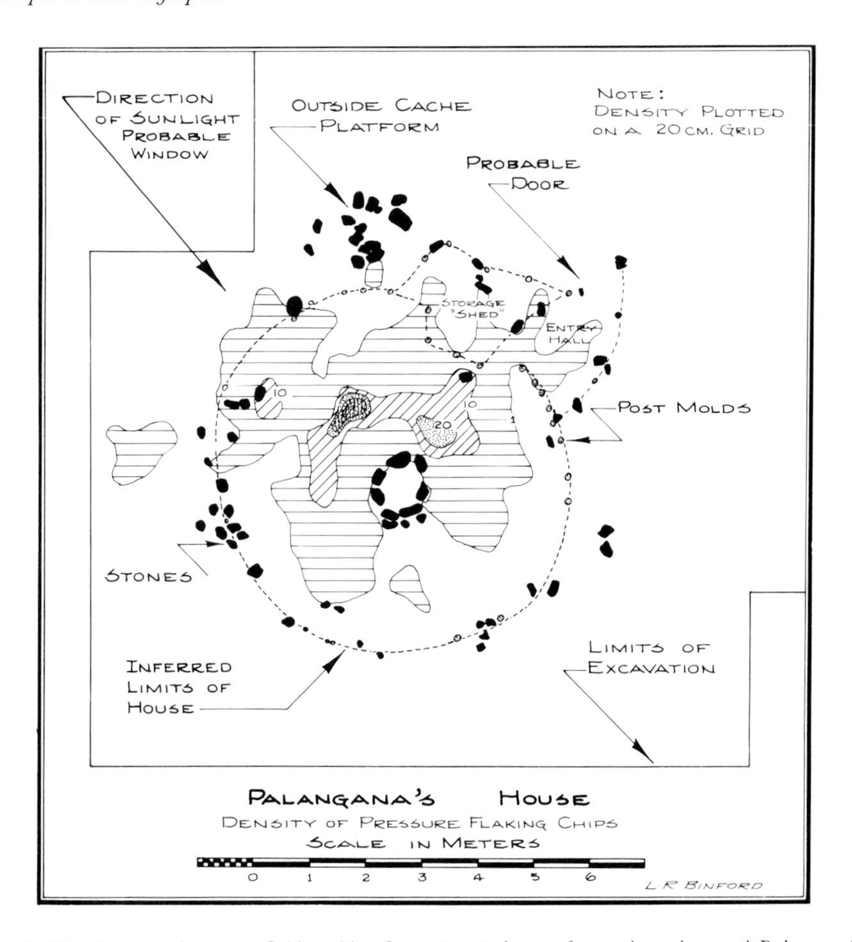

118 *Density map of pressure flaking chips from stone tool manufacture in and around Palangana's House* (cf. ill. 117). The distribution is distinctly window-oriented: that is, it is related to the position of natural light inside the dwelling during the limited hours of daylight in the arctic winter. Two concentrations correspond roughly to dense distributions of bone splinters marked 'A' and 'B' on ill. 117.

By way of comparison, we can also look at the distribution within the house of the small chips produced as a by-product of pressure flaking stone tools. It is clear that these flint chips are densely distributed away from the hearth and are common on the southwest side of the house (upper left in ill. 118), an area where low densities of small bone splinters were observed. This contrast must be understood in terms of the positioning of craftpersons relative to the source of light. People working and repairing stone tools presumably sat so as to take advantage of light coming into the house through the window. The bone splinters, on the other hand,

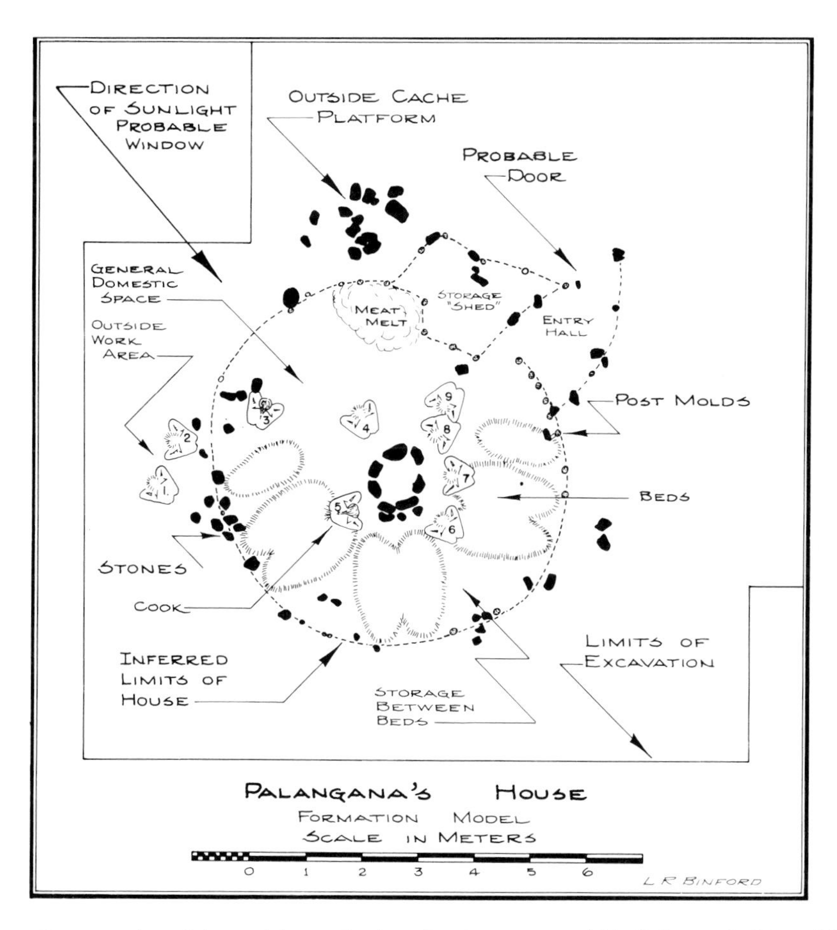

119 *Reconstruction of the spatial organization of major use area within Palangana's House.* The symbols for seated figures indicate the major sitting places identified by the distributions of bone splinters and flint chips (cf. ills. 117, 118). Individuals numbered 8 and 9 represent the same person who adjusts his position to the hearth depending on whether food consumption is going on (8) or craft activities are being conducted (9). The reason he often moves back from the hearth is due to the presence of a roof support which served as a back rest and was located just in front of the stone shown behind person no. 9. In this case he changes his seat when he needs light from the window to facilitate craft activities. Seating positions nos. 3 and 5 are almost certainly those used primarily by the woman of the house: position no. 3 being her 'light-oriented' seat needed for carrying out manufacturing or repair of artifacts, while position no. 5 is the area reserved for the cook's access to the hearth, at which time it is quite likely that she sits on her bed. Note also the table rocks to the right of her sitting position at the hearth (5). Seating places nos. 1 and 2 are located outside the house in the sun where almost certainly men sat on rare warm days during the early and late winter working on crafts and eating snacks.

would be produced primarily during the evening meal which, in winter, is served after the few hours of available light have passed and the house is warmed by the fire used in food preparation; at that time, consumers are seated out of the major work space of the cook but in the light created by the hearth. Thus, differences in the distributions of these two classes of item (bone splinters and flint chips) are governed by where and when the tasks took place. Even so, there are also some features common to both distributions: (1) bone splinters and flint flakes are most densely concentrated at points *A* and *B* (ill. 117) and (2) they share a concentration outside and to the south of the house itself. These correspondences betray the habitual seating position of people repairing tools or eating. The seating arrange- 81, 119 ments I would infer from such data can be summarized in a model of space use inside Palangana's house. The sleeping area shown in ill. 119 (corresponding to Leroi-Gourhan's 'Zone C'[20]) yielded little debris from manufacturing activities and had a lower overall density of artifacts than other areas inside the house, a 120 characteristic anticipated by Leroi-Gourhan. The superimposition of the distribution of industrial debris on the house plan reveals two interesting points.

First, there is a generalized scatter in the quadrant of the house nearest the window (the domestic work space). This area is equivalent to 'Zone B' in Leroi-Gourhan's model, but its breakdown into two subunits, as that model predicts, is not found here. In Palangana's house what we see are: (1) hearth-centered activities derived from, or related to, food consumption and carried out largely during hours of darkness and (2) daylight-centered activities oriented to the source of daylight within the domestic space. The distinction made by Leroi-Gourhan between the 'fine' and 'crude' activities expected to occur on different 74, 75, 89, 90, 115 sides of the hearth is much more likely to be applicable to outdoor hearths, where aggregate materials are dumped to the side of work spaces.

Secondly, the Nunamiut characterize the different use areas around the hearths 119 within a house as the 'women's' side (the light area of domestic space) and the 'men's' side (the darker zone of domestic usage). These terms do not imply any rules for use or exclusive access to these spaces by men or women; they only describe the relative frequencies with which the different sexes do in practice use each area. In fact, most male crafts are conducted in a *men's house*, a special struc- 80, 122 ture common on winter sites. Not infrequently, the men's house is the initial structure erected at a site for use as shelter while the men build the winter houses and before their families move to the site. Here men in groups spend many days working on crafts, often in the company of boys who are learning the techniques of tool manufacture and repair. In the men's house, craft items may be left in place and need not be cleaned up when the woman of the house needs space, for example, to prepare meals or attend to the children before bed. Consequently, it is a special activity area, where tool manufacture and repair can be carried out independently of work space in the residential house. On less permanent sites or

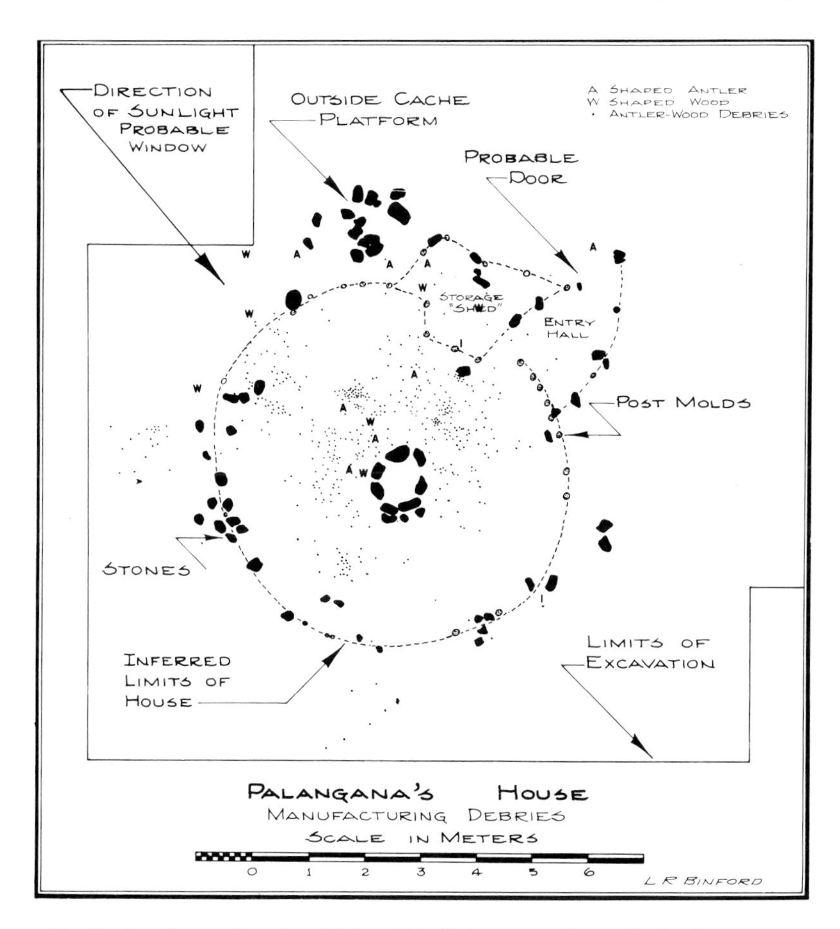

120 *Distribution of manufacturing debris within Palangana's House.* Each dot represents an item whose discrete position was plotted during the excavation of the site. It is clear that there is a concentration of material in the quadrant of the house adjacent to the window (cf. ills. 117, 118).

those occupied in warmer weather, there is usually a men's seating area outside the house, where males carry on crafts and even eat some of their meals; it is usually in a well lit and relatively warm and protected place, quite often along the southern wall of the house, as shown in the generalized Nunamiut residential model in ill. 115. In very warm weather, when women's activities too may move outside, meals are prepared on the outdoor kitchen hearth, near which is usually the women's conversation area, where they sew, manufacture or repair items, or simply keep an eye on the young children playing nearby. In summer, therefore, the house becomes merely a sheltered sleeping and storage area used for other activities only during bad weather.

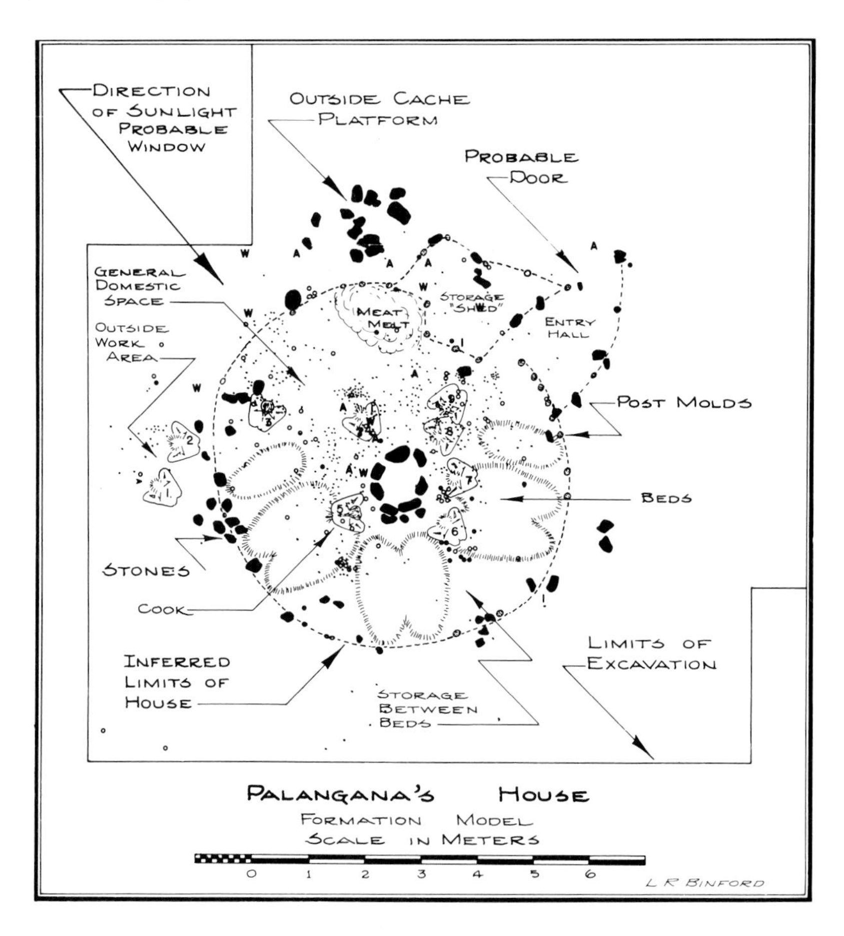

121 *Formation model of activities at Palangana's House.* The distribution of manufacturing debris as shown in ill. 120 and the positions of tools or their parts has been superimposed over the seating and space use model presented in ill. 119. The open circles are stone tools; filled circles represent antler artifacts; the small dots are pieces of lithic manufacturing debris; 'A' represents waste from production of antler tools; and 'W' is debris from manufacture of wooden tools. It should be noted that the tools are grouped in small clusters on the right-hand (north) side of the hearth, as opposed to the isolated and dispersed occurrences to the left and above (south and west of) the hearth. Most of the tools were cached or tucked away and were not seen or were forgotten at the time the site was abandoned. This pattern of tool dispersal is very common in bedding areas of many sites.

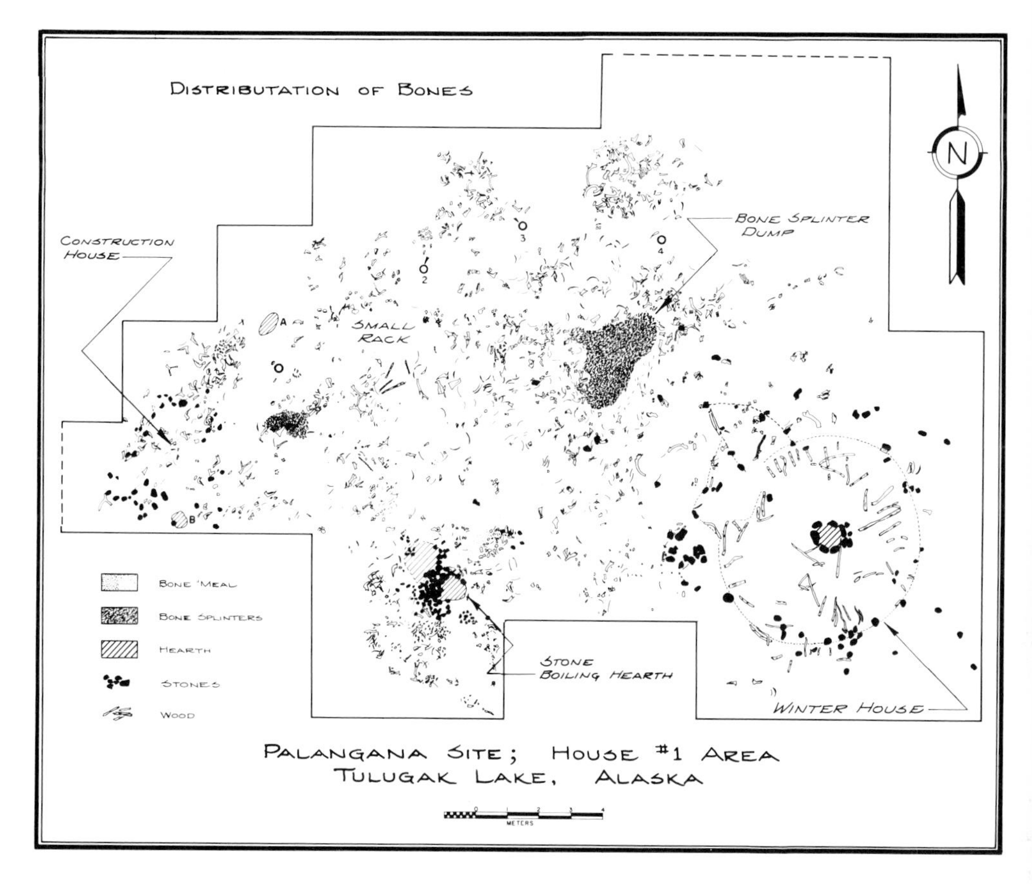

122 *The Palangana site, Tulugak Lake, Alaska showing the distribution of bones* (except within the house itself) (cf. ill. 80). Part of the scatter of bones is related to the feeding of dogs which were tethered along the northwest edge of the site. Additional bone is related to special features such as the stone boiling hearth, but most of it is scattered in the same general area as the bone splinter dump, the most readily recognizable feature on the site.

Returning to the internal organization of space within a house, it is clear that the domestic space is defined by the dense distribution of artifacts and fragments of debris from the manufacture or repair of wood and antler artifacts. Within this area the distribution of artifacts is itself interesting. In the first place, there is a major concentration between the beds and at arm's distance to the right of seating position no. 5 (the cook). Similarly, there are small clusters of artifacts to the rear of, or just beside, all the male seating positions on the dark side of the hearth: these tools are either disassembled items in the process of being manufactured or completed tools in mint condition, which have been stored near the men's habitual seating spots or in sleeping areas. Cached items tend to be found less

121

commonly in the domestic space, because it is regularly cleaned. I have noted that little caches are characteristic of sleeping areas, particularly where housing is permanent, so that the male or 'dark' side of the house is poorly lit at the time of moving; where a tent is taken down, however, the search for lost items on the dark side of the hearth is facilitated by daylight.

Outside an Eskimo House

Turning from the interior of a single house to the site as a whole, we can observe a contrast in the structure of space use between the highly differentiated and intensively used area within the shelter and the more grossly partitioned space in 80, 122 the yard outside the house. In the area along the upper margin of the site plan (ill. 122), four dogs were tethered and between the dogs and the house was a big dump of bone splinters. To the west of the house was a large and extensive feature, a stone boiling hearth used in the rendering of grease from caribou bones. It should be noted that the area occupied by the stone boiling hearth and its associated bone meal dump is almost as large as the house itself.

There are present on this site some special features which would be hard to interpret, were one to ignore the problems which the environment presents to the 119, 121, 122 Eskimo at different seasons. For instance, in ills. 119 and 121 there is shown outside the house a pile of rocks which is designated as a *cache platform*. In the Arctic, items laid on the ground prior to the major snowfalls during the months of October and November become frozen onto the surface and cannot be removed without the expenditure of a great deal of effort in chipping the ice away. For this reason, bundles of rarely used items to be stored over the winter are placed on 123 small platforms made of stones or (if stones are not readily available) of antler. Such special storage areas for goods needing special protection, but for which heat and light are not required, are a common feature around Eskimo houses: for example, a large winter meat storage rack is almost certainly located just south of Palangana's house, in an area which was not excavated.

If we now stand back from the site for an overview of its spatial organization, 122 what generalizations emerge? We can clearly see a core area – in this case the house interior, which was intensively used and internally partitioned in a very fine-grained manner. Immediately adjacent to it are areas more grossly differentiated in spatial terms, areas given over to activities which individually occupy a considerable amount of space: the storage racks and platforms, plus the door dump. Moving still further away from the house, we observe the largest and functionally most specialized areas: the dog tethers and the stone boiling hearth. Such empirical generalizations are useful and interesting, but how can we use these observations about an Eskimo winter settlement to help us interpret the

123 Caribou antlers used as storage facilities at Anaktuvuk Pass village, fall 1969. To prevent items cached outside from freezing to the ground, packages of stored goods are placed on top of antler platforms. This also facilitates access to the goods once the accumulation of snow has become substantial. (Photo courtesy of C. Amsden.)

archaeological record more generally? The answer is that we need to build theory to explain patterns and structures of the sort noted at the site of Palangana's house.

Constraints on the Use of Space: Heat and Light

Palangana's house provides an example of spatial organization constrained by a limited amount of sheltered living space. The house provided shelter for a wide variety of activities distributed differentially in both time and space. Some of these, such as crafts and food preparation, were conducted in the same spaces at different times (*intensive use*), whereas others, for instance domestic activities and sleeping, were more permanently segregated in spatial terms (*extensive use*). In essence, we can consider the organization of space within the house primarily in terms of two dimensions: heat and light. The position of heat within the building was roughly symmetrical while light was distributed asymmetrically relative to the design of the structure. Thus, activities requiring both light and warmth (various craft and food preparation tasks) were localized in the lighted quadrant of the house and were carried out sequentially, largely during the hours of daylight, but within an area of intensive use; other activities requiring only heat and minimal light (e.g.

eating and sleeping) were concentrated in those areas of the house poorly illuminated by outside light.

Against the backdrop of general spatial organization – a compromise in the requirements for heat and light – we must view the effects of the division of labor in society, insofar as it was role differentiated in terms of sex and age. Many of the men's activities, including the manufacture of tools and other useful items, required relatively large amounts of space and sometimes took a long time to complete.[21] This being so, the setting up of specific use areas offered the advantage of not usurping or disrupting the daily cycle of space use in the limited domestic space within the confines of the house.

Site structure, in addition to being affected by limitations on space use, must also be understood in terms of those factors which favor intensification within the utilized space. It is clear from the preceding discussion that the level of the outside temperature is a major factor contributing to site structure, for the colder it becomes, the more activities must be conducted in sheltered spaces. But this raises the problem that the construction of a structure or the use of a sheltered location tends to restrict the quantity and distribution of light within it. Palangana's house illustrates rather well how a limited quantity of light tends to favor intensification in the use of spaces with adequate light. The reverse is also true: when light is more generally available, a more extensive use of space may take place. Limitations on the distribution of heat should also increase the intensification of activities into more restricted spaces. For these reasons the more critical shelter becomes (mainly as a function of environmental conditions), the more differentiation of space use in response to lighting limitations may be anticipated.

The effects of constraints on space use is illustrated by John Yellen's[22] observation that the !Kung Bushmen move around during the day but, depending on the shifting distribution of shade, carry out essentially the same activities in a variety of different places. Such extensive use of space is really only possible if there are no other constraints on the appropriateness of places for doing tasks of short duration and with relatively small requirements for space. Faced only with the problem of maintaining an advantageous relationship between work space and shade, Bushmen workers are able to adapt their work space to take account of the distribution of shade. This example suggests that the more a particular task requires a very specific sort of setting for its performance, the more intense will be the concentration of activity in places which meet those requirements. The domestic space within Palangana's house is a case in point.

Regardless of environmental conditions, individual tasks differ in the degree to which they demand extensive use of space. For instance, a variety of tasks which can be accomplished by a single seated person might all be conducted in the same place, provided they did not overlap in time – a point to which I return below. On the other hand, activities requiring vastly different amounts of space for their execution tend to be independently distributed. We saw earlier in this chapter, for instance, that a roasting pit is a facility dominating about 17 to 24 square meters and its use considerably modifies the land surface (e.g. by the accumulation of charcoal), making it unsuitable for use in many other ways. An activity of this sort, therefore, will usually be given an area all to itself.

Turnover Rates

An additional factor which causes certain activities to take place in special areas is variation in the time required to complete them. Tasks that monopolize space for extended periods are rarely conducted in areas of intensive domestic use, where the normal pattern involves activities of short duration which can be slotted into the daily schedule of eating and sleeping. Many manufacturing tasks require the production of parts which are gradually fitted together as each one is completed, so that any interruption along the way is a real nuisance. We have all experienced as children the frustration of laying out a puzzle or game on the kitchen table, only to be told to pick up our things so that a meal can be prepared – and, of course, the 'picking up of our things' largely destroys the progress already made. For precisely the same reason, those tasks expected to take some time are therefore generally relegated to areas where they can monopolize space, while not interfering with tasks which require shorter periods of time (i.e. those with a more rapid 'turnover' rate).[23]

Effects of Bulk Processing

There is still another consideration to bear in mind when examining the organization of space use: how bulky are the by-products generated by different tasks? Regardless of its duration, any activity which creates a lot of waste takes up space, not only during its execution but also afterwards, for until the waste is removed its presence may make the surface inappropriate for other activities. This is true no matter how fast the task is performed. When a Jemez Indian processes corn for storage at harvest time, for example, a huge mound of debris is generated. It does not take much imagination to realize that, as long as the debris from shucking the corn is left in place, the area is of little use for other purposes.

124

At sites occupied for a short time, activities producing waste products in bulk may be located peripherally to intensively used areas and the debris from them allowed to remain *in situ*. On the other hand, with longer-term occupations, even the activity areas located on the edges of the site may be tidied, so that the same or different activities can be scheduled to take place later in the same place.

124 Jemez Pueblo Indian man processing corn for winter storage, southwestern United States, October 1976. (Photo courtesy of the Maxwell Museum of Anthropology, University of New Mexico.)

Initially, I was surprised to observe the Nunamiut cleaning up their large spring and fall hunting sites, located at great distances from their village. They explained that the large quantities of bones and antler left lying around from previous mass butchering got in the way and were apt to cause accidents. Thus, during the off-season for caribou hunting, they collected the bones at key, repeatedly used sites and burned them.[24] Sites which were used only in response to one specific situation or which were otherwise unrelated to regular land use strategies were not cleaned up in this way. Ill. 125 shows a site which is functionally equivalent to the hunting stand and butchering site at Anavik. The latter was cleaned up, since the site was intended to be used time after time, whereas the former was left in the state shown in the photograph, being judged unlikely to be used again. In short, bulk processing sites illustrate two points. Firstly, the size of the area required and the quantity of debris anticipated may well determine the selection of the place where an activity is to take place. Secondly, the extent to which it is expected that the area will be used again, coupled with the durability of the bulky waste by-products generated there, affects how clean even peripherally located activity areas are kept.

59, 125

125 Caribou kill and butchering site on the north slope of Anaktiqtauk River, Anaktuvuk Pass, Alaska. (See ill. 53 for exact location.) Butchering debris which is scattered on a site not intended for re-use is simply abandoned; but at other sites repeatedly used for similar functions, the large antlers and bones are often gathered up and burned.

Clean-up Strategies

The Eskimo butchering sites emphasize an additional factor which conditions the structure of archaeological sites: *site maintenance.* Perhaps no archaeologist has been more responsible for calling attention to this important aspect than Michael Schiffer.[25] In my experience as an ethnographer, site maintenance involves at least two kinds of tactics: (1) *preventive maintenance* (the disposal of items away from intensively used spaces) and (2) *post hoc maintenance* (the actual cleaning up of areas and the transport of the debris collected to special dumping areas). Generally speaking, preventive maintenance involves some degree of anticipation of the amount of rubbish likely to accumulate in the course of a given activity and this, in turn, affects the differential placement of activities in the first place (as examples discussed earlier clearly indicate).

In the case of activities occurring outside a structure, preventive maintenance commonly takes the form of throwing waste out of the area of immediate action, resulting in the build up of a deposit or toss zone on the edges of the intensively used area. Technically speaking, this debris is *primary refuse* (in Schiffer's terms[26]), because the items have been disposed within the immediate context of their use. Within a house, preventive maintenance is usually linked explicitly with clean-up strategies. For instance, inside an Eskimo dwelling items which otherwise might end up in a toss zone are placed instead in little piles around the hearth[27] or in a bucket which is later taken to an outside dump. Likewise 'aggregate' refuse, such as that contained in a cooking pot, is deliberately carried out of the house to a dumping area, whereas in a more transient or unsheltered situation the same contents might be dumped directly to the side of the hearth. Both the distinct dumps created by preventive maintenance inside the house would be classified by Schiffer as *secondary refuse* (i.e. redeposited waste), yet they could contain exactly the same things as the toss zones around a hearth, which Schiffer would almost certainly recognize as primary refuse. The important difference between these two situations is the scale of the area being intensively used and maintained: In the former case it was quite small (the seating area relative to the peripheral toss zone), while in the latter it was the entire interior of a house, including the areas for seating, domestic work and sleeping. So understanding the organizational relationships among items recovered from the site depends on teasing out structural patterns in the observed data, not on some conventional separation, made on purely formal grounds, between primary and secondary refuse.[28]

I think it is fairly obvious that the care with which an area is maintained is related to the intensity of its use, other things being equal. Areas used intensively are maintained the most thoroughly and will therefore be associated with specialized disposal areas. The degree to which this is true, however, is also a direct function of the length of time that such intensive use lasts – maintenance of areas used intensively only for short periods is minimal. This means we can expect a strong set of relationships in such areas between duration of occupation and the investment of effort in maintenance. Moreover, the longer the occupation, the more diverse are the activities which are likely to be conducted, so there should be a correlation between length of occupation and the numbers of special-purpose activity areas and/or the quantity of carefully maintained, large-scale areas on the periphery of the major activity area. This latter proposition certainly seems to be warranted by Yellen's observations among the !Kung[29] and is sustained by my own research, at least for residential sites.

Building a Theory of Site Structure

Enough has been said to indicate, albeit in a preliminary way, the directions that my attempts at theory building are taking with respect to site structure. Since both light and temperature are factors which vary in regular ways on a global scale, we should therefore be able to begin to suggest correlations between site structure and geographical variations in both seasonal and day-to-day temperatures, as well as in cycles of natural light. Other environmentally conditioned properties of settlement systems, such as mobility,[30] may also be related in functionally determined ways. For instance, the less mobile or more sedentary a group is, the greater the likelihood of conflicts in the scale and duration of activities carried out at any one place. We have already seen that variables of this sort affect the extent to which different activities are likely to be spatially segregated or to which space within sites is intensively or extensively organized. Similarly, the more complex the technology and social organization of a group using a site, the more intricate will be the activities involved in manufacturing and processing materials for use and consumption. This can only lead us to expect yet greater complexity in site structure. If we also add environmental variables – for instance, rain or intense sunlight, both of which have considerable influence on the use of shelter – understanding spatial organization in human behavior becomes a still more challenging and interesting area for research.

I hope I have demonstrated how the investigation of functional relationships[31] can help us develop methods for interpreting accurately observed patterns in the archaeological record. Given some success in the development of interpretive methods with faunal remains and with aspects of site structure, I think we can now tackle the interesting task of trying to understand, in terms of the internal organization of past systems, the variability in assemblage composition illustrated by the 'Mousterian problem'. The interpretive examples and resulting generalizations discussed here should be regarded as illustrations of a particular research strategy and I hope may also demonstrate the potential of this approach for the study of site structure. Needless to say, however, much more has to be done before we can take a scatter of artifacts and begin to reconstruct the dynamic contexts in which such distributions took shape.

Throughout this section of the book I have used the controversy about the Mousterian to illustrate a much more general problem which archaeologists simply have not faced: namely, that criteria based on similarity are insufficient to demarcate the boundaries of past cultural systems. Recall for a moment the different kinds of sites which were illustrated in Chapter 6: they demonstrated repeatedly that a living system is composed of internally differentiated (1) places, (2) labor forces, and (3) sets of tactics. Archaeologists must recognize that different archaeological complexes represent expressions of functional differentiation *within* single systems, not necessarily differences *between* systems. Simply to group things which are similar ensures that we will never see a system in realistic terms. We need ways of reliably bringing together all the different archaeological aspects of a single system.

These represent central challenges to archaeological method. But there are further implications to be drawn from the study of site structure for the discipline as a whole. In Chapter 3 I discussed the difficulties experienced by archaeologists in recognizing the material expression of certain important types of sites in the past, such as base camps. The very notion of a base camp, for instance, carries with it implications about its inhabitants eating and sleeping in one and the same place, about the organization of social roles in terms of age and sex differences, about sharing behavior among those playing different roles, about how adaptive technology was supplied and maintained – all activities centered on discrete 'living places'. Understanding the static spatial consequences of the way these different dynamic dimensions of organization were functionally integrated is a fundamental prerequisite for the accurate recognition of this or any other class of site in the archaeological record. This ability to recognize characteristics which are believed to reflect important, 'pace-setting' transformations is crucial, if we hope to discuss man's evolutionary history in a realistic manner. Current conventions – for instance, arguments about artifact densities or the association of artifacts and bones – stem largely from wishful thinking and do not represent sufficient diagnostic criteria. We must abandon the idea that plausibility itself serves as ample justification for the meanings we give to archaeological observations: better procedures than this are needed.

Confronted with a recognizable pattern in the archaeological record, we have to begin by asking 'What does it mean?'. But then we must follow the *scientific* approach that involves investigating properties of the external world in order to gain better understanding. Investigation of the relationships between dynamics (human behavior) and the resulting statics (artifacts, site structure, faunal remains) must be directed towards the development of reliable and accurate methods for inferring 'what it was like' in the past. In this section, I hope to have illustrated how research must move back and forth between (1) the recognition of patterns in the archaeological record, (2) asking the important question 'What does it mean?', and (3) conducting 'actualistic' studies in order to develop methods which aim to make inferences about 'what it was like' absolutely watertight. Once we know something of the nature of the archaeological record, in terms of how it might have been formed, we will be in a position to make much more accurate statements about certain aspects of past reality.

Part III
WHY DID IT HAPPEN?

Certain events in the past we know must have happened. It is fairly clear, for instance, that at one time we were all hunters and gatherers; then somewhere, somehow, people started to plant crops and to domesticate plants and animals. Similarly, it seems reasonably obvious that all mankind at one time lived in small, mobile groups, with little social superstructure in the form of major political and religious institutions; somewhere, somehow, these modes of life changed and complex political systems came into being. So we can ask 'Why did it happen?', without necessarily knowing much about the archaeological record of the times and places where such events occurred.

To ask such a question is certainly not unique to scientists: cultured man has sought explanations for known or imagined events ever since he has been capable of their cognitive appreciation. One of the main kinds of cultural variability recognizable in the world today, indeed, is the discrepancy among the intellectual biases favored in different styles of explanation. Certain events may be explained by a Marxist as deriving inevitably from the dialectical interplay of social forces; a creationist may see the self-same events as the hand of God at work in all things; those of other cultural persuasions will emphasize the causal role of human choice, population pressure, cybernetic looping, and so on. All such explanatory arguments suggest necessary linkages between one set of conditions and another. They are arguments about the kinds of causes that are thought to be operative.

Once a problem (for instance, the origins of agriculture or the causes of complex society) has been recognized, cultural bias alone can suffice to frame an explanatory argument. Given only some form of received understanding of how the world works, it is possible to organize that understanding so as to provide a post hoc account for the 'problem' facts. In fact this is the commonest mode of argument in which cultural man engages, endlessly advocating this position or that. He justifies his position by citing selected bits of evidence – observations mustered for or against particular views of how the world works. The meanings of these observations are generally assumed or taken to be self-evident. Since all such arguments are based on assumptions about how the world worked at some time in the past, it is impossible to reach a conclusion about the past which is inconsistent with the premises upon which the argument is based. This means, inevitably, that there are as many explanations for past events as there are fundamental differences in the basic assumptions made at the time of inference. All arguments which try to make such inferences plausible by appealing to additional facts which did not figure in the original argument are like advertisements: they are making claims about the 'utility' of the mode of thought being advocated.[1] *Most of the time such appeals to facts are equivocal, in that the meanings attached to the observations cited are not justified independently of the arguments to which they are referred as evidence.*

It is perhaps ironic that many of the general theories which archaeologists employ were generated, or at least stimulated, by the study of contemporary or historically documented cultural phenomena. Since I have in the past urged the crucial role of 'actualistic' studies in the development of our methods for inference,[2] *obviously I do not disapprove of this situation. But it must be stressed that general theory is not middle-range theory. General theory involves arguments advanced to explain why the past was the way it appears to have been. Most of the theoretical propositions generated by the study of contemporary societies involve speculation about the sequences of events that might have characterized the transformation of one form of system into another. They take the form of extrapolations from one state of the system to another, with arguments about how the transformation took place.*[3] *What the theorist observes when viewing a living ethnographic situation, however, is the functioning of a system already in the state for which an explanation is sought.*[4] *For instance, in his classic argument relating irrigation to 'Oriental' forms of state organization, Wittfogel*[5] *suggested irrigation's causal role on the basis of an observed correlation between hydraulic systems and socially stratified political systems. He understood from the functioning of such systems that the monopolistic control of irrigation technology seemed to provide the basis for the maintenance of power within the system. The next step was to suggest that this functional relationship between a productive monopoly and political power also caused the rise of socially stratified societies. A similar relationship must stand behind the essentially functional argument of Marshall Sahlins*[6] *that chiefs, since they function as redistributive agents, come into being under conditions which favor redistribution` Such views are perhaps an inevitable outcome of having only ethnographic experiences to serve as the basis for speculations regarding evolutionary processes.*

Archaeologists (and perhaps some historians) are the only researchers with facts of direct relevance to evolutionary episodes. All ethnographic observations are at best referable to the functioning of relatively stable systems: so why do we use them to prompt our imaginations regarding the evolution of systems? Archaeologists, in general, have not recognized the need for middle-range theory of their own. They have instead adopted the general theoretical arguments advanced by historians and ethnographers and accommodated observations from the archaeological record to them. It is merely an exercise in tautology when (as frequently happens) these observations in turn are cited as proof that the general theories are true!

So archaeologists must abandon this profitless pastime. We need to concentrate on the development of middle-range theory – an area where ethnographic and historical observations are crucial in testing – and to use the methods for inference developed in this way to get answers to questions such as 'What does it mean?' and 'What was it like?'. Only if reliable answers to these questions can be obtained might work on the question 'Why did it happen?' be profitable.

8
On the Origins of Agriculture

A professor of mine once remarked that you can spend your life trying to explain why the earth is flat and be a total failure. He was quite right; if you ask a silly question, you can waste a lot of time. In this chapter, therefore, I begin by briefly sketching some of the basic models and arguments that have commonly been adopted by archaeologists and anthropologists in approaching the problem of the origins of agriculture – a global phenomenon beginning in some areas about 10,000 years ago. I shall point out what I think are some of the weaknesses in these arguments and then proceed to outline a few research directions which seem provocative. These new arguments are by no means finished; they are merely probes. Even so, they indicate some slight but significant changes in the way we may ask a question.

Approaches to the Problem of Agricultural Origins

I suppose there must have been speculation about the origins of agriculture as long as man has been aware of his own history. Within our own cultural tradition, writings by Charles Darwin[1] and by H. L. Roth[2] perhaps represent some of the earliest serious attempts to deal with the problem. For all his insights into biology, Darwin did not have quite such good ones into the origins of agriculture. In a paper speculating about what would prompt man to realize that a plant would grow from a planted seed, he approached the problem with the assumption that the critical and determinant variable for the beginning of agriculture was *knowledge*; he felt, that is, that agriculture was the inevitable consequence of the knowledge that a seed planted in the ground would grow into a plant. This erroneous view did not end with Darwin. There are still many who would argue that agriculture is a mode of production with self-evident advantages and that man will inevitably adopt it if he knows about them.

An early form of mechanistic argument first emerged in England, initially popularized in the writings of Peake and Fleure[3] and later in the works of V. Gordon Childe.[4] It was a Darwinian argument (in the sense of Darwin's biological ideas) since there was some attempt to imagine what conditions in the past might force man to experiment with new means of production. To what degree did man modify his behavior under pressure, because his existing strategies were failing? Did he adopt new strategies as a result of his own insight into what the future might hold? How far did certain pressures force man to cope with new problems, experiment with his environment and, eventually, become an agriculturalist? These important early ideas – ones with which we must still cope – were made popular by Childe and are well-known as the so-called 'Propinquity Theory' or 'Oasis Theory' of agricultural origins. In what now seems a charming but naive scenario, he imagined that as the Sahara Desert and other areas became increasingly desiccated at the end of the last Ice Age, all the animals (including man) progressively began to aggregate in the river valleys. There ensued a 'crunch', rather like catching a commuter train, in which animals and man, now cheek by jowl, had to find some mutual arrangement for working out their problems. In such favored environments where all forms of plants would grow, Childe wrote, men practicing agriculture would obviously provide the grazing animals with great amounts of food in the form of stubble. So there was envisaged a shift from man's parasitic way of life as a hunter and gatherer, to the kind of symbiosis between plants and animals which Childe believed characterized the agricultural way of life.[5]

126

This argument was not really an explanation, but what the philosopher of science Carl Hempel[6] might call an 'explanation sketch'; that is, it included some variables and some ideas of mechanism, but it also included a model of history. Now the problem with successful model-building is that all the imagined events must be accurate (something theories do not demand). Where variables are

126 *The village farming community.* An agricultural village established at the end of World War II on the island of Yaeyama (Ryukyu Islands) by displaced persons from Okinawa, Iwo and Siepan. (Photo taken in June 1953 by E. Santry, on assignment with the author.)

127 *The herders' village.* Navajo settlement of *Ah Tso lige* near Red Lake in Arizona, *c.* November 1935, at the time of counting sheep. (Photo courtesy of the Maxwell Museum of Anthropology, University of New Mexico.)

combined with events, there is the danger of attack on both fronts: your historical facts may be proven to be wrong, or it may be argued that your variables were inappropriate. Frequently, by showing one of these two elements to be ill-conceived, the other one is also rejected. This was exactly the strategy followed by Robert Braidwood (then of the Oriental Institute in Chicago) and his co-workers, in attacking Childe's argument based on mechanistic aggregation.[7] He employed a variety of techniques, such as pollen analysis and sedimentology, to evaluate whether there had, in fact, been an environmental change prior to the appearance of agriculture in the Near East. His conclusion, basically, was that there had been no major period of desiccation.[8] If that was the case, then clearly Childe's model was wrong.[9]

Braidwood's own approach to the question was essentially idealist, since he too shared the perspective that knowledge was a limiting factor. He argued that man became more familiar with environments at the close of the Pleistocene and that this familiarity built up to the point where he realized that he had enough knowledge to manipulate the environment to his own ends. The concept is that of crossing a sort of intellectual Rubicon. To use Braidwood's own phrase, man 'settled in' to his environment,[10] like the chicken getting comfortable on the nest, and then – one must suppose – had great thoughts! If man settled into, and accumulated knowledge about, an environment that contained potentially domesticable plants and animals, then there seemed to be a certain inevitability about the end results of the process.[11] That is, if he settled into an area with wild wheat, he would become a wheat farmer; if he settled into an area with mountain 127 sheep, he would become a sheep herder. This was more or less the level of understanding of mechanism to be found in much of the argument about the origins of agriculture between the end of World War II and the early 1960s. The 'settling in' notion is still with us. I think it underlies much of the work by the late Eric Higgs and his associates,[12] in which they argued essentially that domestication was a protracted learning process, a very gradual dawning on man of the possibilities for manipulation offered by his environment. So the gradualism characteristic of Braidwood's writing is not at all missing from the contemporary literature. In fact, a resurgence of this type of argument is apparent.

It is worth noting, incidentally, that an additional element was often implicit in the idealist literature of pre- and immediately post-war periods. Those theorizing about the origins of agriculture along the lines I have just mentioned would occasionally be confronted with an ethnographic counter-case in which, say, a human group lived in an area where wild corn grew, but did not domesticate corn. One explanation was that they were dull people who did not learn very well. Conversely, a group who practiced agriculture in an area where it did not seem they should had to be regarded as exceptional, since one of the determinant variables upon which the theory depended was a quality of the actor – that is, his ability to learn.

The Childean approach involving the push-and-pull of selection, then, was replaced entirely by Braidwood's view of agriculture as an emergent process – a view to which there were no effective alternatives in the archaeological literature of the 1950s. Indeed, this was a period during which 'The Emergence of . . .' was a common title for articles and there was much discussion of the *incipience* of various phenomena (with definitions of *incipient, epi-incipient* and *post-incipient* phases). The general picture was one of man's gray dawning before illumination: he was floundering around in his environments, trying this or that. My own minor challenge to the Braidwood view, in a paper published in 1968,[13] had some effect on the field. In fact, it appeared contemporaneously with other arguments in which population growth was cited as a major factor conditioning the appearance of technological innovations,[14] as well as more complex forms of socio-political organizations.[15] My argument was adopted for the data from the Near East[16] and for a time enjoyed some popularity. Nevertheless, it suffered from some of the same weaknesses of Childe's earlier arguments – namely, it was a combination of conjectural history and theory, an 'explanation sketch'. I tried to use some variables that I thought were important in a model based on what we thought at the time the past had been like. Unfortunately, I was wrong about what the past had been like; and if that could be demonstrated, then it was also fairly easy to dismiss the variables I had been working with as unimportant. In fact, after the initial popularity of so-called 'demographic' arguments, there set in a reaction.[17] Many authors today simply declare that such arguments are naive or have been proved inadequate.[18]

Regardless of controversy over the importance of demographic factors *per se*, the methodological message coming forth was the following. Agriculture is a way of making a living, a solution to a fundamental human problem – getting enough to eat. Now if agriculture developed in some way out of the practices of non-agricultural people, then it seems reasonable to suppose that it arose to solve a problem that some of them were facing. What on earth could that problem be? Surely it was environmental, because the problems of food procurement for hunters and gatherers must be a by-product of the dynamics of the environment in interaction with man. Are the animals where they are supposed to be? Are they there in the numbers they used to be? Are plant resources being over-exploited? In other words, what is the interaction between man and the environment? Quite justifiably, therefore, there was a period of intense interest in the analysis of environments, with the work becoming more and more detailed. The archaeologists were still gradualists, but they were now working within an ecological context.

It was interesting, then, to see what happened when someone came along to a lecture series and asked, say, 'Why didn't the Californian Indians practice agriculture?'. The lecturer might respond by asking what kinds of plants they had, and the audience would usually supply the data at this point: 'They had lots of acorns'. The question was then brushed aside by observing that the Indians didn't need agriculture in such a lush environment. This exemplifies an argument that increasingly appeared both in lectures and in print. I call it the *Garden of Eden Proposition.* Contrary to the Bible, it seems, there was not just one Garden of Eden, but lots of them (and they are being generated rapidly as a function of the number of people who write about the origins of agriculture!). Let me explain.

128

There are many ethnographic accounts of non-agricultural peoples present in interesting parts of the world during the period of exploration or colonial settlement. Consequently, whenever an argument was advanced about why agriculture was adopted, it was possible to do a quick test of logic by asking 'If that's true, why didn't the So-and-So have agriculture?'. Such continuous testing of hypotheses was possible with the availability of ethnographic material, about which, however, the environmental specialists knew very little. So there came to be a wonderful game played between people who had ethnographic expertise and people who thought they knew about the environmental background of agricultural origins; it was a game I have seen played over and over in recent years.

Someone might be offering an argument about the origins of agriculture, urging the importance, for example, of diminishing quantities of pistachio nuts

128 *'Man and all the animals in the Garden of Eden'*. Many archaeologists have suggested that rich environments such as this, with plentiful food just for the picking, provided the setting for the beginnings of sedentary life and the origins of agriculture. (Drawing by Iva Ellen Morris.)

among the hunters and gatherers of the Near East and pointing out that complex society is dependent on giving up hunting and gathering, when a member of the audience would point out that there were no pistachio nuts in Mesoamerica, yet agriculture was invented there; or, conversely, that there were all those complex societies in California and the Northwest coast of North America which were not agricultural! The speaker might confess that he had not considered those issues, but would point out that in Mesoamerica there was some other resource said to be diminishing, while in California and on the Northwest coast they had so many acorns or salmon that they had no need to invent agriculture. That is, people did not adopt agriculture if they lived in highly productive environments: little 'Gardens of Eden' where food was plentiful. In addition, it has been generally assumed that in such environments people will become sedentary; they will stop moving. For instance, the following summarizes what seems to be the consensus view of many archaeologists: 'We have taken it for granted that, in general, sedentary life has more survival value than wandering life to the human race, and that, other things being equal, wherever there is an opportunity to make the transition, it will be made. . . .'[19]

This proposition is what I like to call the 'Slug Principle': a man doesn't do anything to get a meal unless he has to. If he doesn't have to walk, he will sit. If

129

there is a lot of food in one place, as for example on a shell bank, then he will sit right there. Clearly, in a Garden of Eden man will not move about. These two ideas, the 'Garden of Eden Proposition' and the gustatory 'Slug Principle' have been woven together to make an interesting array of arguments.

For instance, it has recently been suggested that there was a Garden of Eden promoting sedentary life at the top of the Andes![20] Similarly, it has been proposed that in the Great Basin of North America there existed a Garden of Eden along various internal drainages, where big marshes produce vast numbers of edible cat-tails. I don't know how many tons of cat-tails there were supposed to be within a two-hour radius of the site in question; but if you want to eat cat-tails all your life, then perhaps there is a Garden of Eden there. At any rate, it was argued – quite seriously – that this resource was the basis of sedentism and village life in the region.[21]

Another suggestion, recently advanced by Perlman,[22] tries to identify aquatic and estuarine resources as the 'real' Gardens of Eden. It is claimed that any strategy which tends to optimize labor by minimizing effort and risk will be selected. The Slug Principle dictates that there will be a gravitation towards productive Gardens of Eden, which, in this version of the argument, are identified as being coastal environments. I admit that this was something I myself had

129 Rice drying for storage at Hoshino village, Yaeyama island in the southern Ryukyus. Sedentism represents a major investment in facilities and the movement of goods and products to consumers; it is also made possible by bulk storage of products over periods much longer than they are available in nature. (Photo taken in June 1953 by E. Santry, on assignment with the author.)

casually assumed at the time I built my own model of agricultural origins in marginal zones.[23] But I gave up such a position some time ago, since it seemed to me to lead one inevitably to the view that some peoples were 'more perceptive' or 'smarter' than others: why else would they have grasped so early the Great Truth of the Least Effort Principle, while others ignored its self-evident advantages?

Although it does not necessarily follow from these arguments that the idyllic sedentism made possible by a localized Garden of Eden led to agriculture, some archaeologists have made such claims. Kent Flannery found his Garden of Eden in Turkey. After Harlan[24] published his well-known paper on the wild wheat fields there, Flannery[25] suggested that these might indeed have been a sufficient basis for sustaining sedentism and he apparently thought the development of further arguments unnecessary. This suggestion was later linked by Hassan[26] to environmental changes which brought into being in some places a Garden of Eden yielding resources said to be of increased seasonal and spatial predictability.[27] These resources were thought of previously only as starvation foods, but under changed environmental conditions their true value was realized and the use of these 'environmentally stimulated' high-yield resources promoted sedentism and led eventually to agriculture.

Yet another example is provided in recent work by Niederberger.[28] In her excavations at a site on the side of Lake Texcoco in Mexico, she found remains of ducks, deer, cat-tails – in fact, evidence for all the resources a man might need, all in one place. There was no reason to move from such a place. And so here is a whole set of arguments about the origins of agriculture. Man first became sedentary because he found a little Garden of Eden. Once he was accustomed to being sedentary, things began to go sour on him; for instance, perhaps the ducks didn't come as much any more. Man began to foul his nest, so to speak, and was forced to move to supplementary production (i.e. agriculture). But if sedentism leads to agriculture in this way, then we are back where we were earlier. For why didn't the Californians and the peoples of the Northwest coast develop agriculture? Such arguments overlook a very important bit of empirical evidence: while it appears that agriculture *followed* sedentism in the Near East, Mesopotamia, even in Peru, the data available from Mesoamerica and North America are clear in indicating that the adoption of domesticated plants *preceded* the appearance of sedentary ways of life in those areas.[29]

Although there are others, the arguments I have sketched above constitute the essence of the explanations so far offered for agriculture. In the gradualist argument, man develops agriculture because he becomes more knowledgeable. 128 According to the Garden of Eden view, he does so faster in rich environments which encourage sedentism; sedentism, in turn, is seen as encouraging productive intensification, or experimentation with ways of producing sufficient food in the limited space around a permanent settlement (hence, agriculture). An alternative to this view (and one which totally begs the question) is that the adoption of agriculture requires increased sedentism; presumably, therefore, with agriculture people settle down, because it offers that increased reliability which ensures that the decision against mobility will be made according to the Slug Principle.[30]

All the views summarized so far incorporate various forms of gradualism into the argument. In addition, all the ideas are teleological. The continuous but gradual move towards the use of reliable resources, the adoption of techniques which lead towards the assumed absolute goal of sedentism, or the move towards the reduction of effort – all these notions assume that man's evolution is goal-oriented and that it is therefore progressing towards some inevitable end point. It is worth noting that the approaches of structural-Marxists and general systems theorists who consider processes of morphogenesis are not so different from the earlier gradualist views, because change is seen as inevitable. In both of these newer styles of discourse, it is assumed that 'the cultural system has self-transforming properties. . . . Rather than societies being in equilibrium they are always in a state of becoming. . . .'[31] Here transformations of society, we are told, are to be plotted largely as a product of human choices, choices as to how to invest one's time or how to use the fruits of productive investments: '. . . how can one speak of material causation of human actions when the unpredictable and creative powers of the human mind are at work in nearly every situation?'[32]

There is a further form of gradualism which does not see the vital property causing the change to agriculture as coming from within the system, but imagines an external 'prime mover'. This force is thought to be a continuous push from the environment. One might cite as an example the demographic argument of Cohen,[33] who employs a nearly pure form of Malthusian theory about population growth – namely, that since populations continue to grow unabated, there is a continuous and unrelenting pressure operating on a group to favor new methods of increasing the food supply.

It is my opinion that we need to give much more serious thought to Darwinian arguments, where the driving forces of change lie in the interaction between the environment and the adaptive system being considered. Given such a view, the system of adaptation may enjoy relatively stable periods of varying duration, representing times when it is able to cope successfully with the perturbations of the environment. Selection for change occurs when the system is unable to continue previously successful tactics in the face of changed conditions in its environment. The source of such changes may be the accumulated effects of the system's history, but such effects are build-ups of changed ecological relationships rather than the continuous operation either of some inner vital principles or of unrelenting external pressures. Childe made a probe in the direction of a selectionist approach of this sort, but he was knocked down on strictly historical grounds. I feel it might be useful to try to move in that same direction once again.

Mobility as a Security Option among Hunters and Gatherers

Most of the arguments given above share one common assumption: that movement is something man tries to avoid and that sedentism is a desired condition.[34] Is that assumption justified and, if so, why? From the standpoint of a species such as our own, trying to gain a secure living, why should mobility be bad and sitting in one place good?

The first thing that struck me was simply an empirical observation. Over the past decade or more, I and my students have had a variety of experiences living and working with mobile peoples – with Eskimos in north-central Alaska, with 130 Central Desert Australian Aborigines, with !Kung Bushmen in Botswana, with mobile horticulturalists in northern Mexico. None of these peoples believed that mobility was bad; indeed, in the case of 'pure' hunters and gatherers, the idea was quite insane, for a simple reason. As one old Eskimo man expressed it, 'When I'm here in one place, I don't know what's going on over there.' He went on to explain that living a secure life was totally dependent on his making good judgments about where to move next, judgments that were possible only if he knew what was happening throughout an enormous area in which he was not actually living. It was necessary, that is, to monitor a huge amount of territory, in order to have sufficient knowledge to make prudent decisions regarding the resources pulsing through and across that space.

When contemporary Eskimo men are forced by various bureaucratic means to stay in one place, they find it a very traumatic experience. In practice, they sneak away and make long circuitous trips over the territory. They come back with long narrations: how many moose tracks they saw, where the ducks are, how good the firewood resources are in a certain area, whether there have been forest fires, whether the snow drifts are up and over the lakes, how deep the ice is on ice-fishing lakes, and so forth. All this is crucial information, in order to be able to know what to do if something transforms what had appeared to be a secure state – for instance, if grizzly bears get into meat caches and the stores are lost. Unless one can make good judgments about what to do next, based on information gathered from a vast area, one may not survive. So it turns out that most of the moves these Eskimo made were made not because they did *not* have food, but because they *did* have food. If there is plenty of food in one place, it is always possible to return there. It is a low-risk, secure strategy to take a long walkabout in such circumstances, to take chances on the availability of risky foods. In fact, much mobility occurs when there is also the most food. That hardly suggests the operation of the Slug Principle.

I found exactly the same thing in the Central Desert of Australia. I was working with a group in an area of very high density of game: on one four-hour walking trip, for example, we counted as many as eighty-five kangaroos. You might

130 Ngatatjara Aborigines moving camp in the Warburton Ranges in Western Australia, *c.* 1935. In contrast to the sedentary way of life associated with agriculture and other intensive food-getting strategies, hunters and gatherers must continuously reposition themselves within their environment. (Photo taken by N. B. Tindale, courtesy of the Department of Anthropology, University of California at Los Angeles.)

suppose, if the Garden of Eden view were correct, that the group would just sit there and work their way through the kangaroos. On the contrary, however, they realized that the abundance of game gave them the total security they needed to make a trip to see the other end of the territory, which they had not visited for a long time; if anything went wrong, they could always return to the known, secure situation. I think that all hunter and gatherer systems work this way. They do not stay in one place where food resources are nucleated and get nutritionally drunk, but rather they use such circumstances as an opportunity to travel to other areas, most often for purposes of information-gathering. So it seems to me that, if a system is to become a sedentary one, a set of circumstances must arise in which information of this kind is no longer a help and the option of moving around in unoccupied territory is no longer a realistic one.

At this point, I must stress again the *scale* of hunting and gathering systems: they are not all big, but none of them is really small. We saw in Chapter 6 that the caribou hunters I worked with (admittedly, an extreme case) think of their territory in terms of a life cycle. A group of three dozen people will use an area 53

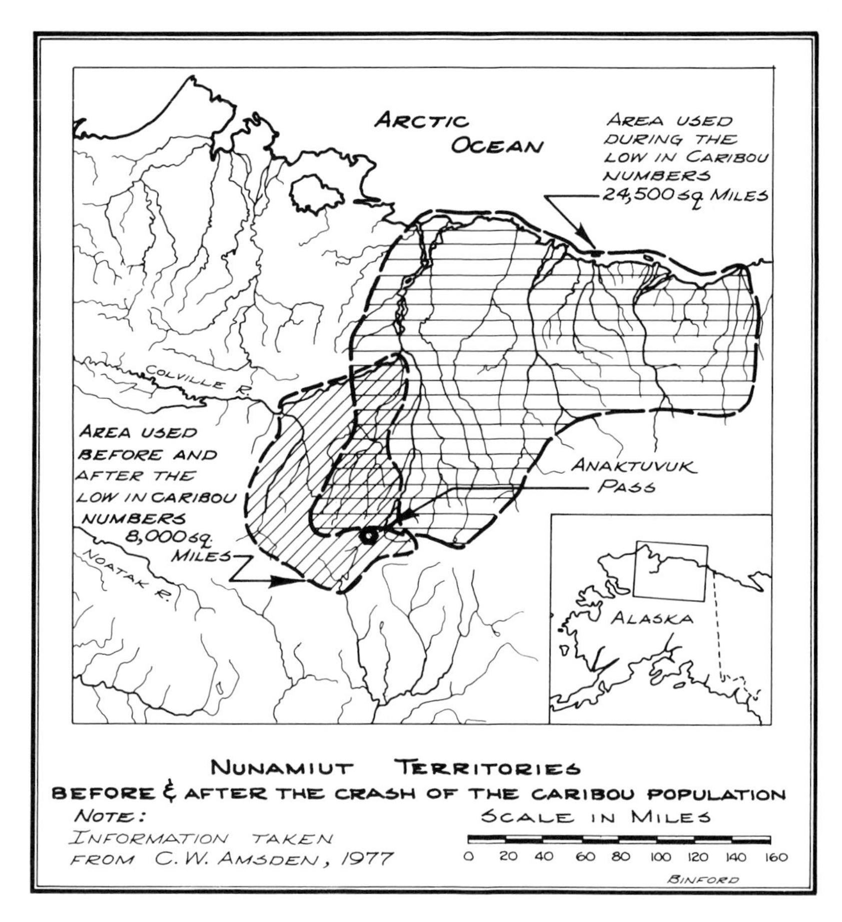

131 Nunamiut territories before and after the 1910 crash of the caribou population. This hunter-gatherer group's response to food stress was to triple the effective territory they covered for extracting food. (Based on Amsden 1977.) Coastal aquatic resources – what some would see as a 'Garden of Eden' – were used as a back-up food supply during the low in caribou numbers, but with the recovery of the herds, the Eskimo returned to mobile hunting in the interior.

of about 22,000 square kilometers during their lifetime. That is a big area, but the men know that much space – where the caches are, where the stream crossings are, where the game trails are, and so on. During my fieldwork, for example, I took an inventory of cached tools and subsequently interviewed the hunters of two overlapping bands about their locations: almost every man could provide me with an accurate list of cached tools dispersed over an area of nearly a quarter of a million square kilometers. Such information was not gained by being sedentary! Their entire educational system, in fact, was designed to teach them about that much space, to give them a series of alternative options.

It is easy to see that in such a huge space there exist plenty of alternative possibilities, if the resources in one particular micro-environment fail. For instance, in north-central Alaska in 1910 the caribou population crashed. Outsiders involved in the Yukon gold mining operations started forest fires which burned off the winter range (an area the Eskimos never saw themselves), contributing to a catastrophic decline in the population density of caribou. But the caribou hunters were not at all at a loss when they found that their primary source of food was gone: they had several other options, all involving mobility, and they knew exactly what they were. Some moved to the Upper Colville River and began putting up stores of fish; others began the seasonal hunting of mountain sheep in the Dietrich Valley, a part of their range in which they had not actually been living; others began to compete with Athapaskan Indians for access to another caribou herd with a different breeding territory and winter range; yet others moved to the coast and started hunting seals. None of these alternative strategies had to be learned. The men already knew and had experienced all the fundamental subsistence strategies of their neighbors and could execute them very well. 131

132 Okinawan man and his wife preparing the soil for planting sweet potatoes, Yanbabu, 1952.

133 Transplanting rice seedlings into ground paddies, Nago Okinawa, 1951.

But the means to their knowledge of these other options was through *mobility* – mobility which led to the accumulation of an information bank, on the basis of which alternatives could be selected.

We may turn back to our initial question about agricultural origins, but from a rather different angle. What would force a group of people to shift from a system based on an *information bank* (hunting and gathering) to one based on a *labour bank* (agriculture)? Staying in one place to tend plants is a totally different 132, 133 way of gaining a livelihood from the mobile strategies I have just outlined. In my opinion, the critical constraint must have been something that prevented mobility as a security option. This leads me back to a set of arguments I advanced some years ago. Although the idea seems to be out of favour in certain quarters, I still think that population growth must somehow be relevant to the problem.

Population Growth and Hunter-Gatherer Subsistence Options

The archaeological record indicates that the widespread shift from hunting and gathering to agricultural strategies is largely a phenomenon of the post-Pleistocene period. If the arguments advanced to account for this involve the loss of mobility options as a consequence of demographic packing, then we must face the problem of why population growth only had some effect so recently in human evolution. This is a subject that is far from being well understood, but I feel that we may have been misled by assuming that explanations we give for events after the emergence of fully *sapiens* man about 30,000 years ago should also be relevant before that time. Pre-modern man may have been very different from ourselves, both biologically and behaviorally, as I have already suggested (Chapters 2 and 3).

Now it is known that every species has zones in which its reproduction is optimal: corn grows better in Iowa, for instance, than almost anywhere else. Why should this not also be true for human hunters and gatherers? I therefore 134 examined how population densities achieved among hunters and gatherers vary in relation to environment throughout the world. Summarizing considerably, the result was that the maximum densities occurred roughly at a mean earth bio-temperature (Mean Effective Temperature)[35] of 14.4°C – that is, right in the temperate zone, not in the tropical rainforest or in the desert. It seems, then, that fully *sapiens* man is reproductively most effective in the temperate zone, something I seriously doubt for pre-*sapiens* man; early man did not exist in the temperate 52 zone and Neanderthal man was not very successful there. So modern man may have very much more reproductive potential in parts of the warm temperate zone than in any other place.

Once man with this potential existed in the temperate zone there would have been a build-up of population. The process, of course, must have been compli-

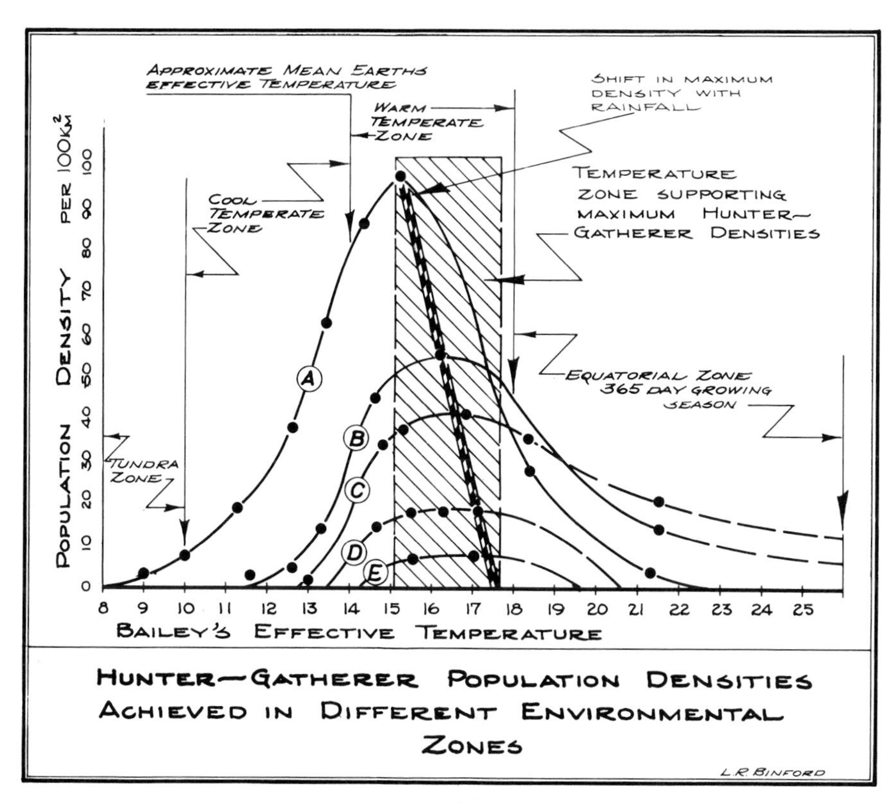

134 *Hunter-gatherer population densities achieved in different environmental zones.* Ethnographic hunter-gatherer societies have been grouped into five ordinal categories (curves A to E) of a 'rainfall index', derived by dividing the potential evapotranspiration at a locality (i.e. the amount of water which would be evaporated and transpired if unlimited water was available, given the amount of solar radiation recorded annually at the locality) by the actual rainfall. By plotting mean hunter-gatherer densities for each effective temperature and rainfall interval, it can be seen clearly that the maximum population densities are achieved within a zone of warm temperate environments (shaded area). The actual maximum density value in each rainfall category shifts with effective temperature (thick checkered bar).

cated by climatic fluctuations during the Ice Age, which resulted in many local extinctions of population. Nevertheless, in some places the build-up would have occurred to the point where density-dependent effects came into operation. This makes some sense in terms of biology: the main regulatory mechanism seems to be mortality in the tropics and fertility in the Arctic, the two coming together in the temperate zone. It is interesting to note that the rate of population growth in comparable equatorial settings was enormously faster in the New World than in the Old World, because in the New World there were no native disease organisms.

By the time man entered the New World he had evolved with these organisms in the Old World; he had gone through a 'disease filter' which allowed a population boom when he entered the equatorial zones of the New World. This accounts for the greatly truncated chronology of cultural development from hunters and gatherers to state societies there, something related both to nutrition and to intrinsically different rates of population growth in different environments (although the mechanisms are not yet known). At any rate, my main point is that we cannot think in terms of a *constant* reproductive potential for man in all environments.

If we accept that discernible population growth would occur among hunters and gatherers in certain environments, we may ask what effects that growth would have on their normal strategy of subsistence. Let us take a typical situation in which we have a group of about thirty people in an annual range *A* which they 52 occupy for about ten years, making a lifetime range of approximately five such units. As the number of persons in the group increases, arguments about meeting kinship obligations sooner or later break out. Perhaps there are simply too many mouths to be fed with the available stored fish and, despite an ethic of generalized reciprocity, someone begins to go back on his obligation to feed a kinsman. One or two angry families decide to move away into the next annual range unit *B*. It is their territory and they certainly have a right to do so, but at this point nobody is yet living there; under normal conditions the whole group would not have moved there for another five years or more, so this segmentary move is, in a sense, premature. When the resources in territory *A* begin to give out, the remaining people there, since they are still angry with their kinsmen, move into territory *C*, rather than *B*. In a very short space of time, in place of one kinship group there come to be two, both quite legitimately using different parts of the same lifetime range simultaneously. Instead of the territory being used serially, as it would be without population pressure, competition within the system tends to separate and segment people, resulting in the utilization of territory in leap-frog fashion. With further population growth, fights continue to occur (and I have some good examples documented ethnographically). The group in territory *B* may move on to *D*, while that in *C* might split into two mutually avoiding groups in *E* and *F*. When the group in *D* comes full circle and moves back into *A*, many of the resources necessary for living there will not yet have recovered: in the Arctic, for instance, willows used for firewood need about forty-five years before they are ready for use again. This presents no problem under normal conditions, since a group would not expect to return to the same territory for well over forty years. When they return in twelve, difficulties will obviously occur.

As the region fills up, then, a band comes to have little or no option about where it can move next. By packing the region with people, mobility is restricted and resource exploitation becomes concentrated. Packing, in fact, thwarts the normal strategy of hunters and gatherers to use mobility as a source of security. Among the interesting set of responses to this problem is an increase in interregional visiting by individuals (since whole groups cannot move between regions as they once did). This may represent an attempt both to get through difficult times and to educate the children about the territory as a whole, but the attempt is totally unrealistic, given that the children will have no opportunity to move away into other parts of the territory. A far more significant response, however, occurs in terms of the *kinds* of food resources utilized.

There exists a simple relationship between the body size of an animal and the amount of space it requires to feed itself. The space needed to feed an animal in the 120 to 300 pound body size range is fairly extensive (and in the Arctic is very large indeed). If a hunter has an area of about 20,000 to 25,000 square kilometers, he will probably be able to kill moose and caribou on a regular basis. If, however, he is restricted to an area with sides of only 80 kilometers, he may still be able to get caribou, assuming his territory lies on a migration route; but he will certainly no longer get moose, because their range is bigger than his by a substantial margin. The hunter who formerly killed moose and put up the meat for storage now finds he must make do with animals of smaller body size – ducks, or fish, or in coastal areas even shellfish. In short, he is progressively forced to move down the chain of animal body sizes, as he is constrained spatially. Eventually, inevitably, he is drawn away from animals and towards plants, because plants are aggregated in small amounts of space. A very different set of strategies now comes into play. In the first place, there is a switch to alternative animal species, often aquatic ones (and, indeed, the first response to packing in the temperate zone seems to have been the move to aquatic resources). Secondly, dependence on plants increases. Thirdly, as population continues to grow in an environment which offers no budding-off options, consumer demand increases within a space that is now constrained: some form of intensive production system (i.e. agriculture) now becomes mandatory.

This *packing model* is not necessarily an easy one to work with from the methodological point of view. How can archaeologists measure population growth or packing? In a sense, the situation is rather like that of a medical doctor observing the symptoms and trying to determine what the disease is. One of the interesting 'symptoms' that the packing model would lead us to expect is that hunters' attempts at herd management and animal domestication should precede plant domestication. In the archaeological sequences from Peru, where domesticated camelids and guinea pigs appear some 2,000 years before any domesticated plants, that certainly seems to be true. Similarly, the work of Dexter Perkins and others in the Near East suggests that domesticated sheep and goats precede plants in that region also.[36] A few facts of this kind, which could not be adequately dealt with before, begin to make a little more sense.

The beginning of a sedentary lifestyle constitutes another interesting symptom. I have already noted that one major contrast between the Old World and Peru on the one hand, versus Mesoamerica and North America on the other, is the difference between the historical appearance of sedentism relative to evidence for the use of domesticated plants; in the latter areas, domesticated plants precede by some considerable time the appearance of sedentary settlements, while in the former the reverse is the case. If it is accepted as likely that animal protein is important both nutritionally and in terms of human reproduction,[37] then plant agriculture itself *never* solves the packing problem. Alternative non-plant foods such as aquatic resources[38] and the actual domestication of animals help intensify production for human use of non-plant foods. Under such conditions, moves toward sedentism may precede the adoption of agriculture, which – while it may increase in importance as a 'calorie-seeking' strategy – never solves the nutritional imbalance between animal and plant foods. In Mesoamerica and North America, as well as in some regions of temperate Europe, increased sedentism facilitated by aquatic exploitation seems to have anticipated the adoption of agriculture. On the other hand, where aquatic alternatives were not present and where domestication of animals did not occur, agriculture continued to be a calorie-seeking strategy and mobility remained the only means of ensuring the acquisition of animal foods largely from terrestrial sources. In these circumstances, sedentism is only forced into being long after the adoption of agriculture as a 'back-up' strategy and at a much greater packing threshold.

Yet another symptom is what Flannery[39] called the 'broad spectrum revolution'. But in fact this was a broad spectrum *depression*, not a revolution. As hunters and gatherers were packed in a region, they were forced to move down the animal body-size chain, to exploit a wider variety of species, to make use of increasing numbers of smaller and smaller food packages, to compensate for the more specialized (and no longer viable) strategies they employed as spatially unfettered hunters. This change is itself perhaps one of our best clues to the processes involved in the origins of agriculture. Using the ratio of species diversity against body size as an index, I think it will not be long before we can predict with some precision at what point in the archaeological sequences we should see the first signs of labor-intensive strategies. For eastern North America, certainly, such procedures show signs of working well. It can be shown, for example, that any group of hunters which was forced to subsist on shellfish as early in the year as February was only a short step away from adopting agriculture. In other words, where pressure on resources resulted in such limited stores in the fall and such poor winter hunting that shellfish were the only available foodstuff from so early in the spring, it regularly seems to be the case that the growing of corn begins within a short time.

The development of the ideas suggested above may be profitable. But there is an important additional point to be made: all such theories or models for why something happens cannot be tested in any direct sense against the archaeological record. Almost all the different theories touched upon earlier in this discussion assigned different meanings to the archaeologically demonstrable fact that smaller and more stationary food sources were increasingly used through time. I have already noted that Flannery termed this pattern the 'broad spectrum revolution', a response by game hunters living outside their Garden of Eden. Hassan saw it arising from a realization of the advantages of reliable resources triggered by environmental changes. Cohen regarded these same facts as good evidence for a linkage between subsistence strategies and population pressure in general; that is, a decreasing ratio between available food and consumer demand resulted in an increased use of less 'desirable' foods. Hayden considered that the greater use of 'r-selected' resources – those that reproduce themselves rapidly and in great abundance – stemmed from the accumulated wisdom of populations who have suffered continuous and unrelenting stress.[40] I myself have argued here that these facts reflect an intensification tactic. The operation of the homeostatic mechanisms which tend to maintain hunter-gatherer local groups at optimally small sizes results in decreased effective territory for any given local group. As more groups are generated, the locational options of all of them are reduced, thus forcing the intensified use of smaller and smaller segments of habitat.

All these archaeologists' theories are ways of giving different meanings to the same empirical pattern demonstrable in the archaeological record; and I am sure that many other interpretations could be offered besides. I am equally sure that there could be developed additional arguments about quite different causes for agriculture, citing other empirical patterns (equally subject to ambiguous interpretation). How do we choose among these alternative interpretations of the same facts? How do we decide between theories and between their different biases?

In the cases illustrated here, the rules for cognition generally derive from the theories being advocated. That is, the meaning given to archaeological observations are *consistent* with the assumed mechanisms of causation built into the theories. This means that any appeal to the empirical materials of the archaeological record will represent merely a '*post hoc* accommodative argument', whereby the theory is necessarily supported. In order to move away from this wholly unsatisfactory situation, we must develop an appropriate language and instruments for measuring variables which we observe in the archaeological record; but we must achieve some operational objectivity when evaluating theories.[41] This means that in order to make inferences archaeology needs to develop middle-range theory[42] which has been devised and tested in intellectual contexts divorced from the theories about past behavior which we seek to evaluate. Archaeology, in general, has failed to realize that in order to refute or support theories it requires a strong body of inferential techniques, warranted independently of its theories about past dynamics.

9
Paths to Complexity

Complex societies and civilizations arose at different times in different parts of the world nearly always after the development of agriculture. How they came into being is an area of research in which I have long had an interest. My own doctoral thesis, in fact, written over twenty years ago, was concerned with the appearance of complex social systems in eastern North America,[1] but since then I have not worked directly on the problem. I have tried, however, to keep up with the fast-growing literature, for my interest continues to be strong from a methodological and procedural standpoint – that is, what strategies have archaeologists followed in trying to explain such phenomena? I have to say that I cannot concur with much of what I have read on the subject. So it will perhaps

135 A corner of the 'palace' at Labná, Yucatan, Mexico. The impressive investment of labor and craftsmen's skills, as well as the elaborate symbolism underlying a structure such as this, challenge our explanatory powers: why did it happen? (From the files of the late Professor Fay-Cooper Cole, now in author's possession.)

be not without interest to consider briefly some of what seem to me to be limitations in the patterns of thought that are currently prevalent.

We should first dismiss entirely some ideas about the origins of complex systems which were very influential in their day (and are still to be found in the contemporary literature). Earlier generations of anthropologists, for instance, used to argue that knowledge – as with the origins of agriculture – must somehow have been a critical limiting factor: explaining the emergence of civilization simply involved trying to imagine what would lead man to invent art, philosophy, complicated legal systems, and the like. Even in comparatively recent times some historians and archaeologists have tried to claim that such wonderful achievements are possible only when leisure time becomes available to free man for 'thoughtful' activities. That too is quite wrong. If anything it is the other way around, for hunter-gatherer groups seem typically to have more free time than do complex societies. Then there are arguments of the orthogenetic variety, which claim that certain human cultures had a sort of built-in dynamic, an inherent tendency for progressive growth. People who started out in the right direction, so to speak, had a much better chance of becoming civilized than those who squandered their lives doing something not on the direct path to western civilization! The total inadequacy of such arguments is not hard to see and they need not detain us further.

135

Monopolists, Altruists and Big-Men

When I first began to learn about the origin of complex systems – and I did so from a strongly American perspective which has no doubt colored my views – two main lines of argument were current. In our respective doctoral theses, as it turned out, I followed one line and Marshall Sahlins[2] followed the opposite one.

I believed that power derived from productive *monopolies* and that monopolies were to a large extent a functional response of societies which were very dependent on storage and whose food resources were patchy or highly aggregated in space. On the basis of ethnohistoric and archaeological data from eastern North America, it seemed clear that anadromous fish (i.e. fish, such as salmon, that live in saltwater but run up river to spawn in fresh water) constituted a critical resource for some human groups dependent on storage. Access to such a foodstuff, however, was virtually 'point-specific': the fish cannot be caught readily in deep waters, yet by the time they reach really shallow waters they are in such a poor nutritional state they are not worth taking. So they are available only at certain points in the environment. And the people who lived near 'access windows' of this kind had an effective monopoly over a critical resource which they were able to manipulate for their own political advantage throughout the region.

136

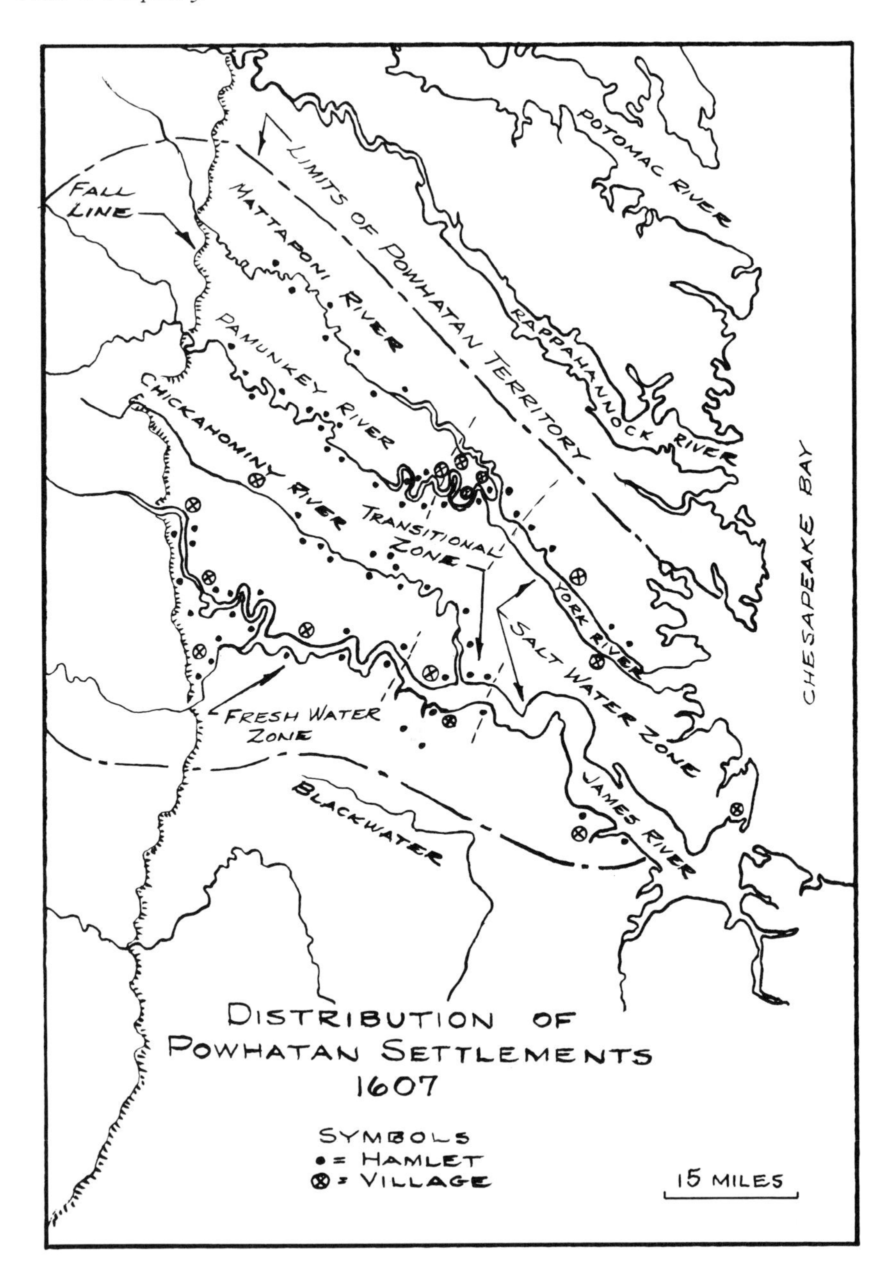

136 Distribution of Powhatan settlements in Chesapeake Bay, Virginia, 1607. Note the clusters of hamlets and villages in the fresh- to salt-water transitional zone, that which yielded most anadromous fish taken in impounding weirs; these fish provided critical foods during the least productive periods of the year (e.g. the month of April). Most power rested with the chiefs of the villages of the transitional zone.

This simple model, I still believe, works very nicely for nearly all known North American societies with high levels of sociopolitical ranking and a clear despotic base. Interestingly, most of them were small political units, rarely exceeding 3,000 people.[3] Those that were much larger were integrated quite differently, by confederacies or other more 'democratic' political forms. The truly dictatorial powers of life and death exercised by the chiefly individuals of the small systems based on resource monopolies were not found in other types of native North American society. Decisions about warfare or the adjudication of disputes in the large political alliances usually depended on the unanimous consent of councils made up of representatives from various social segments and kin groups.[4] Some of the systems organized in this way could be very large indeed, with political hegemonies covering over three-quarters of a million square kilometers and integrating up to 200,000 people. Big contrasts, then, exist in the ethnographic record of North America. One sees, on the one hand, the politically extensive confederacies, with power vested in council organizations rather than individually filled status positions; on the other are the small, classic, internally ranked systems based on productive monopolies over critical subsistence resources.

Now Sahlins adopted a different viewpoint. With rather simplistic Marxist notions in mind, he supposed initially that in emergent complex societies all chiefs must be despotic entrepreneurs exploiting the masses; his now famous fieldwork in Polynesia was designed to prove the point. What he actually found there was something quite different. The chiefs seemed not to be nasty entrepreneurs, but nice guys acting altruistically – in fact, they were somewhat harried individuals forever trying to serve the constituency they represented by making alliances in terms of external trade links. This necessitated the development by Sahlins of a very different notion about the growth of power. He had to argue that chieftainships and potentially powerful statuses came into being largely as a result of *altruistic* behavior, whereby chiefly individuals redistributed goods (or served to organize their distribution) so that all members of the population would have equal access to products that were differentially produced in different parts of the landscape. The model, of course, presupposes the existence of sedentary populations. Sedentism, in turn, combined with environmental diversity was seen as the mechanical basis for productive diversity at the regional level (since individuals in different places will be unable to produce the same things). In the short term, this diversity may put some people at an advantage over others; but if the system is to maintain itself without competition there must be a 'benign altruist' at the top, someone with overriding powers to take the excess production of one area and disperse it in other areas which either produce something else or are naturally less productive.[5]

137

This classic *redistributive model*, then, came into being, in part, because Sahlins discovered he liked the Polynesian chiefs instead of hating them! After his ideas

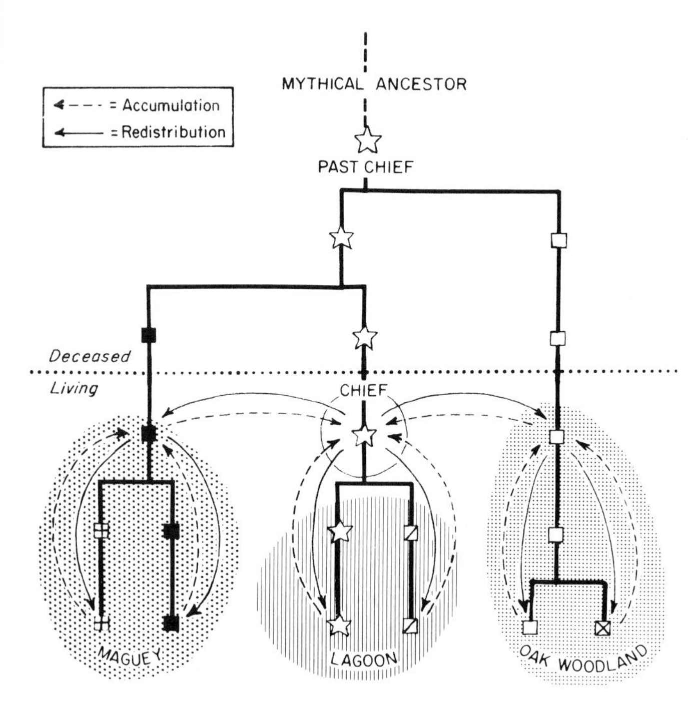

137 Model of redistribution of goods among kinsmen occupying different environmental zones; redistribution results in symbiotic linkage among productively diverse areas. (Reproduced with permission from Flannery and Coe 1968, fig. 4, p. 280.)

had been submitted as a doctoral thesis to Columbia University, critical articles began to appear,[6] in which it was argued that the model was nonsensical in terms of the data Sahlins had himself used. These critics pointed out that on the high islands of the Pacific where environmental diversity is great (an implicit element in the argument) political territories ran from coast to interior rather than parallel to the coast, so that each polity included within its domain the full range of ecological variability present in the region. This being so, it could hardly be argued that the main function of chiefs and the alliances among chiefs was to generate regional symbiosis and to ensure equal access for everybody to all products. The assumptions Sahlins had made about Polynesia, it seemed, were not met at the factual level.

Of course, this did not deter archaeologists in the least and they quickly embraced Sahlins' model wholeheartedly.[7] All over the world, there were identified prehistoric redistributive systems organized by central chiefly agents, nice people who passed out the goods and generally made life secure for their followers.

Meanwhile, a number of anthropologists noted that certain areas of the Pacific (notably Melanesia) offered some interesting ethnographic cases to which one could turn in testing the model. In New Guinea and Borneo, they pointed out, high status persons certainly exist, but *not* in association with redistributive economic systems. According to Sahlins, altruistic redistributive agents devoted themselves to the greater good of the larger community, achieved status by virtue of such selfless behavior, and by virtue of status gained power; so the presence of redistributive systems in conjunction with high status positions is crucial to the argument. Yet this did not seem to be the case in certain areas of Melanesia.

Sahlins' response to such challenges was to play a semantic game; in essence, he defined the problem away. In his ingeniously titled paper 'Poor man, rich man, big-man, chief...',[8] he argued that these New Guinea societies are not truly ranked or power-based redistributive systems and that their hierarchical organization is more apparent than real. His conclusion, in fact, was that they represent another very different sort of system altogether, something called a *big-man system.* Nevertheless, the main interest of Sahlins and most archaeologists has continued to focus on redistributive chiefdoms. Yet I feel that it is to societies organized around big-men that we should look for the origins of social complexity.

A big-man system, in brief, works as follows. As a man becomes mature, he begins to compete with his peers to establish negotiable alliances outside his own group with individuals in other social units distributed across the landscape. What is involved is effectively a form of delayed reciprocal exchange. A would-be big-man makes an alliance by giving his new alliance partner a token or symbol of their agreement – a carved boar's tusk, or a great shell from the coast, or some such object that he has himself obtained via some other alliance. As long as the partner wears or keeps that token, he has some call on the big-man for food or hospitality for himself and members of his group. His followers get security and the big-man gains prestige. Now if the big-man occupies a favored and productive position in the environment and is successful in negotiating alliances with individuals spread widely throughout the region, he may rarely need to use his alliances and 'cash in' his tokens to get food for his group in return. He builds up a great deal of security which he can offer to those who ally themselves with him and live in his village. In big-man systems, the competition is for *persons* and the result is the actual residential gravitation of people to the neighborhoods of big-men. Status, however, accrues to those who can offer others security on account of the number of alliances they have. When the crops do fail, the followers of a big-man are protected in the short run because he can use his alliances to get food to support them; but as soon as he begins to cancel alliances by calling them in, he loses status (which really means the ability to offer security). His followers drift away to other aspiring big-men who seem to offer greater security.

The result of this effective and interesting system is an unending movement of population through the habitat in almost perfect adjustment to changing patterns of differential production. In contrast to Sahlins' hypothetical chiefdom system, where status results in the redistribution of consumer goods, in a big-man system it is not *goods* that move, but *people.* Short-term fluctuations in production are buffered by patterns of status differential, which have the effect of continuously up-dating the distribution of population across the environment in relation to its actual production.

Stable environments, of course, with more or less permanent, ecologically determined production differentials, ought to favor the emergence of high-status individuals who never need to call in their alliances. That, one might suppose, could be the basis for getting some continuity in the differential distribution of status and population in a region – the beginnings, that is, of a complex society with institutionalized power and wealth disparities. This seems not to be so, however. A big-man's alliances, negotiated at the individual level, cannot be passed on to someone else; they are not transferable to his sons, who must negotiate their own. Consequently, when a successful big-man dies, his alliances die with him and his competitors gain in status as a result of his death. So there is an inevitable outflow of population associated with the death of high-status persons. If there exists marked environmental variability in a region, it will probably take little time for a big-man's offspring to negotiate favorable new alliances and attract followers back again. Over time one would see a recurrent pattern of inflow and outflow around centers of secure production and the continuous presence there from one generation to another of high-status individuals. This, I suppose, is a sort of monopoly, but one of a very different kind from monopolies based on point-specific access to critical resources.

How, then, could a system of this kind evolve into a classic complex society based on true power? I have always thought that power really starts when one can renege on a social relationship with impunity. You and I may have an agreement: what's mine is yours and what's yours, mine. If, when life gets rough, I can simply ignore that agreement and not suffer the consequences, then I have taken my first step towards power. This is a rather negative notion of power, which has normally been thought of as *making* rules to suit oneself; in practice, at least from an evolutionary point of view, it seems to me that it has to do with *breaking* rules to suit oneself and getting away with it. Perhaps we should focus our attention rather more on the conditions under which that might occur in the context of big-man types of organization.

It is important, at any rate, to have some idea of the differences between a so-called redistributive system and a big-man system. The former is not something we can readily detect when we look at the world of primitive culture: perhaps it never existed, except in Sahlins' imagination. The institutionalized movement of goods in bulk is, after all, a characteristic of industrial state societies, not primitive ones.[9] On the other hand, systems involving the continuous adjustment of the distribution of consumers (rather than goods) to productive differentials seem from the ethnographic record to be very widespread indeed and we do in fact know quite a lot about them. Might they not have been equally common in the prehistoric past?

Intensification and Specialization

Let us turn to consider another currently popular idea about the origins of complex societies. The argument is a simple one. In certain systems of subsistence production it is possible to increase the input of labor in order to increase the marginal output, or to change and enhance the technology of production in order to improve the effectiveness of the labor input, or in other ways to modify the character of production itself.[10] The effect of such changes is to facilitate production beyond the simple demands of the producers themselves. Once that becomes possible, the way is open to support persons who are not themselves directly engaged in subsistence production – metallurgists, ceramicists, political specialists, etc.[11] Role specialization of this kind, it is claimed, provides the natural basis for the growth of further complexity. In this model, then, understanding complex systems involves focusing on two crucial questions: (1) what kinds of incentives exist for production beyond immediate subsistence needs, and (2) how are such surpluses actually used in the formation of complex societies?

138–40

I find it extremely difficult to deal with this kind of reasoning. I am essentially a Darwinist. I believe that cultural systems change under conditions of natural selection, that they are pushed and pulled in different directions, and that the way in which change occurs is a function of how people actually solve problems. The 'adaptationists' – no matter whether they operate in an idealist paradigm like Bennett,[12] or the materialist mode as does Harris,[13] or are fascinated with the principles of 'least effort'[14] or 'risk reduction'[15] or 'optimal foraging theory'[16] – all attempt to build a teleological explanation for trends seen or imagined in the history of evolution. Yet I think that the most practical principle for us to adopt in theory building is an analog to the principle of inertia.[17] A system will remain stable until acted upon by forces external to its organization as a system. When I am faced with a question such as why complex systems come into being, my first reaction is to ask what problem people were attempting to solve by a new means. Experimenting with novel ways of doing things is surely worthwhile only if some fresh problem has emerged for which no previous solution appears satisfactory.

Thus, the idea that increased production is fundamental to the origins of social complexity leads me to ask what problem is solved by increasing production. What difficulties that a group of people might face give a direct pay-off, in terms of security, to technological change, labor intensification and growth in production? What is driving them to develop these and other new strategies? I don't think the motivation is simply psychological, a sort of prehistoric attempt to keep up with the Jones. Nor are vitalistic explanations acceptable – that a society just 'wants to grow' or is 'ready to become civilized'.

Even the less objectionable forms of vitalism are none the less orthogenetic in that they assume an inner driving principle or 'prime mover'. In the case of approaches such as optimal foraging theory, it is argued that minimizing energy expenditures relative to energy returns will automatically increase 'fitness' and hence be favored selectively. Such assumptions amount to vital principles of internal dynamics which are cited as moulding evolutionary trajectories.[18] The system, I would maintain, must be under stress in some way, must face some problem. The proponents of intensification-specialization arguments have yet to come up with any adequate suggestions about what these stresses and problems might have been. The assumption seems to be that any 'rational' man will seek a profit!

This is just another way of pointing to the fact that almost all our theories about why complex sociopolitical systems emerged are overblown arguments taken largely from differing brands of economic philosophy. We are committing the methodological *faux pas* of offering functional arguments of how modern systems work internally as explanations of how systems change or have changed in the past. While this is a fundamental problem, there exist additional problems, even if one takes a gradualist position and adopts various forms of economic functionalism as a theory. For instance, the appearance of craft specialization is frequently cited as a major step forward on the path to complex systems; yet it is not at all clear to me why craft specialization need necessarily play any significant role. In Africa, for example, metal-working (about which we have much interesting information) is principally practiced by outcasts. Those involved in the specialized production of pottery, such as the technical ceramicists of the Tarascan area of Mexico, are often the disenfranchised and disadvantaged members in society, people who have no land and are cut off from food production. In fact, most instances of specialization with which I am familiar from the ethnographic record of the New World, Asia and Africa suggest that these specialists are individuals

138 *(Left)* Young woman of Miyako, Ryukyu islands, making items of adamba grass for exchange. (Photo taken in June 1953 by E. Santry, on assignment with the author.)

139 *(Right, above)* Navajo woman weaving at *Ah Tso lige*, near Red Lake in Arizona, *c.* November 1935. (Photo courtesy of the Maxwell Museum of Anthropology, University of New Mexico.)

140 *(Right, below)* Potter at work, Naha Okinawa, Ryukyu islands, 1952.

scrambling to gain a foothold in society in any manner they can. This is a situation [141] quite different from the one envisaged by many archaeologists, who see the organization of society itself changing in such a way as to make possible and encourage the support of specialists, almost in a renaissance fashion. These sorts of observations from the developing Third World may, or may not, be relevant [142] to the problem; but I have yet to be convinced that archaeologists understand how to set about modelling the conditions under which craft and other specialists became causally important in the development of cultural complexity.

I have always thought that a major shift in social forms, such as those represented by the appearance of ranking and stratification, must represent some kind of major break with earlier patterns of growth.[19] For instance, among hunter-gatherer groups the growth pattern involves duplication of the basic unit of co-operative production – the band or the family, depending on how the group was [143]

organized. Population growth produces an increase in the size of the local unit, until such a group splits into two or more similar units, with the daughter units taking up independent activities in independent locations. Even among horti- 144 culturalists, where the basic units of production are frequently family or extended family units, growth appears to consist of the duplication of these basic units. More families are formed and more 'spaces' are sought for these families to act as units of production. It is this general structure of growth which results in packing problems (as indicated in Chapter 8); and the consequences of this pattern of growth are the selective contexts favoring various tactics of intensification. It seems to me that at some point in the trajectory of intensification a major structural break with earlier forms of growth appears. These basic units of production and generalized reciprocity (in Sahlins' terms), instead of duplicating themselves, 145 begin to develop conventions for *excluding* individuals: that is, persons are excluded from them so that the unit remains basically the same in size and also remains located in space in a stable manner. Population growth under such conditions results in an increasing class of disenfranchised persons which changes appreciably the arena of competition and the units of competition.[20]

141 A peddler in the market at Naha Okinawa (Ryukyu islands). By hawking his wares for a small cash profit, this man ekes out a marginal and very uncertain existence.

142 *A market street in Hong Kong, 1952.* 'Our course lay through the long street, which was a fair specimen of Chinese streets . . . Here were to be seen the artisans of the various branches of native industry pursuing their busy work, and vending the products of their labor, in one and the same room which served the triple object of workshop, warehouse and counter. Here were crowded together, in their narrow dwellings, amid the din of forges and hammer, little groups of wire-drawers, braziers, button-makers, and smiths, with four men alternating their rapid blows on the sounding anvil. Here again were to be seen image-makers, carpenters, shoe-makers, tailors, gold and silver leaf-beaters, umbrella-makers, cotton-beaters, grocers, druggists, jade-stone cutters, seal-engravers, and decorators, with the professors of the numerous arts which supply the necessities or luxuries of Chinese life. Further on were to be seen picture-shops hung out with the tawdry performances of native artists. . . . At every corner were to be seen portable kitchens, steaming away, and supplying to hungry expectants the savory materials of a hasty meal. For the more wealthy a succession of cook-shops, wine-shops, and tea-shops lined the way. A little farther on, a crowd of gamblers disputed a few square feet of ground with the holders of orange-stands or venders of sweetmeats. Near to these were the well stored shops of pawn-brokers . . .' (Smith 1847, p. 289).

Some of my colleagues and students have worked in recent years with hunter-gatherer groups in Botswana, who, for various reasons, are becoming sedentary and self-sufficient as agriculturalists or herders. There is a spectrum from hunting and gathering to fully sedentary adaptations, but it is the people in the middle – those who are neither one thing nor the other – who are the most interesting in the present context. They are in a quandary. In hunter-gatherer societies, generalized reciprocity is the guiding ethic of behavior: that is, people share freely with their relatives without expecting an exact or immediate return from them. Yet, if a man is to maintain a herd of goats and build up his property as he becomes increasingly sedentary, he must refuse his relatives when they come to him to ask

143 *(Above) A complete band of hunter-gatherers:* the Nharo Bushmen living between Sanfontein and /Gam, Namibia. Such a group can be considered the unit of production; growth results in the multiplication of roughly identical units. (Photo taken *c.* 1927 by L. Fourie, courtesy of the Africana Museum, Johannesburg.)

144 *(Left)* The extended family of Tanahara Gensho in the village of Fatima, Okinawa (Ryukyu islands), 1952.

145 A scene in the squatter community of El Porvenir, Panama City, Panama in 1967. Individuals migrate to such communities from more stable social units elsewhere; growth results in increased numbers of persons cut off from the social units into which they were born. (Photo courtesy of W. Salvador.)

for a goat for supper. Anthropologists find that the only successful individuals are the ones who sever their social ties, the ones who can stand up to the social pressures for them to share their wealth and not be stingy. In order to capitalize on their own production, they must be mavericks in their own society. But once isolated in this way, they have a kind of freedom to manoeuver which is impossible for those still playing by society's rules; once they have turned their backs on generalized reciprocity, their security comes from their wits, not from the relatives they have now rejected. In fact, they quickly become entrepreneurs and begin to negotiate in a variety of ways with people *outside* the system. They are always the first ones who want to make deals with the anthropologists when they arrive, or with the government agents who want to drill wells. In other words, their security is something that must now be organized by means external to the system of which they were originally a part.

Gew-Gaws and Trade-Goods

Does trade and exchange really *cause* social and political development, as archaeologists have so often suggested?[21] Perhaps returning the discussion briefly to the big-man systems described earlier might help put this question in some perspective.

Nearly everyone must have seen photographs in the pages of magazines like *National Geographic* of big-men in the New Guinea Highlands. They are weighed down with shell beads, pendants, paint, feathers and every conceivable sort of 146

146 New Guinea Big Men displaying the gew-gaws for which they have exchanged and which represent their high status in the local group. (Photo courtesy of M. Strathern.)

gew-gaw: they look rather like some garishly decorated Christmas tree. The material items they wear are tokens of social relationships and they circulate exclusively in terms of those negotiated alliances between individuals to which I have already referred. They are not trade-goods, but symbols. They are not exchanged for their intrinsic value, but are worn because they carry information about the number and variety of alliances an individual has made. Objects and raw materials that are easily obtained and occur widely throughout a region obviously do not convey much information. So in all big-man systems there is a real push to gain access to exotic items – shells from the coast, different kinds of colorful feathers, various kinds of raw materials that are available only at very particular places. The more rare and specific they are, the more information they can carry.

We seem to see something similar in the archaeological record of eastern North America. A developmental sequence beginning *c.* 6000 BC culminated during the

147

147 Goods included in two separate burials (top, burial 79; bottom, burial 57) from the Rankin Site, Cocke County, Tennessee (see Smith and Hodges 1968); over half the items illustrated are exotic to the site's region. (Photo courtesy of the Department of Anthropology, University of Tennessee.)

period *c.* 250 BC–AD 250 in a system of exchange involving the circulation of an astonishing variety of goods on a truly continental scale. *Busycon* shells from the Gulf Coast are commonly found 1,500 kilometers from their source and in large numbers in burials throughout the Great Lakes region. There is native copper from the north side of Lake Superior in the village sites and burials throughout the Midwest.[22] Mica from mines in Virginia found its way all the way up and down the Mississippi valley. Galena from lead mines in northern Illinois occurs in burials in the Southeast, North and South Carolina to Florida.[23] Little buttons and other trinkets made of meteoric iron from the margins of the Plains turn up at sites all over the Midwest.[24] Obsidian from Yellowstone National Park in the Rocky Mountains is found from Wisconsin to Ohio.[25] This is an enormous and complex system for the circulation of material goods, a system whose geographical scale is commensurate with all of western and central Europe put together.

If trade does indeed stimulate political complexity, then – to judge from the scale and volume of the documented circulation network – we should expect the development of something akin to Rome in areas such as Ohio already by 100 BC! Yet exchange systems as extensive as this are quite unknown in those areas of the world in which the so-called 'great civilizations' developed: there is nothing comparable in the Near East, in the Aegean, in the Valley of Mexico or in Highland Peru, before the emergence of what are generally accepted as complex societies.[26] So *any* model that attempts to explain the rise of complex society by appealing to the importance of trade and monopolistic exchange modes must also be capable of accounting for the evidence from eastern North America. None can so far do so, yet exchange models are currently being applied to the archaeological record in many areas of the world.

Consider, for example, the American Southwest where some remarkable, large sites developed during the period *c.* AD 900–1200. They are not just residential locations: there is a great variety of complex architecture (kivas, great rooms, etc.) associated with social and religious ritual. The most prevalent explanation for these pueblo systems attributes their complexity to the important functions they must have served as nodal points in wide-ranging exchange networks.[27] But the hard evidence on which this view is based proves to be remarkably slight – a little turquoise from the Southwest trickles down into Mexico; a few shells from the Baja coast eventually work their way up into northern New Mexico; Mexican motifs on Southwestern pots indirectly reflect connections of some sort. This hardly amounts to a great trade network, yet network-node models of this kind are currently rife in the Southwest and beyond. Ultimately, they rest on Sahlins' original argument that redistribution is the route to power. Such complex achievements as these big pueblo sites could only have originated and been organized – or so the argument goes – under the guidance of some central authority.[28] A central authority could only come into being by virtue of the redistributive roles it played. And what was being redistributed? Not much more than a few lumps of turquoise per century . . . in total probably fewer exotic materials than occur in a single Middle Woodland burial a millennium earlier!

Paths to Complexity

What I am saying, in effect, is that archaeologists still do not know what causes complex societies, what brings them into being. The argument for redistribution has no obvious factual basis: at least, I know of no redistributive agents who are not operating in what are already societies based on political power and I doubt that power comes from being nice. Arguments involving economic incentives for the intensification of production required to support a complex system have a certain chicken-and-egg flavor. It is far from clear, in any case, why anyone should 'want' a complex system to the extent of investing effort in over-production; there must exist some pressures for change in the Darwinian sense. However, we have yet to identify what they are and how they operate. Arguments in which trade is claimed as the necessary basis for power generally founder, because most of the instances cited as evidence relate to the exchange of social tokens rather than economically valued consumer goods: they tell us about social alliances between individuals, not about the economic articulation of social groups.

The problem here is the very limited number of models that archaeologists have considered. If all we have is the ideas I have touched on, when in fact there might well be many different stages and characteristic patterns of change associated with different paths to complexity, then archaeology is in great trouble. Until archaeologists have some idea of the range of variability that can exist in complex systems and in their developmental trajectories, they are at an enormous disadvantage.

Another major limitation is that almost all the approaches to modelling change were developed from varying perceptions of functional dynamics (that is, the operation of living systems as seen by an observer or participant). As suggested earlier, functional insights have been used to model transformational changes when (1) the nature of the transformation was not accurately known, and (2) there was nothing but the criterion of plausibility used to justify the use of a functional argument as relevant to evolutionary processes. Perhaps the most obvious and probably the most misleading instance is the use of various 'profit-seeking', vitalistic economic arguments in modelling evolutionary processes. All ecological processes are non-rational in that there is no guiding intellect or sentient being controlling the dynamics, as all economic arguments generally assume.

As in the cases discussed in previous chapters, I am appealing for the development of reliable methods of inferring past conditions from the archaeological record. If we can develop such methods, then we may gain a secure knowledge of at least some of the characteristics answering the question 'What was it like?' At the same time, we must be alert to recognize patterning for which we may seek to understand 'What does it mean?' Both these approaches need and are dependent upon the development of middle-range research.

The reader may well enquire about the numerous philosophical positions in archaeology for which there are skilled advocates all about us.[29] I have suggested that most such positions involve giving meaning to the archaeological record by the use of '*post hoc* accommodative arguments'.[30] No objectivity is achievable with such approaches nor is real learning possible, but merely the fascination of endless debate.[31] Only when we can evaluate such views by appeal to the properties of the external world can we obtain some idea of the utility of differing intellectual positions. Those appeals must be through a scientifically built observational language, whereby meaning is given to observations and justified independently of the intellectual positions said to be under evaluation.

No matter how we approach the problem, the conclusion is the same: we require stronger methods for inference. We cannot just follow the Muse of Curiosity and speculate about how things happened. We must develop methods for evaluating ideas we have generated and also face the real possibility that sometimes we may be asking a bad question. We need simultaneously to investigate the questions 'What does it mean?' and 'What was it like?', if we ever hope to make progress with the really big question: 'Why did it happen?'

Notes on the Text

Preface (pp. 13-18)

1 This trip was both initiated and made possible through the efforts of Colin Renfrew. Colin invited me to come and was unfailing during the period of our joint search for funds which would make the trip possible. In the long run it was Colin who found the money and extended to me unending challenge, courtesy and warmth. I am most grateful to him.
2 Binford 1977a.
3 Fritz and Plog 1970.
4 Watson *et al.* 1971.
5 This is well illustrated by the contents of Brothwell and Higgs 1969.
6 Binford 1978a.
7 Binford 1981a.
8 E.g. attempts to reconstruct the age and sex structure of the parent herd on the basis of bones found in residential sites, or to reconstruct the number of living animals represented by bones on sites whose function is unknown.
9 See Binford 1981a, pp. 69–72, 478–9 for criticisms of the use of MNI (i.e. minimum number of individuals) estimates.
10 E.g. the development of radiocarbon dating.
11 Hawkes 1954.
12 See O'Kelly 1968, 1982; Van Wijngaarden-Bakker 1974.
13 A good example of the type of argument used by the 'social philosophers' can be found in Adams 1981. Particular attention should be given to the comments and author's rebuttal.
14 There is a considerable amount of confusion among archaeologists as to both how a science grows and what constitutes 'progress'. Many basically accept the thesis of Kuhn 1962, 1970 that progress is largely the result of the operation of irrational forces which tend to condition the world views of scientists. (Trigger 1981 represents an attempt to use this belief to interpret the history of archaeological thought.) This irrationalist position has been further elaborated and argued by many: e.g. Feyerabend 1978. *The present book and essentially everything I have ever written represent a quite different view of what science is and how it works.*

I have always been strongly committed to the position that the development of robust methods for inference are basic to the development of modern science. It should therefore be no surprise to anyone that I should not be upset by the recent claims of Meltzer 1979 that no Kuhnian paradigm shift has occurred in archaeology and that my own contributions have been mainly methodological rather than theoretical. The call for revolutionary changes in paradigms is all right, I suppose, but the field is already rich in diverse points of view and yet no progress occurs. On the contrary, these intellectual fads rise and fall much like the hemlines of women's fashions. Only with the development of scientific epistemologies and the accompanying methods for achieving relative objectivity when evaluating novel ideas will knowledge begin to be accumulated as the product of scientific endeavour.
15 Binford 1981a.
16 Hodder 1982, pp. 191–2.
17 Binford in press.

Chapter 1 (pp. 19-30)

1 E.g. Hawkes 1980.
2 See Binford 1968c.
3 For a description of radiocarbon dating techniques see Michels 1973; Fleming 1976.
4 E.g. Gould 1980; Hayden 1979.
5 E.g. Yellen 1977.
6 Rathje 1974, 1978; Rathje and McCarthy 1977.
7 Binford 1976, 1978a, 1978b, 1979, 1980, 1981c, 1982.
8 Binford and Bertram 1977.
9 For additional examples of 'ethnoarchaeological' research, see Gould (ed.) 1978; Kramer (ed.) 1979.
10 Coles 1973, 1979.

11 Winter and Bankhoff 1979.
12 E.g. Witthoft 1957; results of recent replication experiments for stone tools can be found in the newsletter *Flintknapper's Exchange.*
13 See South 1977a, 1977b for an explicit use of historic site archaeology as a form of control over archaeological methodology.
14 Isaac 1978.
15 Leakey and Hay 1979.

Part I (Introduction) (pp. 31-2)

1 Taylor 1948.
2 Taylor 1972.
3 Taylor 1948, p. 131.
4 *Ibid.*, p. 193.
5 Binford 1981b; Dunnell 1980b.
6 Taylor 1948, p. 193.
7 I have recently discussed methods for inference in Binford 1981a, particularly pp. 21–34.

Chapter 2 (pp. 33–59)

1 See Dart 1959; LeGros Clark 1967, pp. 1–40.
2 Dart 1925, 1948. Dart's reasoning was based on the best evidence available to him at the time; it seemed to indicate that bones from Makapan Limeworks had been burned. When fossils of *Australopithecus* were found at Makapansgat, Dart put the observations together and concluded that *Australopithecus* was a fire-user and hence a true man. For a good review of subsequent research see Oakley 1954, 1961.
3 Dart 1926. From the earliest days of the discoveries at Taung, Dart argued that *Australopithecus* was a hunter and thus the agent responsible for the accumulation of associated bones which he viewed as middens. Central to these early ideas were depressed fractures noted on the skulls of baboons. The initial statement that animal bones recovered from the deposits yielding fossils of *Australopithecus* were tools is found in Dart 1949. Dart 1957, 1960 further developed his argument for the tool-making and using habits of *Australopithecus.* For a more recent view see Wolberg 1970; Binford 1981a.
4 Dart 1953.
5 Dart 1957, p. 85.
6 Dart 1926, 1949, 1957, 1960.
7 Ardrey 1961.
8 Lorenz 1966.
9 Washburn 1957.
10 Hughes 1954.
11 Dart 1956 includes a discussion of classical descriptions of hyena behavior.
12 Dart 1958.
13 Vincent 1978.
14 Leakey 1979.
15 This interpretation was widely reported in the press at the time but I have failed to uncover the actual statement made at the press conference.
16 Washburn and Howell 1960, p. 40.
17 Leakey 1959a, 1959b, 1960.
18 Leakey 1971, particularly pp. 49–58 and fig. 24.
19 Isaac 1971, 1975, 1976b, 1976c, 1978. A more focused statement on meat eating can be found in Isaac and Crader 1981.
20 Isaac 1976a, pp. 483–5.
21 Brain 1981 is the major summary of his work and should be consulted by anyone interested in the issues discussed here.
22 See Washburn 1957; Bartholomew and Birdsell 1953. The early interpretations by Dart and others were influenced by the fauna associated at the Taung site where only small animals such as rock rabbit, birds' eggs, small rodents, baboons and hominids were present. These data were not thought to be indicative of the actions of hyenas or other large carnivores. For instance Robert Broom (1933, p. 137) wrote:

'From the study of the bone breccia associated with the Taung skull we get some idea of the habits of *Australopithecus* . . . I agree with Dart in regarding it as the kitchen midden of *Australopithecus* . . . The breccia is mainly composed of bones of an extinct dassie or rock rabbit. All the skulls are broken, often into small fragments. It could be no large carnivore like a leopard or jackal that fed on these dassies. Such would have chewed up the skulls and swallowed them . . . Then we have many baboon skulls all broken as if by some creature that wanted to get at the brain . . .'

This view of early man was gradually accepted and dominated the literature until the early 1950s. Sites were thought to be middens from *Australopithecus* who was a minor predator taking small game, birds' eggs, etc. See for instance Oakley 1953. Once Dart began finding a very different fauna, one dominated by antelope, at Makapansgat, he began to argue for a much more active hunting way of life for early man. Those who had accepted the arguments based on the Taung data saw the new data as inconsistent and Dart's interpretations as extreme. Similarly, those who were simply repulsed by the notion of our ancestors as bloodthirsty killers reacted against the interpretations of the Makapansgat material; since more robust fauna was present, arguments favoring large carnivores as the agents of accumulation now seemed realistic.

23 Brain 1968.
24 Dart 1959, p. 121.
25 Brain 1981, figs. 50, 221.
26 Brain 1967.
27 Binford and Bertram 1977.
28 Binford 1978a.
29 Binford 1981a.
30 Hill 1972.
31 Klein 1975.

Chapter 3 (pp. 60-76)

1 Brain 1981, pp. 271–3. This remark applies particularly to the robust forms of *Australopithecus*.
2 See Bunn *et al.* 1980.
3 In Binford 1981a, pp. 83–9, 181–90, 244–6 and 283–99, I have discussed the role of '*post hoc* arguments' in some detail.
4 Isaac 1971, p. 278.
5 Isaac and Crader 1981.
6 *Ibid.*, p. 83.
7 During the months of July and August 1981, I was given the opportunity to visit many sites and areas in South Africa and neighboring regions by virtue of a grant from the University of Cape Town, where I also lectured to a dedicated group of students.
8 For a good example of what I have in mind see Schaller 1972, pls. 1 and 2.
9 Dating of the site is based on an estimate by Vrba 1975.
10 For discussion of the site of Elandsfontein see the following: Singer and Wymer 1968; Klein 1978; Deacon 1975.
11 Although all Acheulian sites are not densely covered by artifacts, there are enough to render this impression interesting; for instance a classic example is Horizon B and the main site (DE/89) at Olorgesailie. See Isaac 1977.
12 While I would argue with the specific interpretations presented in a recent paper by Munday 1976 and discussion by Marks and Freidel 1977, their work illustrates the value of studying the relationships between raw material sources, the forms in which materials are introduced to a site, and the disposition of both lithic waste and tools produced from raw materials. In the case of the Mousterian sites located by springs in the Negev, Israel, it was shown that the size of the cores and flakes were smaller when the lithic raw materials did not outcrop in the vicinity. The investigators interpreted this as a reflection of economizing behavior on the part of the makers of the Mousterian tools. It is my guess, however, that instead we are seeing the consequences of the behavior of occupants who arrived at a site unequipped with an adequate tool kit (an essentially 'non-curated' technology). They then searched around the site for raw materials and finding artifacts which had been introduced by previous occupants, they reduced them into tools. Such a condition would account for the observed patterning and would not require the unlikely proposed inference that the Mousterian population lived in sedentary settlements at which raw materials, introduced to the site from elsewhere, were utilized in an economical manner.

Regardless of this controversial point, tools and introduced debris rarely survive as pristine items on sites which have been occupied over substantial periods of time. In marked contrast, the mean length of cores on Acheulian sites tends to increase as a function of the degree to which the assemblage is dominated by bifaces. (This observation applies, for instance, to the materials from Olorgesailie.) These items had to be transported and disposed of in their context of use, which had to be one in which they were not reduced to flakes and flake tools but were used as bifaces. It is hard to imagine a base camp being an end point of tool use or occupants of such base camps ignoring immediately available raw materials in the form of previously introduced bifaces.
13 I am fully aware that there are sites with different assemblage composition than that depicted in my imaginary scenario; I am simply using this 'reconstruction' to illustrate that we do not understand the formation processes. It is not unlikely that some of the assemblage variability in the Acheulian may well reflect distinctly different kinds of locations used by the early hominids; home bases might even have been present.

14 I have been conducting some investigations into the characteristics of faunal assemblages viewed from the perspective both of anatomical part frequencies and of patterns of cutting and chop marks and combinations of such marks with the tooth scoring and pitting produced by gnawing carnivores. While this research is incomplete, it seems quite likely that scavenging was the major source of parts from relatively large-bodied animals found at Middle Stone Age sites of Klasies River in South Africa. Similar behavior may be represented by the remains of aurochs and horses in the Mousterian sites of western Europe. I will report on this research in the near future.
15 When questioned on the direct evidence for hunting in the Lower Pleistocene, most researchers mention a number of sites where stone tools are associated with a single carcass of a large animal (elephant at Olduvai FLK N6, hippopotamus at Koobi Fora, and Deinotherium at Olduvai FLK NII) or where tools are associated with a large number of carcasses of animals of a single species. While the former situation is frequently acknowledged as possibly representing the scavenging of food from the death site of a large animal, the latter is often presented as evidence of early man's hunting skills, suggesting that he drove the animals to their death or that he was at least instrumental in obtaining large quantities of a single species. See e.g. Isaac 1977; Shipman *et al.* 1981. For contrary views, see Binford 1977b; Binford and Todd 1982.
16 For a description of the research situation see Leakey 1981, pp. 76–88.
17 See Binford 1981a, pp. 83–6 and 246–7 for a discussion of such methods of inference.
18 Keeley and Toth 1981.
19 Binford 1977a, p. 7.

Part II (Introduction) (pp. 77-8)

1 Popper 1972, p. 198.
2 Sonneville-Bordes 1975a, p. 35 (translation from the original French).
3 Popper 1972, p. 30.
4 Black, in Popper 1959, p. 82.

Chapter 4 (pp. 79-94)

1 The evidence for the use of pigments is the presence of worked or abraded fragments of red ochre and of manganese. Although the abrasions are interpreted as deriving from use of these fragments as crayons for drawing, thus far no colored artifacts have been recovered from Mousterian deposits.
2 Evidence for the burial of the dead in the Mousterian period has been summarized by S. Binford 1968 and Harrold 1980.
3 For a critical discussion of Neanderthal cave bear ritual see Binford 1981a; Kurten 1976.
4 Klindt-Jensen 1975.
5 Myres, 1906, p. 29.
6 *Ibid.*, pl. III.
7 Quennell and Quennell 1922, pp. 102–5.
8 Weiner 1980.
9 Osborn 1927, p. 73.
10 Bordes 1969, pp. 2–3.
11 Clarke 1979, p. 17.
12 Mason 1883, p. 403.
13 Nelson 1938, p. 148.
14 For a good example of views in the early years of the 20th century see Osborn 1916.
15 For discussions of the 'artifact and assemblage period' from slightly different perspectives see Binford 1981a, 1982.
16 Childe 1929, p. vi.
17 For another discussion of the situation in archaeology just prior to 1930 see Trigger 1980, particularly Chapter II.
18 E.g. Breuil 1931, 1932a, 1932b.
19 Garrod 1938, p. 1.
20 Breuil and Lantier 1965, p. 115.
21 Burkitt 1963, pp. 129–30.
22 For examples of a relatively recent treatment of these views see Hoebel 1949; Movius 1956; Herskovits 1955; there are, of course, many additional examples.
23 Peyrony 1930, 1933, 1936.
24 Movius 1953. For a more recent discussion see Laville *et al.* 1980.
25 See Bordes 1950, 1953b, 1961a. Also compare Sonneville-Bordes 1975b.
26 Bordes 1953a.
27 Bordes 1972.
28 For a description see Sonneville-Bordes 1975b.
29 *Ibid.*
30 Peyrony 1930.
31 Bordes 1972.
32 The early formulations of parallel phyla were beginning to be questioned by the late 1940s and early 1950s: e.g. Braidwood 1946; Movius 1948.
33 Modified versions of Breuil's views continue to dominate some research even today. See Collins 1969; Ohel 1979.

34 Sackett 1981, p. 90.
35 Wissler 1914, 1923; Klimek 1955; Kroeber 1939; Milke 1949; Hodder 1977.
36 Bordes 1972, pp. 148–9.
37 Wissler 1914, pp. 468–9.
38 For the basic literature on the debate regarding the 'functional argument' see Binford and Binford 1966, 1969; Binford 1972a, 1973. The opposing point of view is represented by Bordes 1961b; Sonneville-Bordes 1966; Collins 1969, 1970; Bordes and Sonneville-Bordes 1970; Mellars 1970; Bordes *et al.* 1972.

Chapter 5 (pp. 95-108)

1 A major breakthrough with regard to the search for stratigraphy was made by Coe 1964.
2 Taylor 1948.
3 See particularly Willey 1953.
4 See Brown (ed.) 1971.
5 At the time that I began searching the literature, the two most important publications known to me treating the manufacture of stone tools were Pond 1930 and Witthoft 1957; in addition, a provocative study had appeared in Witthoft 1952.
6 Some of my early investigations into lithic analysis include Binford 1963; Binford and Papworth 1963; Binford and Quimby 1963.
7 Binford and Papworth 1963.
8 Binford 1964b.
9 See Binford 1968a.
10 See Binford and Binford 1966.
11 For a short history of the early work with multivariate statistical techniques see Binford and Binford 1966, p. 293, fn. 1.
12 My former wife, Sally Binford, and I received a research grant from the National Science Foundation. We were assisted in France by Georges Bordes, Gerald Eck, Nicholas Gessler, Cathy Read-Martin, Dwight Read, Michèle Lenoir, and Polly Wiessner. The team was also continuously aided and encouraged by François Bordes, Jean Phillippe Rigaud and the staff of Bordes' laboratory.
13 At the time I assumed, as did most researchers, that these were 'living floors' with near-perfect integrity and with high resolution. Today such assumptions seem very naive.
14 Research among the Nunamiut Eskimo was supported by the Wenner-Gren Foundation for Anthropological Research and by the National Science Foundation. Works stemming directly from the Nunamiut research include the following: Binford 1976, 1978a, 1978b, 1979, 1980, 1981a, 1981b, 1981c, 1982.
15 Both travel to and fieldwork in Australia was supported by the Institute of Aboriginal Studies, Canberra.
16 E.g. Binford 1981b.
17 Binford 1967; see also Binford 1968b.
18 A similar point was made in Binford 1969.

Chapter 6 (pp. 109-43)

1 Silberbauer 1972.
2 The approach was developed for more sedentary systems by Flannery, 1972.
3 See MacNeish 1958, p. 137 or for a more expanded version MacNeish, Peterson, and Neely 1972, especially p. 355.
4 For a more complete description of this argument see Binford 1981c.
5 Binford 1978a, pp. 306–12.
6 See Downs 1966.
7 For a further description of the Anavik Springs site see Binford, 1978a, pp. 171–8.
8 *Ibid.*, pp. 235–45.
9 I refer here to features interpreted by P. P. Yefimenko as *zemlyanka* or 'sleeping pits'. Examples include 'dwelling number 1' in the upper level of Kostienki I and 'pit U' at Avdejevo, an unpublished site. For descriptions of Kostienki and other major Russian Palaeolithic sites, see Klein 1973. My information about these specific features is based on personal communication with Professor Grigoryev at the University of Leningrad.
10 Klein 1973, p. 70, fig. 8.
11 Similar features have been described among the Kalahari San Bushmen by Crowell and Hitchcock 1978, pp. 37–51.
12 Binford 1978b, pp. 330–61.
13 Yellen 1977, pp. 113–30.
14 *Ibid.*, particularly pp. 125–31.
15 Williams 1968, 1969.
16 Patricia Draper, personal communication.
17 Binford 1982.
18 It should be pointed out that the basis of the Mousterian debate was the nature of stone tool assemblages. I have not mentioned stone tools in discussing land use, because the Nunamiut Eskimo I observed were no longer

using stone artifacts; however, there is little chance that the kinds of lithic artifacts used by the Eskimo would have been comparable to those of the Mousterian. Once again I must stress that I do not consider the Nunamiut as providing an analogy for Palaeolithic groups.
19 Binford 1978a.

Chapter 7 (pp. 144-92)

1 Binford 1978b.
2 Binford 1978a, particularly pp. 265–320.
3 *Ibid.*, pp. 321–7.
4 Whitehead 1953, pp. 158–9.
5 Wagner 1960, p. 91.
6 Leroi-Gourhan and Brézillon 1966, pp. 361–4.
7 Van Noten 1978.
8 Schiffer 1972; Schiffer and Rathje 1973.
9 Binford and Binford 1966.
10 A major confusion exists in the recent archaeological literature with regard to some of these ideas. From the days at the University of Chicago when I and my students explored the concepts of activity areas and tool kits, we clearly recognized the dual problem of developing techniques for identifying patterning in the archaeological record and for interpreting the results of such pattern recognition studies. Robert Whallon took up the challenge and investigated techniques and approaches which might be useful in this respect; he demonstrated clearly that he appreciated the difference between an archaeological pattern and the meanings which might be attached to it:
(1) '. . . at least *some* human activities will be spatially separated within *most* places of occupation and . . . the areal differentiation of activities will result in the differential distribution of tool types over an occupation area as a consequence of their different uses in the various activities carried out at the site.' (Whallon 1973a, p. 116.)
(2) '. . . our arguments do not necessitate the constant spatial separation of all activities into mutually exclusive areas, only that some activities must, at least some of the time, be spatially distinct.' (*Ibid.*: p. 117.)
(3) 'Spatial clusters of tools do not necessarily have to represent items left in a place of use . . . but are the results, nonetheless, of regular human behavior associated with the embeddedness of the technology in, or its articulation with, the rest of a total cultural system. They should therefore be perfectly susceptible of explanation by the prehistorian within the proper frame of reference.' (*Ibid.*: p. 119.)
Whallon followed these basic statements with a discussion of the techniques known to him for recognizing patterning in spatial distributions. He has continued to refine old techniques for detecting patterning and to develop new ones. See Whallon 1973b, 1974 and the additional work along these lines by Newell and Dekin 1978.

Against this background, it is difficult to comprehend how the kind of criticism which Schiffer (1974) levelled against Whallon could be justified. Perhaps the strangest misstatement of Whallon's work has been made by Yellen (1977, especially p. 134), who suggests that we assumed that every activity must occur in independent spatial locations and that tools found in association therefore refer to a single activity. These kinds of arguments simply betray a total misunderstanding of the issues and the history of the development of archaeological methods.
11 My work in Australia was conducted as a guest of James O'Connell while he worked with the Alyawara. Financial support was extended by the Australian Aboriginal Institute, Canberra.
12 Leroi-Gourhan and Brézillon 1966, 1972.
13 Leroi-Gourhan and Brézillon 1966, fig. 58.
14 Gould 1977, fig. 22.
15 Velder 1963, fig. 2.
16 Movius 1975, 1977.
17 Pat Draper, personal communication.
18 Binford 1978a, pp. 142–5.
19 *Ibid.*, pp. 435–57.
20 The pattern of alternating beds and hearths noted earlier applies only to unsheltered sleeping areas or for structures and rock shelters, whose primary function is to provide protection from rain and sun. When structures are used to retain heat, group sleeping arrangements are more common. Furthermore, the alternating beds and hearths are not employed because the fuel, which is used to heat the entire shelter rather than just the areas directly adjacent to the fire, is conserved.
21 In an Eskimo context, the manufacture of boats, sleds, or house frames and the sewing of tents are examples of large-scale manufacturing tasks which are generally done in

areas specially set aside for the purpose. See Binford 1978a, p. 348, fig. 7.5 for a photograph of a kayak which was manufactured in its own activity area outside, but next to, the house.

22 Yellen 1977, p. 92.

23 Among the Eskimo it was observed that older men tended to be more regularly engaged in craft activities than other people. They would frequently congregate in the house of an elderly couple with no children or with married offspring living elsewhere. Such childless houses sometimes functioned in the same way, in terms of craft activities, as men's houses. There the men could lay out their work and leave it in areas peripheral to the domestic space of the woman of the house, where it would be unmolested.

24 See Binford 1978a, p. 462, fig. 9.1 for a photograph of debris being burned on a butchering/processing site.

25 Schiffer (1972, 1976) has proposed the conceptual distinction between *primary* and *secondary* refuse and has stressed the need for archaeologists to distinguish between these two types of deposit. While I accept that Schiffer's intention was based on a valid premise and was constructive, the distinction is not adequate, at least given my understanding of formation processes.

26 Schiffer 1972.

27 Binford 1978a, pp. 145–7 gives a description of an Eskimo meal in a winter house.

28 Schiffer 1976, p. 57 provides some formal criteria for the recognition of secondary refuse: 'Secondary refuse consists of worn-out and broken materials and usually occurs in deposits of high material density and diversity.' Compare this statement with the descriptions by Yellen 1977, p. 109 of *primary refuse* seen in his *nuclear areas*!

29 Yellen 1977, pp. 81–3. It should be pointed out that, while Yellen has made valuable observations, his attribution of 'rigid' site typologies to Whallon and myself is completely erroneous. Cf. note 10 above.

30 Binford 1980, pp. 4–20.

31 The dispute about *functional variation* linked to the Mousterian controversy does not concern tool use, as many have tried to argue: e.g. Collins 1969; Tringham 1978, p. 174; Cahen *et al.* 1979. I reasoned that forms of variability in the organization of human-hominid systems of adaptation, as well as the factors which conditioned them, were important, whereas traditional archaeology had denied that such variability existed. Because of this denial it is therefore not surprising that investigations of the type discussed here have not previously been conducted. Many modern investigators have misinterpreted my point completely: they have assumed I was arguing that there was a necessary relationship between particular tool designs and the anticipated use of the tool (i.e. that considerations of tool use determined the design of the tool). I certainly never made such a statement, nor did I imply one. I did, however, suggest that tools with different designs could be expected to play different roles within the technology. Thus the study of variation in frequency from place to place among identical morphological classes with differing sets of designs should tell us something about organizational variability within a cultural system. Just as there is no necessary determinant relationship between use and design, similarly, there is no such relationship between use and organization (although there are certainly mutual interactions in both cases). Knowing the use of an item will not allow one to infer the organized patterns for the maintenance of the technology through time (i.e. curation), nor the patterned modes of disposal, including the investment of effort in maintaining places where the technology was used. The latter must be considered in conjunction with the reconstruction of the particular actions conducted by tool-using actors, before any realistic understanding of patterned associations actually observed in the archaeological record can be understood in accurate and historically meaningful ways. In short, there is much more to the functional argument than merely questions of tool use.

Part III (Introduction) (pp. 193-4)

1 This weakness has been recognized by others (e.g. Lamberg-Karlovsky 1975 – with whose suggested solutions to the problem, however, I do not agree). For the bizarre idea that one can deduce 'test implications' for a procedure which seeks to give meaning to archaeological observations by referring to archaeological observations, see Binford 1977a.

2 Binford 1981a, especially pp. 21–30.

3 I do not mean to imply that this approach is restricted to the study of complex societies: there are many examples from the literature dealing with much earlier time ranges (e.g. Isaac and Isaac 1975). Leakey and Lewin 1978, for instance, argued (by analogy with the !Kung San) that gathering was very important for early man and that the carrying bag was therefore one of the most important early tools; shortly after reading that, I saw a television interview with Pat Shipman (John Hopkins University), in which she explained that the reason there were so many cut marks found on ungulate metapodials from early African sites was that the hominids sought tendons for making . . . carrying bags! (cf. Potts and Shipman 1981; Bunn 1981; *Science News* 1981). This is a classic example of observations from the archaeological record being accommodated to one's beliefs and then cited as proof that those original ideas were correct: mere tautology.

4 Radcliffe-Brown recognized the weakness of 'conjectural history'. He pointed out (1958, p. 41): 'The hypothetical reconstruction of the past inevitably assumes certain general principles but does not prove them; on the contrary its results depend upon their validity.' Although he was objecting to the reconstruction of history from ethnographic observations, the methodological point is just as sound for archaeologically generated observations. His criticism of historically-oriented ethnology is equally applicable to those who adopt theories guiding the interpretation of archaeological observations and somehow suppose that these same facts can confirm or refute the theories (for a good example, see Mellen 1981).

5 Wittfogel 1957.

6 Discussed in Chapter 9.

Chapter 8 (pp. 195-213)

1 Darwin 1875.

2 Roth 1887.

3 Peake and Fleure 1927.

4 Childe 1928.

5 *Ibid.*, p. 2.

6 Hempel 1965.

7 Braidwood 1963.

8 Braidwood and Howe 1960.

9 Braidwood and Willey (eds.) 1962, pp. 132–46.

10 Braidwood and Reed 1957.

11 Braidwood 1963, p. 110.

12 Higgs and Jarman 1969; Higgs (ed.) 1972, 1975.

13 Binford 1968a. Anticipating arguments later in this chapter, I should point out that one major flaw in these early ideas was the concept of little 'Gardens of Eden' which served to concentrate population and offer the potential for more secure population growth. I was operating with some of the assumptions of my predecessors and adding arguments for selective stress arising through the structure of population dynamics.

14 Dumond 1965; Boserup 1965.

15 Smith and Young 1972.

16 Flannery 1969.

17 Bender 1975; Bronson 1975; Cowgill 1975; Hassan 1974, 1979; Hayden 1981.

18 Cf. the attitude of Flannery 1973.

19 Beardsley 1956, p. 134.

20 Rick 1980.

21 Madsen 1979.

22 Perlman 1980.

23 Binford 1968a.

24 Harlan 1967.

25 Flannery 1969.

26 Hassan 1977; also discussion in Hassan 1981, especially pp. 213–14.

27 It makes no sense to regard *reliability* and *predictability* as environmental characteristics which came to be increasingly recognized (cf. Hassan 1977; Hayden 1981): both are properties of tactical procedures, not characteristics of the environment itself. Given enough information about an environment, almost any resource is rendered predictable (and hence reliable). What Hayden describes as reliable 'r-selected' resources are precisely those which can be exploited with minimal information about the environment, since they tend to be stationary and aggregated in clumps; so it is curious that these are the very resources which Hayden thinks man exploits as he becomes more 'knowledgeable' about his environments.

28 Niederberger 1979.

29 MacNeish 1964, 1971, 1972. This important observation was acknowledged by Flannery 1973 and Bender 1978, yet ignored in a work as recent as Hassan 1981. Hassan no doubt would claim that his models for food production apply only to Palestine and that other areas each require their own particularistic explanations.

30 E.g. Hayden 1981, p. 544: 'It seems self-evident to me that all else being equal, hunter-gatherers will adopt strategies involving the least amount of movement.'

31 Bender 1978, p. 207.

32 Bennett 1976b, p. 848.

33 Cohen 1977.
34 Cf. notes 19 and 28 above.
35 Bailey 1960.
36 Perkins 1964; cf. Reed 1969.
37 Binford and Chasko 1976; additional information on this point may be found in Lee 1972.
38 Osborn 1977 has sought to demonstrate that aquatic resources do not constitute 'Gardens of Eden'. Yesner 1980 realizes that there is an historical problem: if aquatic resources are to be considered 'Gardens of Eden', why did early populations apparently not realize this fact? Nevertheless, he tends to cite coastal hunter-gatherers as examples of adaptations to exceptionally productive settings, which he believes were more common in the past. His suggestion that increased sedentism in such settings is tied to greater resource diversity relates to the notion of the 'broad spectrum revolution'.
39 Flannery 1965.
40 The references are given in notes 17, 26, 33 and 39.
41 This was the topic of another lecture delivered during my stay in Great Britain, but not included in the present volume (Binford 1981c).
42 Binford 1977a, p. 7.

Chapter 9 (pp. 214-32)

1 Binford 19164a
2 Sahlins 1958.
3 The pattern of small power-based 'chiefdoms' referred to here has a coastal distribution in North America, beginning at Chesapeake Bay, continuing south along the Atlantic coast (including such groups as the Guale) and around the Florida area into the Gulf of Mexico. Similar systems extended up the Mississippi valley, but became much rarer along the Gulf coast west of the mouth of the Mississippi.
4 E.g. Gearing 1962.
5 Sahlins never dealt adequately with the latter point (differential productivity). His concept of 'imbalanced' reciprocity, for example, related only to short term conditions of exchange. Popular discussions of a redistributive mode of organization have not yet satisfactorily addressed the more likely situation in which there exist much more permanent imbalances within a region which would serve to ensure a fairly permanent imbalance in the flow of goods.
6 See Finney 1966; Earle 1977.
7 Flannery and Coe 1968; also Sanders and Price 1968.
8 Sahlins 1963, 1965.
9 See Sanders *et al.* 1979, especially pp. 400–1, for a discussion of this point.
10 Boserup 1965.
11 This model, like so many others, assumes a teleological explanation: that is, the existence of some form of principle that man, if given the chance, will seek to raise his standard of living, will invest in culture building, will explore new ways of investing his time. These views are all forms of what Trigger (1981, p. 150) has characterized as the 'Enlightenment belief that technological innovation is an autonomous process of rational self-improvement and the driving force behind cultural evolution.'
12 Bennett 1976a.
13 Harris 1979. After laying out many principles with which I can find little to disagree, Harris' actual illustrations of cultural materialism take the form of various cost-benefit arguments which assume a vital evolutionary 'good' for increasing the 'standard of living', or at least decreasing the cost of maintaining it (see particularly Harris 1979, pp. 85–114). This, once again, is a gradualist view.
14 The Principle of Least Effort has been most explicitly stated by Zipf 1949.
15 'The law of minimal risk means that when faced by choices the decision will be to adopt that solution which produces the minimal risk' (Sanders *et al.* 1979, p. 360).
16 Pyke *et al.* 1977; Charnov 1976.
17 I do not wish to imply that I have not operated from time to time with propositions from economics as if they were principles of evolution, for I think almost all of us who have ever addressed the issue of process have thought in economic terms about ecological processes. What I am suggesting here is that we should become increasingly aware of this 'functionalist' approach. Economics, even if the principles are valid, refers to the behaviour of participants within a system, rather than the patterns of interaction between a system and its environmental field, which is in my opinion the most profitable way of thinking about the locus of evolutionary processes. Those who would see the dynamics of a system as simply a generalization about the normative behaviour of participants within it have, I fear, largely

missed the point regarding the organization of ecological articulations among systems.

18 The assumption of an inner dynamic has been a basic and fundamental part of most philosophical positions associated with the word 'evolution' in the social sciences. See Dunnell 1980a. For my own much earlier argument in favour of a selectionist position see Binford 1972b.

19 I am suggesting here that there are major organizational characteristics in the evolutionary history of culturally integrated systems. This means that there are apt to be dramatic kinds of changes or 'punctuations', with seeming lack of continuity of the type to be expected if one adopted a gradualist view of evolutionary process.

20 Dunnell's (1980a) recent survey of evolutionary ideas in anthropology makes an argument against vitalism and in favour of a selectionist view, as advocated here. On the other hand, he rejects some paradigmatic distinctions which he does not admit may be well founded. For instance, he states critically: 'The view that the subject is culture has led to isolation of cultural evolution from evolution in general. Culture is to be explained, not by evolutionary principles and mechanisms demonstrated to be operative in the world at large, but by processes unique to culture itself.' (p. 48) These statements, which Dunnell takes to be a devastating pronouncement, to me seem silly posturings which would lead, if taken seriously, to that masquerade for productive thought currently parading under the rubric of sociobiology. In the example I have just given the situation is analogous to a species previously interacting competitively with its conspecifics suddenly being able to shift the dynamics of selection to an 'unwanted' organ – a little finger, for instance – and by doing so ensure not only the future security of the original species but also a real competitive scrap between the new 'disembodied' little fingers! If an organization is capable of that type of restructuring (as culture certainly is), then I think it might be well to investigate some of the properties of that domain of phenomena, rather than attempting to reduce it to a simple analog of genes with fitness guiding reproductive success at the species level in the literal sense of the word species. Dunnell's argument entirely misses the point of interest about human adaptations: they are truly extra-somatic and must be understood in terms of extra-somatic processes. Culture refers to that organizational domain.

21 See Renfrew 1969; Parsons and Price 1971; Rathje 1971.

22 Fogel 1963.

23 Walthall *et al.* 1979.

24 Prufer 1961.

25 Griffin *et al.* 1969.

26 See Struever and Houart 1972.

27 E.g. Judge 1979; also Cordell and Plog 1979, particularly pp. 419–24.

28 It is not infrequent to see claims made for complex societies in areas such as the American Southwest phrased as a step toward achieving intellectual 'freedom' from the 'oppression' of the ethnohistoric past where only 'egalitarian' societies were described. It is of course possible, indeed almost a certainty, that there were forms of society in the past which are not represented in the relatively recent descriptions from the colonial era. Nevertheless, I fear that the criteria being cited in favour of centralized authorities and major redistributive functions are largely the size and architectural sophistication of the ruins. Are we really to believe that mankind can only accomplish substantial acts of coordinated labour if 'organized' by a powerful central government authority?

29 See Gould and Lewontin 1979. For a review of currently active philosophical positions, see Wenke 1981.

30 Binford 1981a, especially pp. 83–5 and 184–97.

31 Binford in press.

Bibliography

Adams, R. N. 1981 'Natural selection, energetics, and "cultural materialism"', *Current Anthropology* 22 (6), 603–24.

Almeida, A. de 1965 *Bushmen and other Non-Bantu Peoples of Angola*, Johannesburg.

Amsden, C. W. 1977 *A Quantitative Analysis of Nunamiut Eskimo Settlement Dynamics: 1898 to 1969* (Ph.D. Dissertation, Department of Anthropology, University of New Mexico), Ann Arbor.

Ardrey, R. 1961 *African Genesis*, London and New York.

Ascher, R. 1962 'Ethnography for archaeology: a case from the Seri Indians', *Ethnology* 1, 360–9.

Bailey, H. P. 1960 'A method of determining the warmth and temperateness of climate', *Geografiska Annaler* 43 (1), 1–16.

Bartholomew, G. A. and Birdsell, J. B. 1953 'Ecology and the protohominids', *American Anthropologist* 55, 481–98.

Beardsley, R. K. *et al.* 1955 'Functional and evolutionary implications of community patterning', in R. Wauchope *et al.* (eds.), *Seminars in Archaeology* (Memoirs of the Society for American Archaeology, 11), Salt Lake City, 129–55.

Bender, B. 1975 *Farming in Prehistory*, London.

1978 'Gatherer-hunter to farmer: a social perspective', *World Archaeology* 10 (2), 204–22.

Bennett, J. W. 1976a *The Ecological Transition: Cultural Anthropology and Human Adaptation*, New York.

1976b 'Anticipation, adaptation and the concept of culture in anthropology', *Science* 192, 847–53.

Binford, L. R. 1963 'The Pomranky site. A late archaic burial station', *Anthropological Papers, Museum of Anthropology, University of Michigan* 19, 149–92.

1964a *An Archaeological and Ethnohistorical Investigation of Cultural Diversity* (Ph.D. Dissertation, Department of Anthropology, University of Michigan), Ann Arbor.

1964b 'A consideration of archaeological research design', *American Antiquity* 29 (4), 425–41.

1967 'Smudge pits and hide smoking: the use of analogy in archaeological reasoning', *American Antiquity* 32 (1), 1–12.

1968a 'Post-pleistocene adaptations', in S. R. Binford and L. R. Binford (eds.), *New Perspectives in Archaeology*, Chicago, 313–41.

1968b 'Some comments on historical versus processual archaeology', *Southwestern Journal of Anthropology* 24 (3), 267–75.

1968c 'Archaeological perspectives', in S. R. Binford and L. R. Binford (eds.), *New Perspectives in Archaeology*, Chicago, 5–32.

1969 'Comment on D. Collins' "culture traditions and environment of early man"', *Current Anthropology* 10 (4), 297–9.

1972a 'Contemporary model building: paradigms and the current state of paleolithic research', in D. L. Clarke (ed.), *Models in Archaeology*, London, 109–66.

1972b 'Comments on evolution', in L. R. Binford, *An Archaeological Perspective*, New York and London, 105–13.

1973 'Interassemblage variability – the Mousterian and the "functional" argument', in C. Renfrew (ed.), *The Explanation of Culture Change*, London, 227–54.

1976 'Forty-seven trips: a case study in the character of some formation processes of the archaeological record, in E. Hall (ed.), *Contributions to Anthropology: The Interior Peoples of Northern Alaska* (National Museum of Man Mercury Series, 49), Ottawa, 299–351.

1977a 'General introduction', in L. R. Binford (ed.), *For Theory Building in Archaeology*, New York, 1–10.

1977b 'Olorgesailie deserves more than the usual book review', *Journal of Anthropological Research* 33 (4), 493–502.

1978a *Nunamiut Ethnoarchaeology*, New York.

1978b 'Dimensional analysis of behavior and site structure: learning from an Eskimo hunting stand', *American Antiquity* 43 (3), 330–61.

1979 'Organization and formation pro-

cesses: looking at curated technologies', *Journal of Anthropological Research* 35 (3), 255–73.
1980 'Willow smoke and dogs' tails: hunter-gatherer settlement systems and archaeological site formation', *American Antiquity* 45 (1), 4–20.
1981a *Bones: Ancient Men and Modern Myths*, New York.
1981b 'Behavioral archaeology and the "Pompeii premise"', *Journal of Anthropological Research* 37 (3), 195–208.
1981c 'Long term land use patterns: some implications for archaeology', Paper presented at the 46th Annual Meeting of the Society for American Archaeology, San Diego.
1982 'The archaeology of place', *Journal of Anthropological Archaeology* 1 (1), 5–31.
in press 'Objectivity-explanation-archaeology 1980', in C. Renfrew, M. Rowlands, B. Abbot-Seagraves (eds.), *Theory and Explanation in Archaeology: the Southampton Conference*, New York and London.
BINFORD, L. R. AND BERTRAM, J. B. 1977 'Bone frequencies – and attritional processes', in L. R. Binford (ed.), *For Theory Building in Archaeology*, New York, 77–153.
BINFORD, L. R. AND BINFORD, S. R. 1966 'A preliminary analysis of functional variability in the Mousterian of Levallois facies', *American Anthropologist* 68 (2), Pt 2, 238–95.
1969 'Stone tools and human behavior', *Scientific American* 220 (4), 70–84.
BINFORD, L. R. AND CHASKO, W. J. 1976 'Nunamiut demographic history: a provocative case', in E. B. W. Zubrow (ed.), *Demographic Anthropology*, Albuquerque, 63–143.
BINFORD, L. R. AND PAPWORTH, M. L. 1963 'The Eastport site, Antrim County, Michigan', *Anthropological Papers, Museum of Anthropology, University of Michigan* 19, 71–123.
BINFORD, L. R. AND QUIMBY, G. I. 1963 'Indian sites and chipped stone materials in the northern Lake Michigan area', *Fieldiana, Anthropology* 36, 277–307.
BINFORD, L. R. AND TODD, L. C. 1982 'On arguments for the "butchering" of giant Geladas', *Current Anthropology* 23 (1), 108–10.
BINFORD, S. R. 1968 'A structural comparison of disposal of the dead in the Mousterian and the Upper Paleolithic', *Southwestern Journal of Anthropology* 24 (2), 139–54.
BORDES, F. 1950 'Principes d'une méthode d'étude des techniques de débitage et de la typologie du Paléolithique ancien et moyen', *L'Anthropologie* 54 (1–2), 19–34.
1953a 'Levalloisien et Moustérien', *Bulletin de la Société Préhistorique Française* 50 (4), 226–35.
1953b 'Essai de classification des industries "moustériennes"', *Bulletin de la Société Préhistorique Française* 50 (7–8), 457–66.
1961a *Typologie de Paléolithique Ancien et Moyen*, Bordeaux.
1961b 'Mousterian cultures in France', *Science* 134 (3482), 803–10.
1969 'Reflections on typology and techniques in the Paleolithic', *Arctic Anthropology* 6 (1), 1–29.
1972 *A Tale of Two Caves*, New York.
BORDES, F., RIGAUD, J. P. AND SONNEVILLE-BORDES, D. DE 1972 'Des buts, problèmes et limites de l'archéologie paléolithique', *Quaternaria* 16 (1), 15–34.
BORDES, F. AND SONNEVILLE-BORDES, D. DE 1970 'The significance of variability in Paleolithic assemblages', *World Archaeology* 2 (1), 61–73.
BOSERUP, E. 1965 *The Conditions of Agricultural Growth*, London.
BRAIDWOOD, R. J. 1946 'The interrelations, core and flake tool traditions in Europe', in R. Braidwood (ed.), *Origins: An Introductory Course in General Anthropology*, Chicago, 145–52.
1963 *Prehistoric Man* (6th edn), Chicago.
BRAIDWOOD, R. J. AND HOWE, B. 1960 *Prehistoric Investigations in Iraqi Kurdistan* (Oriental Institute Studies in Ancient Oriental Civilization, 31), Chicago.
BRAIDWOOD, R. J. AND REED, C. A. 1957 'The achievement and early consequences of food production: a consideration of the archaeological and natural-historical evidence', *Cold Springs Harbor Symposia on Quantitative Biology* 22, 19–31.
BRAIDWOOD, R. J. AND WILLEY, G. R. (eds.) 1962 *Courses Toward Urban Life* (Viking Fund Publications in Anthropology, 32), Chicago.
BRAIN, C. K. 1967 'Hottentot food remains and their meaning in the interpretation of fossil bone assemblages', *Scientific Papers of the Namib Desert Research Station* 32, 1–11.
1968 'Who killed the Swartkrans ape-man?', *South African Museum Association Bulletin* 9 (4), 127–39.

1981 *The Hunters or the Hunted? An Introduction to African Cave Taphonomy*, Chicago.

Breuil, H. 1931 'Pleistocene sequence in the Thames Valley', *South-Eastern Naturalist and Antiquary* 36, 95–8.

1932a 'Les industries à éclats du Paléolithique ancien, I. Le Clactonien', *Préhistoire* 1 (2), 125–90.

1932b 'Le Paléolithique ancien en Europe Occidentale et sa chronologie', *Bulletin de la Société Préhistorique Française* 29 (3), 570–8.

Breuil, H. and Lantier, R. 1965 *The Men of the Old Stone Age*, London.

Bronson, B. 1975 'The earliest farming: demography as cause and consequence', in S. Polgar (ed.), *Population, Ecology and Social Evolution*, The Hague, 53–71.

Broom, R. 1933 *The Coming of Man*, London.

Brothwell, D. and Higgs, E. (eds.) 1969 *Science in Archaeology* (2nd edn), London and New York.

Brown, J. A. (ed.) 1971 *Approaches to the Social Dimensions of Mortuary Practices* (Society for American Archaeology, Memoir 25), Washington D.C.

Bunn, H. T. 1981 'Archaeological evidence from meat-eating by Plio-Pleistocene Hominids from Koobi Fora and Olduvai Gorge', *Nature* 291, 577.

Bunn, H. T. *et al.* 1980 'FxJj50: an early Pleistocene site in northern Kenya', *World Archaeology* 12 (2), 109–36.

Burkitt, M. 1963 *The Old Stone Age* (4th edn), London.

Cahen, D., Keeley, L. H. and van Noten, F. L. 1979 'Stone tools, toolkits, and human behavior in prehistory', *Current Anthropology* 20 (4), 661–83.

Charnov, E. L. 1976 'Optimal foraging: the marginal value theorem', *Theoretical Population Biology* 9, 129–36.

Childe, V. G. 1928 *The Most Ancient East: The Oriental Prelude to European Prehistory*, London.

1929 *The Danube in Prehistory*, Oxford.

Clark, J. G. D., 1979 'Archaeology and human diversity', *Annual Review of Anthropology* 8, 1–20.

Coe, J. L. 1964 *The Formative Cultures of the Carolina Piedmont* (Transactions of the American Philosophical Society n.s., Volume 54, Number 5), Philadelphia.

Cohen, M. N. 1977 *The Food Crisis in Prehistory*, New Haven.

Coles, J. M. 1973 *Archaeology by Experiment*, London.

1979 *Experimental Archaeology*, London.

Collins, D. M. 1969 'Cultural traditions and environment of early man', *Current Anthropology* 10, 267–316.

1970 'Stone artefact analysis and the recognition of culture traditions', *World Archaeology* 2 (1), 17–27.

Cordell, L. S. and Plog, F. 1979 'Escaping the confines of normative thought: a re-evaluation of Puebloan prehistory', *American Antiquity* 44 (3), 405–29.

Cowgill, G. L. 1975 'Population pressure as a non-explanation', in A. Swedlund (ed.), *Population Studies in Archaeology and Biological Anthropology* (Society for American Archaeology, Memoir 30), Washington, D.C.), 127–31.

Crowell, A. L. and Hitchcock, R. K. 1978 'Basarwa ambush hunting in Botswana', *Botswana Notes and Records* 10, 37–51.

Dart, R. A. 1925 'A note on Makapansgat: a site of early human occupation', *South African Journal of Science* 22, 371–81.

1926 'Taung and its significance', *Natural History* 26, 315–27.

1948 'The Makapansgat proto-human *Australopithecus prometheus*', *American Journal of Physical Anthropology* 6, 259–83.

1949 'The predatory implemental technique of Australopithecus', *American Journal of Physical Anthropology* 7 (1), 1–38.

1953 'The predatory transition from ape to man', *International Anthropological and Linguistic Review* 1.

1956 'The myth of the bone-accumulating hyena', *American Anthropologist* 58, 40–62.

1957 *The Osteodontokeratic Culture of Australopithecus Prometheus* (Memoir of the Transvaal Museum, 10), Pretoria.

1958 'The minimal bone-breccia content of Makapansgat and the Australopithecine predatory habit', *American Anthropologist* 60, 923–31.

1959 *Adventures with the Missing Link*, New York.

1960 'The bone tool-manufacturing ability of *Australopithecus prometheus*', *American Anthropologist* 62, 134–43.

Darwin, C. R. 1875 *The Variation of Animals and Plants under Domestication*, Volume 1 (2nd edn), London.

Deacon, H. J. 1975 'Demography, subsistence, and culture during the Acheulian in southern Africa', in K. Butzer and G. Isaac (eds.), *After the Australopithecines*, The Hague, 543–69.

Downs, J. F. 1966 *The Two Worlds of the Washo*, New York.

Dumond, D. E. 1965 'Population growth and cultural change', *Southwestern Journal of Anthropology* 21 (4), 302–24.

Dunnell, R. C. 1980a 'Evolutionary theory and archaeology', in M. B. Schiffer (ed.), *Advances in Archaeological Method and Theory, Volume 3*, New York, 35–99.

1980b 'Americanist archaeology: the 1979 contribution', *American Journal of Archaeology*, 84, 463–78.

Earle, T. K. 1977 'A reappraisal of redistribution: complex Hawaiian chiefdoms', in T. K. Earle and J. E. Ericson (eds.), *Exchange Systems in Prehistory*, New York, 213–29.

Feyerabend, P. 1978 *Against Method: Outline of an Anarchistic Theory of Knowledge* (2nd edn), New York.

Finney, B. 1966 'Resource distribution and social structure in Tahiti', *Ethnology* 5 (1), 80–6.

Flannery, K. V. 1965 'The ecology of early food production in Mesopotamia', *Science* 147, 1247–56.

1969 'Origins and ecological effects of early domestication in Iran and the Near East', in P. J. Ucko and G. W. Dimbleby (eds.), *The Domestication and Exploitation of Plants and Animals*, London and Chicago, 73–100.

1972 'The origins of the village as a settlement type in Mesoamerica and the Near East: a comparative study', in P. J. Ucko, R. Tringham, and G. W. Dimbleby (eds.), *Man, Settlement and Urbanism*, London, 23–53.

1973 'The origins of agriculture', *Annual Review of Anthropology* 2, 271–310.

Flannery, K. V. (ed.) 1976 *The Early Mesoamerican Village*, New York.

Flannery, K. V. and Coe, M. D. 1968 'Social and economic systems in formative Mesoamerica', in S. R. Binford and L. R. Binford (eds.), *New Perspectives in Archaeology*, Chicago, 267–83.

Fleming, J. 1976 *Dating in Archaeology: A Guide to Scientific Techniques*, New York.

Fogel, I. L. 1963 'The dispersal of copper artifacts in the late archaic period of prehistoric North America', *The Wisconsin Archaeologist* 44 (3), 129–80.

Fritz, J. M. and Plog, F. T. 1970 'The nature of archaeological explanation', *American Antiquity* 35 (4), 405–12.

Garrod, D. A. E. 1938 'The Upper Palaeolithic in the light of recent discovery', *Proceedings of the Prehistoric Society* 4, 1–26.

Gearing, F. 1962 *Priests and warriors* (American Anthropologist 64 (5), Pt 2).

Gould, R. A. 1977 *Puntutjarpa Rockshelter and the Australian Desert Culture* (Anthropological Papers, American Museum of Natural History, 54, Pt I), New York.

1980 *Living Archaeology*, Cambridge and New York.

Gould, R. A. (ed.) 1978 *Explorations in Ethnoarchaeology*, Albuquerque.

Gould, S. J. and Lewontin, R. C. 1979 'The spandrels of San Marco and the Panglossian paradigm: a critique of the adaptationist program', *Proceedings of the Royal Society of London, Series B*, 205, 581–98.

Griffin, J. B., Gordus, A. A. and Wright, G. A. 1969 'Identification of the sources of Hopewellian obsidian in the Middle West', *American Antiquity* 34 (1), 1–14.

Harlan, J. R. 1967 'A wild wheat harvest in Turkey', *Archaeology* 20 (3), 197–201.

Harris, M. 1979 *Cultural Materialism: The Struggle for a Science of Culture*, New York.

Harrold, F. B. 1980 'A comparative analysis of Eurasian Paleolithic burials', *World Archaeology* 12 (2), 195–211.

Hassan, F. 1974 'Population growth and cultural evolution', *Reviews in Anthropology* 1, 205–12.

1977 'The dynamics of agricultural origins in Palestine: a theoretical model', in C. Reed (ed.), *Agricultural Origins*, The Hague, 589–609.

1979 'Demography and archaeology', *Annual Review of Anthropology* 8, 137–60.

1981 *Demographic Archaeology*, New York.

Hawkes, C. 1954 'Archaeological theory and method: some suggestions from the Old World', *American Anthropologist* 56 (1), 155–68.

Hawkes, J. 1980 *A Quest of Love*, London.

Hayden, B. 1979 *Palaeolithic Reflections: Lithic Technology and Ethnographic Excavations among the Australian Aborigines*, Canberra.

1981 'Research and development in the stone technological transitions among hunter-gatherers', *Current Anthropology* 22 (5), 519–48.

Hemming, J. E. 1971 *The Distribution Movement Patterns of Caribou in Alaska* (Alaska Department of Fish and Game, Wildlife Technical Bulletin, 1), Fairbanks.

Hempel, C. G. 1965 *Aspects of Scientific*

Explanation, New York.

HERSKOVITS, M. J. 1955 *Cultural Anthropology*, New York.

HIGGS, E. S. (ed.) 1972 *Papers in Economic Prehistory*, Cambridge.

(ed.) 1975 *Palaeoeconomy*, Cambridge.

HIGGS, E. S. AND JARMAN, M. R. 1969 'The origins of agriculture: a reconsideration', *Antiquity* 43, 31–41.

HILL, A. P. 1972 *Taphonomy of Contemporary and Late Cenozoic East African Vertebrates* (Unpubl. Ph.D. Dissertation, University of London), London.

HODDER, I. 1977 'Some new directions in the spatial analysis of archaeological data at the regional scale (macro)', in D. L. Clarke (ed.), *Spatial Archaeology*, London, 223–351.

1982 *Symbols in Action*, New York and Cambridge.

HOEBEL, E. A. 1949 *Man in the Primitive World*, New York.

HUGHES, A. R. 1954 'Hyaenas versus Australopithecines as agents of bone accumulation', *American Journal of Physical Anthropology* 12, 467–86.

ISAAC, G. 1971 'The diet of early man: aspects of archaeological evidence from Lower and Middle Pleistocene sites in Africa', *World Archaeology* 2 (3), 278–99.

1975 'Early hominids in action: a commentary on the contribution of archaeology to understanding the fossil record in East Africa', *Yearbook of Physical Anthropology* 19, 19–35.

1976a 'The activities of early African hominids: a review of archaeological evidence from the time span two and a half to one million years ago', in G. Isaac and E. McCown (eds.), *Human Origins: Louis Leakey and the East African Evidence*, Menlo Park, 483–514.

1976b 'Early stone tools – an adaptive threshold?', in G. Sieveking, I. Longworth and K. Wilson (eds.), *Problems in Economic and Social Archaeology*, London, 39–47.

1976c 'Stages of cultural elaboration in the Pleistocene: possible archaeological indications of the development of language capabilities', in S. Harnard, H. Steklis and J. Lancaster (eds.), *Origins and Evolution of Language and Speech* (Annals of the New York Academy of Sciences, 280), New York, 275–88.

1977 *Olorgesailie: Archaeological Studies of a Middle Pleistocene Lake Basin in Kenya*, Chicago.

1978 'The food-sharing behavior of protohuman hominids', *Scientific American* 238 (4), 90–108.

ISAAC, G. AND CRADER, D. C. 1981 'To what extent were early hominids carnivorous? An archaeological perspective', in R. Harding and G. Teleki (eds.), *Omnivorous Primates*, New York, 37–103.

ISAAC, G. AND ISAAC, B. 1975 'Africa', in R. Stigler (ed.), *Varieties of Culture in the Old World*, New York, 8–48.

JUDGE, W. J. 1979 'The development of a complex cultural ecosystem in the Chaco Basin, New Mexico', in R. Luin (ed.), *Proceedings of the First Conference of Scientific Research in the National Parks* 3 (National Park Service Transactions and Proceedings, 5), 901–5.

KEELEY, L. AND TOTH, N. 1981 'Microwear polishes on early stone tools from Koobi Fora, Kenya', *Nature* 293, 464–5.

KLEIN, R. G. 1973 *Ice Age Hunters of the Ukraine*, Chicago.

1975 'Paleoanthropological implications of the nonarchaeological bone assemblage from Swartklip I, Southwestern Cape Province, South Africa', *Quaternary Research* 5, 275–88.

1978 'The fauna and overall interpretation of the "cutting 10" Acheulean site at Elandsfontein (Hopefield), Southwestern Cape Province, South Africa', *Quaternary Research* 10, 69–83.

KLINDT-JENSEN, O. 1975 *A History of Scandinavian Archaeology*, London.

KLIMEK, S. 1955 'The structure of Californian Indian culture', *University of California Publications in American Archaeology and Ethnology* 37, 1–70.

KRAMER, C. (ed.) 1979 *Ethnoarchaeology: Implications of Ethnography for Archaeology*, New York.

KROEBER, A. L. 1939 *Cultural and Natural Areas of Native North America* (University of California Publications in American Archaeology and Ethnology, 38), Berkeley.

1948 *Anthropology*, New York.

KUHN, T. 1962 'The historical structure of scientific discovery', *Science* 136, 760–4.

1970 *The Structure of Scientific Revolutions* (2nd edn), Chicago.

KURTEN, B. 1976 *The Cave Bear Story. Life and Death of a Vanished Animal*, New York.

LAMBERG-KARLOVSKY, C. C. 1975 'Third millennium modes of exchange and modes of production', in J. A. Sabloff and C. C.

Lamberg-Karlovsky (eds.), *Ancient Civilization and Trade*, Albuquerque, 341–68.

LAVILLE, H., RIGAUD, J. P. AND SACKETT, J. *Rock Shelters of the Perigord*, New York.

LEAKEY, L. S. B. 1959a 'The first men: recent discovery in East Africa', *Antiquity* 33, 285–7.

1959b 'A new fossil skull from Olduvai', *Nature* 184, 491–3.

1960 'Finding the world's earliest man', *National Geographic Magazine* 118, 420–35.

LEAKEY, M. D. 1971 *Olduvai Gorge, Volume 3, Excavations in Beds I and II, 1960–1963*, Cambridge.

1979 *Olduvai Gorge: My Search for Early Man*, London.

LEAKEY, M. D. AND HAY, R. L. 1979 'Pliocene footprints in the Laetolil, northern Tanzania', *Nature* 278, 317–23.

LEAKEY, R. E. 1981 *The Making of Mankind*, London and New York.

LEAKEY, R. E. AND LEWIN, R. 1978 *Origins*, London and New York.

LEE, R. B. 1972 'Population growth and the beginnings of sedentary life among the !Kung Bushmen', in B. Spooner (ed.), *Population Growth: Anthropological Implications*, Cambridge, 329–42.

LEGROS CLARK, W. E. 1967 *Man-apes or Ape Men?*, New York.

LEROI-GOURHAN, A. AND BREZILLON, M. 1966 'L'habitation Magdalénienne No. 1 de Pincevent près Montereau (Seine-et-Marne)', *Gallia Préhistoire, Fouilles et Monuments Archéologiques en France Métropolitain, Tome 9, Fascicule 2*, Paris, 263–385.

LEROI-GOURHAN, A. AND BREZILLON, M. 1972 *Fouilles de Pincevent Essai d'Analyse Ethnographique d'un Habitat Magdalénien* (Supplément à Gallia Préhistoire, 7), Paris.

LORENZ, K. 1966 *On Agression*, New York.

MACNEISH, R. S. 1958 *Preliminary Archaeological Investigations in the Sierra de Tamaulipas, Mexico* (American Philosophical Society, Proceedings, 48, Part 6), Philadelphia.

1964 'Ancient Mesoamerican civilization', *Science* 143, 531–7.

1971 'Speculation about how and why food production and village life developed in the Tehuacán Valley, Mexico', *Archaeology* 24, 307–15.

1972 'The evolution of community patterns in the Tehuacán Valley of Mexico and speculations about the cultural processes', in P. J. Ucko, R. Tringham and G. W. Dimbleby (eds.), *Man, Settlement and Urbanism*, London, 67–93.

MACNEISH, R. S., PETERSON, F. A. AND NEELY, J. A. 1972 'The archaeological reconnaissance', in R. S. MacNeish (ed.), *The Prehistory of the Tehuacán Valley, Volume 5, Excavation and Reconnaissance*, Austin, 341–495.

MADSEN, D. B. 1979 'The Fremont and the Sevier: defining prehistoric agriculturalists north of the Anasazi', *American Antiquity* 44 (4), 711–22.

MARKS, A. E. AND FREIDEL, D. A. 1977 'Prehistoric settlement patterns in the Avdat/Aqev area', in A. Marks (ed.), *Prehistory and Paleoenvironments in the Central Negev, Israel, Volume II*, Dallas, 131–58.

MASON, O. 1883 'The birth of invention', *Annual Report of the National Museum 1882*, Washington, D.C.

MELLARS, P. 1970 'Some comments on the notion of "functional variability" in stone tool assemblages', *World Archaeology* 2 (1), 74–89.

MELLEN, S. L. W. 1981 *The Evolution of Love*, San Francisco.

MELTZER, D. J. 1979 'Paradigms and the nature of change in American archaeology', *American Antiquity* 44 (4), 644–57.

MICHELS, J. N. 1973 *Dating Methods in Archaeology*, New York.

MILKE, W. 1949 'The quantitative distribution of cultural similarities and their cartographic representation', *American Anthropologist* 51, 237–52.

MOVIUS, H. I. 1948 'Old World prehistoric archaeology, 1948' (Preliminary report to the Committee on Interrelations of Pleistocene Research, National Research Council, Peabody Museum, Harvard University), Cambridge, Mass.

1953 'Old world prehistory: paleolithic', in A. L. Kroeber (ed.), *Anthropology Today: An Encyclopedic Inventory*, Chicago, 163–92.

1956 'The old stone age', in H. Shapiro (ed.), *Man, Culture and Society*, Oxford, 49–64.

1975 *Excavation of the Abri Pataud, Les Eyzies (Dordogne)* (American School of Prehistoric Research, Peabody Museum, Harvard University Bulletin, 30), Cambridge, Mass.

1977 *Excavation of the Abri Pataud, Les Eyzies (Dordogne), Stratigraphy* (American School of Prehistoric Research, Peabody Museum, Harvard University, Bulletin 31), Cambridge, Mass.

MUNDAY, F. 1976 'Intersite variability in the Mousterian occupation of the Avdat/Aqev area', in A. Marks (ed.), *Prehistory and Paleoenvironments in the Central Negev, Israel, Volume I, The Avdat/Aqev Area Part I*, Dallas, 113–40.

MYRES, J. L. (ed.) 1906 *The Evolution of Culture and Other Essays by the Late Lt.-Gen. A. Lane-Pitt-Rivers*, Oxford.

NELSON, N. C. 1938 'Prehistoric archaeology', in F. Boas (ed.), *General Anthropology*, New York, 146–237.

NEWELL, R. R. AND DEKIN, A. A. 1978 'An integrative strategy for the definition of behaviorally meaningful archaeological units', *Palaeohistoria* 20 (1), 7–38.

NIEDERBERGER, C. 1979 *Zohapilco* (Instituto Nacional de Antropologia e Historia, Coleccion Cientifica, 30), Mexico City.

OAKLEY, K. P. 1953 'Culture and the Australopithecines', in S. Tax, L. Eisely, I. Rouse, C. Voegelin (eds.), *An Appraisal of Anthropology Today*, Chicago, 28–31.

1954 'Evidence of fire in South African cave deposits', *Nature* 174, 261–2.

1961 'On man's use of fire, with comments on tool-making and hunting', in S. L. Washburn (ed.), *Social Life of Early Man* (Viking Fund Publications in Anthropology, 31), New York, 176–93.

OHEL, M. Y. 1979 'The Clactonian: an independent complex or an integral part of the Acheulean?', *Current Anthropology* 20 (4), 685–726.

O'KELLY, M. J. 1968 'Excavations at New Grange, Co. Meath', *Antiquity* 42 (1), 40–2.

1982 *Newgrange: Archaeology, Art and Legend*, London (New York 1983).

OSBORN, A. J. 1977 'Strandloopers, mermaids and other fairy tales: ecological determinants of marine resource utilization – the Peruvian case', in L. R. Binford (ed.), *For Theory Building in Archaeology*, New York, 157–205.

OSBORN, H. F. 1916 *Men of the Old Stone Age*, New York.

1927 *Man Rises to Parnassus: Critical Epochs in the Prehistory of Man*, Princeton.

PARSONS, L. A. AND PRICE, B. J. 1971 'Mesoamerican trade and its role in the emergence of civilization', in R. F. Heizer and J. A. Graham (eds.), *Observations on the Emergence of Civilization in Mesoamerica* (Contributions of the University of California Archaeological Research Facility, 11), Berkeley, 169–95.

PEAKE, H. J. AND FLEURE, H. J. 1927 *Peasants and Potters* (The Corridors of Time, 3), Oxford.

PERLMAN, S. M. 1980 'An optimum diet model, coastal variability, and hunter-gatherer behavior', in M. B. Schiffer (ed.), *Advances in Archaeological Theory and Method, Volume 3*, New York, 257–310.

PERKINS, D. 1964 'Prehistoric fauna from Shanidar, Iraq', *Science* 144, 1565–6.

PEYRONY, D. 1930 'Le Moustier, ses gisements, ses industries, ses couches geologiques', *Revue Anthropologique* 40, 48–76; 155–76.

1933 'Les industries aurignaciennes dans le bassin de la Vezere. Aurignacien et Périgordien', *Bulletin de la Société Préhistorique Française* 30, 543–59.

1936 'Le Périgordien et L'Aurignacien (nouvelles observations)', *Bulletin de la Société Préhistorique Française* 43, 616–19.

POND, A. W. 1930 *'Primitive Methods of Working Stone, Based on Experiments of H. L. Skavlem'* (Logan Museum Bulletin 2, Number 1), Beloit.

POPPER, K. R. 1959 *The Logic of Scientific Discovery* (Torchbook edn), New York.

1972 *Objective Knowledge: An Evolutionary Approach*, Oxford.

POTTS, R. P. AND SHIPMAN, P. 1981 'Cutmarks made by stone tools on bone from Olduvai Gorge, Tanzania', *Nature* 291, 577.

PRUFER, O. H. 1961 'Prehistoric Hopewell meteorite collecting: context and implications', *The Ohio Journal of Science* 61 (6), 341–52.

PYKE, H. G., PULLIAM, H. R. AND CHARNOV, E. L. 1977 'Optimal foraging theory: a selective review of theory and tests', *Quarterly Review of Biology* 52, 137–54.

QUENNELL, M. AND QUENNELL, C. H. B. 1922 *Everyday Life in the Old Stone Age*, New York.

RADCLIFFE-BROWN, A. R. 1958 'Historical and functional interpretations of culture in relation to the practical application of anthropology to the control of native people', in M. N. Srinivas (ed.), *Method in Social Anthropology*, Chicago, 39–41.

RATHJE, W. L. 1971 'The origin and development of Lowland Classic Maya civilization', *American Antiquity* 36 (3), 275–85.

1974 'The Garbage Project: a new way of looking at the problems of archaeology', *Archaeology* 27 (4), 236–41.

1978 'Archaeological ethnography . . . because sometimes it is better to give than receive', in R. A. Gould (ed.), *Explorations in Ethnoarchaeology*, Albuquerque, 49–75.

RATHJE, W. L. AND MCCARTHY, M. 1977 'Recycling and variability in contemporary garbage', in S. South (ed.), *Research Strategies in Historical Archaeology*, London and New York, 261–86.

REED, C. A. 1969 'The pattern of animal domestication in the prehistoric Near East', in P. Ucko and G. W. Dimbleby (eds.), *The Domestication and Exploitation of Plants and Animals*, London and Chicago, 361–80.

RENFREW, C. 1969 'Trade and culture process in European prehistory', *Current Anthropology* 10 (2), 151–69.

RICK, J. W. 1980 *Prehistoric Hunters of the High Andes*, New York and London.

ROTH, H. L. 1887 'On the origin of agriculture', *Journal of the Royal Anthropological Institute of Great Britain and Ireland* 16 (2), 102–36.

SACKETT, J. R. 1981 'From de Mortillet to Bordes: a century of French Paleolithic research', in G. Daniel (ed.), *Towards a History of Archaeology*, London, 85–99.

SAHLINS, M. D. 1958 *Social Stratification in Polynesia*, Seattle.

1963 'Poor man, rich man, big-man, chief: political types in Melanesia and Polynesia', *Comparative Studies in Society and History* 5 (3), 285–303.

1965 'On the sociology of primitive exchange', in M. Banton (ed.), *The Relevance of Models for Social Anthropology* (Association for Social Anthropology, Monograph 1), London, 139–236.

SANDERS, W. T., PARSONS, J. R. AND SANTLEY, R. S. 1979 *The Basin of Mexico: Ecological Processes in the Evolution of a Civilization*, New York.

SANDERS, W. T. AND PRICE, B. J. 1968 *Mesoamerica: The Evolution of a Civilization*, New York.

SCHALLER, G. B. 1972 *The Serengeti Lion*, Chicago.

Science News 1981 120, 2.

SCHIFFER, M. B. 1972 'Archaeological context and systemic context', *American Antiquity* 37 (2), 156–65.

1974 'On Whallon's use of dimensional analysis of variance at Guila Naquitz', *American Antiquity* 39 (3), 490–2.

1976 *Behavioral Archeology*, New York.

SCHIFFER, M. B. AND RATHJE, W. L. 1973 'Efficient exploitation of the archaeological record: penetrating problems', in C. L. Redman (ed.), *Research and Theory in Current Archaeology*, New York, 169–79.

SHIPMAN, P., BOSLER, W. AND DAVIS, K. L. 1981 'Butchering of giant *Geladas* at an Acheulian site', *Current Anthropology* 22 (3), 257–68.

SILBERBAUER, G. B. 1972 'The G/wi Bushmen', in M. G. Bicchieri (ed.), *Hunters and Gatherers Today*, New York, 271–326.

SINGER, R. AND WYMER, J. 1968 'Archaeological investigations at the Saldanha Skull site in South Africa', *South African Archaeological Bulletin* 23 (91), 63–74.

SMITH, D. C. AND HODGES, F. M., JR. 1968 'The Rankin site, Cocke County, Tennessee', *Tennessee Archaeologist* 24 (2), 37–91.

SMITH, G. 1847 *A Narrative of an Exploratory Visit to each of the Consular Cities of China, and to the Islands of Hong Kong and Chusan*, New York.

SMITH, P. E. L. AND YOUNG, T. C. 1972 'The evolution of early agriculture and culture in greater Mesopotamia: a trial model', in B. Spooner (ed.), *Population Growth: Anthropological Implications*, Cambridge, 1–59.

SONNEVILLE-BORDES, D. DE 1966 'L'évolution du Paléolithique superieur en Europe Occidentale et sa signification', *Bulletin de la Société Préhistorique Française* 63 (1), 3–34.

1975a 'Discours de Mm. Denise de Sonneville-Bordes, président entrant', *Bulletin de la Société Préhistorique Française* 72 (2), 35–9.

1975b 'Les listes types observations de methode', *Quaternaria* 18 (1), 9–43.

SOUTH, S. 1977a *Research Strategies in Historical Archaeology*, London and New York.

SOUTH, S. (ed.) 1977b *Method and Theory in Historical Archaeology*, London and New York.

STRUEVER, S. AND HOUART, G. L. 1972 'An analysis of the Hopewell interaction sphere', in E. N. Wilmsen (ed.), *Social Exchange and Interaction* (Anthropological Papers, Museum of Anthropology, University of Michigan, 46), Ann Arbor, 47–79.

TAYLOR, W. W. 1948 *A Study of Archaeology* (Memoirs of the American Anthropological Association, 69), Menasha.

1972 'Old wine and new skins: a contemporary parable', in M. Leone (ed.), *Contemporary Archaeology*, Carbondale, 28–33.

Trigger, B. G. 1980 *Gordon Childe: Revolutions in Archaeology*, New York.
1981 'Anglo-American archaeology', *World Archaeology* 13 (2), 138–55.
Tringham, R. 1978 'Experimentation, ethnoarchaeology, and the leapfrogs in archaeological methodology', in R. A. Gould (ed.), *Explorations in Ethnoarchaeology*, Albuquerque, 169–99.
van Noten, F. 1978 *Les Chasseurs de Meer* (Dissertationes Archaeologicae Grandensis, 18), Brugge.
van Wijngaarden-Bakker, L. H. 1974 'The animal remains from the Beaker settlement at Newgrange, Co. Meath: first report', *Proceedings of the Royal Irish Academy* 74C, 313–83.
Velder, C. 1963 'A description of the Mrabri camp', *Journal of the Siam Society* 51 (2), 185–8.
Vincent, A. S. 1978 *East Meets West: an Analysis of the Development of Early Man Studies in East Africa 1919–1978* (Undergraduate Honours Thesis, Australian National University), Canberra.
Vrba, E. S. 1975 'Some evidence of chronology and palaeoecology of Sterkfontein, Swartkrans and Kromdraai from the fossil Bovidae', *Nature* 254, 301–4.
Wagner, P. L. 1960 *The Human Use of the Earth*, Glencoe.
Walthall, J. A., Stow, S. H. and Karson, M. J. 1979 'Ohio Hopewell trade: Galena procurement and exchange', in D. S. Brose and N. Greber (eds.), *Hopewell Archaeology*, Kent, 247–50.
Washburn, S. L. 1957 'Australopithecines: the hunters or the hunted?', *American Anthropologist* 59, 612–14.
Washburn, S. L. and Howell, F. C. 1960 'Human evolution and culture', in S. Tax (ed.), *Evolution After Darwin, Volume II, The Evolution of Man*, Chicago, 33–56.
Watson, P. J., LeBlanc, S. A. and Redman, C. L. 1971 *Explanation in Archaeology: an Explicitly Scientific Approach*, New York.
Weiner, J. A. 1980 *The Piltdown Forgery*, New York.
Wenke, R. J. 1981 'Explaining the evolution of cultural complexity: a review', in M. B. Schiffer (ed.), *Advances in Archaeological Method and Theory, Volume 4*, New York, 79–127.
Whallon, R. 1973a 'Spatial analysis of palaeolithic occupation areas', in C. Renfrew (ed.), *The Explanation of Culture Change*, London, 115–30.
1973b 'Spatial analysis of occupation floors I: application of dimensional analysis of variance', *American Antiquity* 38 (3), 266–78.
1974 'Spatial analysis of occupation floors II: the application of nearest neighbor analysis', *American Antiquity* 39 (1), 16–34.
Whitehead, A. N. 1953 *Science and the Modern World: Lowell Lectures 1925*, New York.
Willey, G. R. 1953 *Prehistoric Settlement Patterns in the Viru Valley, Peru* (Bureau of American Ethnology, Bulletin 155), Washington, D.C.
Williams, B. J. 1968 'Establishing cultural heterogeneities in settlement patterns: an ethnographic example', in S. R. Binford and L. R. Binford (eds.), *New Perspectives in Archaeology*, Chicago, 161–70.
1969 'The Birhor of Hazaribagh', in D. Damas (ed.), *Contributions to Anthropology: Band Societies* (National Museums of Canada, Bulletin 228), Ottawa, 142–52.
Winter, F. and Bankhoff, H. A. 1979 'A house burning in Serbia', *Archaeology* 32, 8–14.
Wissler, C. 1914 'Material cultures of the North American Indians', *American Anthropologist* 16 (3), 447–505.
1923 *Man and Culture*, New York.
Wittfogel, K. A. 1957 *Oriental Despotism: A Comparative Study of Total Power*, New Haven.
Witthoft, J. A. 1952 'A Paleo-Indian site in eastern Pennsylvania: an early hunting culture', *Proceedings of the American Philosophical Society* 96 (4), 464–95.
1957 'The art of flint chipping', *Ohio Archaeologist* 6 (4), 138–42; 7 (1), 17–20; 7 (2), 42–6; 7 (3), 80–7; 7 (4), 122–7.
Wolberg, D. L. 1970 'The hypothesized osteodontokeratic culture of the Australopithecinae: a look at the evidence and the opinions', *Current Anthropology* 11, 23–37.
Yellen, J. E. 1977 *Archaeological Approaches to the Present*, New York.
Yesner, D. R. 1980 'Maritime hunter-gatherers: ecology and prehistory', *Current Anthropology* 21 (6), 727–50.
Zipf, G. K. 1949 *Human Behavior and the Principle of Least Effort*, Cambridge.

Index

Numerals in italics refer to illustration numbers